Caring Responsibilities in European Law and Policy

This book explores the emerging engagement of EU law with care and carers.

The book argues that the regulation of care by the EU is crucial because it enables the development of a broad range of policies. It contributes to the sustainability of society and ultimately it enables individuals to flourish. Yet, to date, the EU approach to regulating the caring relationship remains piecemeal and lacks the underpinning of a cohesive strategy. Against this backdrop, this book argues that the EU can and must take leadership in this area by setting principles and standards in accordance with the values of the EU Treaty, in particular gender equality, human dignity, solidarity and well-being. The book further makes a case for stronger protection for carers, who not only need to be protected against discrimination, but should also be supported, valued and put in a position to make choices and lead full lives. In order to achieve this, a proactive approach to rebalancing the relationship between paid and unpaid work is necessary. Ultimately, the book puts forward a series of legal and policy recommendations for a holistic approach to care in the EU.

Eugenia Caracciolo di Torella is an Associate Professor of Law at the University of Leicester, UK.

Annick Masselot is Professor of Law at the University of Canterbury, New Zealand.

This book could not be more timely. With health and social care systems at breaking point, more people than ever are needing to take on the responsibility of caring as we live longer and with multiple conditions. The need for caring will not go away and it will affect us all. Every one of us will be either the carer or the person being cared for, and in some cases both. For the caring role to be valued as much as the role of parenting, there is a lot of catching up to do. How is it that those that give up so much to help others are so much worse off as a result (physically, financially, emotionally and socially)? Nothing sums the situation up more than the first two sentences: if you believe them, read on; if you don't, this book is definitely for you.

Melanie Gray, Deputy CEO, Caring Together
(Carers Trust Network Partner)

Caring Responsibilities in European Law and Policy
Who Cares?

Eugenia Caracciolo di Torella and
Annick Masselot

LONDON AND NEW YORK

First published 2020
by Routledge
2 Park Square, Milton Park, Abingdon, Oxon OX14 4RN

and by Routledge
52 Vanderbilt Avenue, New York, NY 10017

Routledge is an imprint of the Taylor & Francis Group, an informa business

© 2020 Eugenia Caracciolo di Torella and Annick Masselot

The right of Eugenia Caracciolo di Torella and Annick Masselot to be identified as authors of this work has been asserted by them in accordance with sections 77 and 78 of the Copyright, Designs and Patents Act 1988.

All rights reserved. No part of this book may be reprinted or reproduced or utilised in any form or by any electronic, mechanical, or other means, now known or hereafter invented, including photocopying and recording, or in any information storage or retrieval system, without permission in writing from the publishers.

Trademark notice: Product or corporate names may be trademarks or registered trademarks, and are used only for identification and explanation without intent to infringe.

British Library Cataloguing-in-Publication Data
A catalogue record for this book is available from the British Library

Library of Congress Cataloging-in-Publication Data
A catalog record has been requested for this book

ISBN: 978-0-415-52971-6 (hbk)
ISBN: 978-0-203-79582-8 (ebk)

Typeset in Galliard
by Swales & Willis, Exeter, Devon, UK

Printed and bound in Great Britain by
TJ International Ltd, Padstow, Cornwall

Pour Jo et Berny, parents extras et grands-parents extraordinaires.

Per i miei genitor, Emanuela e Giuseppe, per tutta la cura che hanno sempre prodigato.

Contents

Foreword   x
Acknowledgements   xii

Setting the scene: "Everyone cares. Everyone is cared for"   1
  Concepts of care   3
    The markers of the caring relationship   7
    Childcare vs. other types of care   11
    The demographic of care   13
  Should the EU care about care?   19
    Care cannot be confined to domestic borders   20
    The business case   22
    The moral case   24
  Structure of the book   25

1 Conceptualising care   27
  Introduction   27
  Rights and care   29
    Rights, care and the EU: uneasy bedfellows?   31
    A feminist analysis of care: the sameness/difference debate   33
  Beyond the sameness/difference debate: an alternative perspective on rights   38
    Rights, care and capabilities   41
    The ethic of care   44
  Conclusion   52

2 The emerging EU childcare strategy   53
  Introduction   53
  Defining childcare   54
    The diversity of childcare arrangements in the EU Member States   54
    Challenges and shifting rationales   55
    Gender equality and childcare   56

viii *Contents*

    The economic rationale of childcare 57
    Children's rights: reducing child poverty and social exclusion 60
    The governance of childcare 61
  The development of the EU childcare strategy   67
    The first phase: early developments 67
    The second phase: the Treaty of Amsterdam 68
    The third phase: the Work-Life Balance Package and the 2008 financial crisis 73
    The fourth phase: childcare post-2010 – an emerging children's rights framework? 75
  Conclusion   81

3 The EU and long-term care   83
  Introduction   83
  Long-term care: the main features   86
    LTC challenges … 89
    … and opportunities 91
    The rationale for EU involvement 92
  LTC policy development in the EU and in the Member States   93
    Recent policy development on long-term care 97
  Conclusion   98

4 The EU and carers   100
  Introduction   100
  Carers, non-discrimination and equality provisions   104
    Gender equality 107
    Other grounds for discrimination 110
    Discrimination by association 112
  Carers and the work-family reconciliation provisions   116
    The leave provisions 117
    The time provisions 123
  Conclusion   127

5 Reframing the debate   130
  Introduction   130
  Using the EU fundamental principles and values to underpin a legal framework for care   132
  A rights-based strategy for carers   137
    The legal base 137
    In search of the personal scope: who has caring responsibilities? 138
    The material scope: rights for carers 144
    A comprehensive set of leave provisions 146
    Flexible working arrangements 148
    Other initiatives 150
  Conclusion   151

Final remarks	**153**
Identifying the challenges	154
The future of care in the EU: towards a holistic approach?	156
Table of legislation	158
Table of case law	161
Bibliography	165
Index	192

Foreword

It is seen as a hallmark of being an adult and a good citizen that one is self-sufficient, independent and not reliant on the state. Yet the truth is that we are all profoundly vulnerable and deeply dependent on other people to meet our most basic needs. We need others to grow the foods we eat, prepare the medicines we need, and provide us with the emotional support we depend on. Caring relationships are at the heart of humanity. It is by working together that we are able to survive. Ever has it been so. It is why humanity has evolved so successfully.

Yet, perhaps because of its pervasive nature, caring has widely been taken for granted. It has been ignored and invisible. It has received little attention from lawyers, despite its enormous importance to human survival. It might be thought that the lack of any legal intervention is a good thing. Caring should be spontaneous, voluntary and unregulated. But the lack of effective legal acknowledgement of care means that its costs lie where they fall. That is particularly problematic because caring is not spread fairly across the population. In particular it is women who have borne the majority of the care-work and suffered the resulting economic disadvantages. Indeed, it is becoming increasingly apparent in contemporary society that it is care-work that is a major cause of economic gender inequality. It is also becoming clear that caring relationships are currently under considerable strain. Competing demands on people's time, changing demographics and increasing mobility have all made traditional models of care unsustainable.

This important book provides a timely and significant contribution to the debate around the legal response to caring. It focuses, in particular, on the response of EU law to caring. It argues that the EU has a central role to ensure the rights of those in caring relationships are protected. As the authors note, caring is becoming an international phenomenon. The market in care services is now a global one. Any attempt to provide an effective legal framework for caring relationships must be an international one.

The authors welcome the fact that the EU has started to incorporate the importance of care into its policy approaches. However, this has not been comprehensive, with greater strides being made in relation to childcare than other long-term caring relationships. This book provides an invaluable set of concrete proposals to put a holistic approach to caring relationships at the heart of the response of EU law. It demonstrates that there is a powerful economic, equality and moral case for doing so.

This book offers a provocative picture of how law can play its part in prioritising the valuing and nurturing of caring relationships as a key societal goal. As the authors indicate, the light at the end of the tunnel may be the growing recognition that a thriving society does not need to be maximally economically productive. GDP is but one marker of a successful society. Any broader vision of a successful society will recognise the importance of care. After all, it is more important that citizens are happy, have caring relationships that are nurtured, and their basic needs met, than that they are rich.

Jonathan Herring
DM Wolfe-Clarendon Fellow in Law, Exeter College,
University of Oxford
Professor of Law, Faculty of Law,
University of Oxford.

Acknowledgements

Vulnerability and the need for care that comes with it are hallmarks of humanity. Caring for a loved one, whether a child, an elderly parent or a spouse, is a normal occurrence in many people's everyday life. It can be done out of love, it can be a rewarding experience, but will often be a challenging and lonely one.

In this book, we ask ourselves what the law, specifically EU law, and us, as a society, can do to protect these individuals. Are we doing enough? Are we protecting the very people that support the most vulnerable in society?

For us, these questions were not only triggered by academic interest but also by personal experience that is by no means unique. As Professor Herring states in his book *Caring and the Law*, "Everyone cares. Everyone is cared for." Caring for others has meant that writing this book has been a long and complex personal and professional journey for both of us. As lawyers we have encountered a thorny issue whilst writing this book in that we have sought to offer a legal solution to a problem that is not necessarily legal. Where possible we have suggested practical solutions but, in reality, we are aware that we have ended up with more questions than when we started this project. If anything, we hope to have made a meaningful contribution to the debate on the value of the caring relationships and carers.

Along the way, many people have helped us and cared for us in different ways: by patiently reading drafts, by discussing concepts or simply by listening and sometimes questioning our line of reasoning (and at times our sanity). They have all helped to shape our arguments. In no particular order, we would like to thank Nuno Ferreira, Grace James, Petra Foubert, Rachel Horton, Michelle Weldon-Johns, Helen Stalford, Pascale Lorber, Mark Bell, Jonathan Herring, Stephen Riley, Melanie Grey, Arabella Stewart, Vanessa Munro, Miguel de la Corte Rodríguez and Susanne Burri. We are also grateful to the European Commission's network of legal experts on gender equality and the staff of the European Commission Unit for Gender Equality for thoughtful discussions on work-life balance. Thanks are also due to the late Dr Melinda Jone for efficient editing.

Our students have been an invaluable source of inspiration: we thank Ruksar Sattar, PhD candidate, as well as the students in "Caring and the Law" at the University of Leicester, and the students in "Gender and the Law" at the University of Canterbury.

Finally, to the very people that we care for and that in turn care for us: Will, Cecilia, Giacomo, Jo, Berny, Julia and Soeren – this is for you!

This book states the law as of the end of July 2019.

Setting the scene
"Everyone cares. Everyone is cared for"[1]

At some point in their life, either because of age or illness, everybody will require care. Equally, at some point in their life most people are likely to become carers, either as parents or for dependent adults. Care and caring are compelling issues that affect people from all walks of life on a daily basis. Thus, caring relationships are not an exception to the norm but rather a universal experience,[2] an inalienable element and a central concern[3] in the life of most human beings. Yet, perhaps because it has traditionally been perceived as a private matter, the caring relationship has hardly been a concern for the legislator. The European Union (EU) is no exception. The original European Economic Community (EEC) Treaty prioritised economic over social issues.[4] Although social issues and human rights have increasingly been recognised, "care", at least in the sense of this book, is mentioned only once in the Treaty on the Functioning of the European Union (TFEU) and sporadically in the EU Charter of Fundamental Rights (CFR or the Charter).[5] Nevertheless, care underpins and is crucial to the development of a broad range of EU policies.

Against this background, over the years, a care discourse, or rather a care rhetoric, has permeated the EU agenda, which has resulted in some intervention from the EU policy makers in this area. For example, the Commission has adopted several policy documents, such as the Recommendation on Childcare[6]

---

1 Jonathan Herring, *Caring and the Law* (Hart Publishing 2013) 1.
2 See, *inter alia*, Virginia Held, *The Ethic of Care: Personal, Political, and Global* (OUP 2006).
3 Joan Tronto, *Moral Boundaries: A Political Argument for an Ethic of Care* (Routledge 1993). See also the discussion in Chapter 1.
4 Wolfgang Streeck, "Neo-Voluntarism: A New Social Policy Regime" (1995) 1 *European Law Journal* 31.
5 Care is referred to in Article 168(7) TFEU on the responsibility of Member States in relation to medical and health care and in Article 35 of the CFR on the right of access to preventive health care. In addition, Protocol 7 TFEU on the privilege and immunities of the EU addresses the relationship between tax and care in its Article 13. Article 14(1) CFR states that children have the rights to be protected and to receive care necessary for their well-being.
6 Council Recommendation 92/241/EEC of 31 March 1992 on child care, O.J. [1992] L123/16.

2 Setting the scene

and the Recommendation on Investing in Children[7] as well as numerous Communications, reports and staff working documents on long-term care (LTC).[8] The recently adopted European Pillar of Social Rights (EPSR)[9] gives prominence to both childcare and LTC.[10] Furthermore, both the Council of the EU[11] and the European Parliament[12] have contributed to the development of an emerging "care policy". Finally, the Court of Justice of the European Union (CJEU or the Court) has also, in the main, been proactive in the wider area of gender equality and care-work.[13] However, so far, little legally binding legislation has been adopted and the judicial intervention has been largely *ad hoc*. Accordingly, it has not led to the creation of a coherent set of principles, let alone the devising of satisfactory solutions.[14] As a result, to date, care at EU level remains predominantly unregulated. Equally, although there is a growing interest,[15] care is still a largely under-explored topic in the academic legal debate, particularly in the EU context.

The situation is no longer sustainable: the caring relationship should be clearly addressed and be central to legal protection. In this book, we explore the emerging engagement of EU law with the caring relationship. Many questions remain unanswered: to what extent has the EU addressed care? How has the EU addressed

---

7 European Commission Recommendation 2013/112/EU of 20 February 2013, Investing in children: breaking the cycle of disadvantage, O.J. [2013] L59/5.
8 See for example European Commission's "Joint Report on Health Care and Long-term Care Systems and Fiscal Sustainability" (European Commission Directorate-General for Economic and Financial Affairs, Institutional Paper 037, October 2016) https://ec.europa.eu/info/publications/economy-finance/joint-report-health-care-and-long-term-care-systems-fiscal-sustainability-0_en. Accessed 21 January 2019. See more generally Chapter 3.
9 Interinstitutional Proclamation on the European Pillar of Social Rights, O.J. [2017] C428/10.
10 Respectively Principle 11 (Childcare and Support to Children) and Principle 18 (Long-Term Care).
11 European Council, Council conclusions of 7 March 2011 on European Pact for Gender Equality (2011–2020), (2011/C 155/02), O.J. [2011] C155/10.
12 The European Parliament has been active through the European Platform for Investing in Children (EPIC) by releasing evidence-based reports on childcare. See http://europa.eu/epic/. Accessed 25 July 2019.
13 See further Chapter 4.
14 However, see the Commission Proposal for a Directive of the European Parliament and of the Council on work-life balance for parents and carers and repealing Council Directive 2010/18/EU, COM(2017) 253 final, further discussed in Chapters 4 and 5.
15 Nicole Busby, *A Right to Care? Unpaid Care Work in European Employment Law* (OUP 2011); Charlotte O'Brien, "Confronting the Care Penalty: The Cause for Extending Reasonable Adjustment Rights along the Disability/Care Continuum" (2012) 34(1) *Journal of Social Welfare & Family Law* 5; Jonathan Herring, *Caring and the Law* (Hart Publishing 2013), Julie Wallbank and Jonathan Herring (eds), *Vulnerability Care and Family Law* (Routledge 2014); Rachel Horton, "Caring for Adults in the EU: Work-Life Balance and Challenge for EU Law" (2015) 37 *Journal of Social Welfare & Family Law* 356; Eugenia Caracciolo di Torella, "Shaping and Re-shaping the Caring Relationship in European Law: A Catalogue of Rights for Informal Carers?" (2016) 28 *CFLQ* 261.

the fact that women, who traditionally have provided the vast majority of care, are now less available because they are increasingly involved in paid employment? Is the level of engagement sufficient to respond to the fast-changing needs of an ageing society? Perhaps more importantly, should the EU, rather than the Member States, be concerned with care in the first place?[16] This latter question is particularly pertinent in light of the UK process to exit the EU,[17] as well as the increasing unpopularity of EU project in many Member States. Indeed, European citizens appear to want less EU involvement, or possibly a different kind of EU action, in particular in those areas that are not strictly economic.

We argue that it is now time for the EU to take leadership in this area; to place care firmly on the agenda and ultimately to devise a policy and normative framework. This can only be done by promoting and valuing the caring relationship, by adopting a more proactive approach to rebalancing the relationship between paid and unpaid work for carers, and by protecting carers against discrimination and unfavourable treatment at work.

Concepts of care

> [N]ot everything that can be counted counts, and not everything that counts can be counted.[18]

There is no statutory definition of care because it is not a traditional legal concept. A clear definition is, however, important in order to make the concept visible. In turn, this will enable the framing and shaping of legal debate and support the development of an appropriate policy and normative strategy. The task is not easy because this concept is multifaceted and dependent upon contextual considerations.[19] In our quest for a definition of care, we rely on a number of sources outside the legal realm. This section starts by unpacking the concept of care, its main characteristics and its demographic, before moving on to analyse why it should be a concern for EU law.

The caring relationship touches upon many aspects of any legal system.[20] It is a broad and fascinating topic that is increasingly discussed by academic policy

---

16 See also more generally: Jürgen Habermas, "Democracy in Europe: Why the Development of the EU into a Transnational Democracy is Necessary and How It is Possible" (2015) 21 *European Law Journal* 546.
17 Eugenia Caracciolo di Torella, "The Unintended Consequences of Brexit: The Case of Work-Life Balance" in Moira Dustin, Nuno Ferreira and Susan Millns (eds), *Gender and Queer Perspectives on Brexit* (Palgrave Macmillan 2019).
18 William Cameron, *Informal Sociology, A Casual Introduction to Sociological Thinking* (Random House 1963).
19 Jonathan Herring, *Caring and the Law* (Hart Publishing 2013) 13; Janet Finch and Dulcie Groves (eds), *A Labour of Love* (Routledge 1983).
20 Jonathan Herring, *Caring and the Law* (Hart Publishing 2013).

4 *Setting the scene*

and social literature.[21] Such literature is important as it helps our understanding of what care is and the reasons why such an essential element of everybody's life remains to date undervalued and under-explored. However, in order to build upon these findings and to take the discussion further, it is essential to engage with a legal analysis. Although legal academic literature on this topic is growing,[22] arguably, it is still limited. This book aims to fill this gap. Broadly, there are three main areas where connection and interaction between care and the law appears. The first area is where care and caring are found to be within an individual relationship. The most obvious example is that of family law where the vast majority of caring relationships take place.[23] Employment[24] and medical law[25] are also arenas that affect and are affected by the existence of individual caring relationships. The second area is where the state plays a direct role as the carer. This entails the organisation of care when the state takes responsibility for vulnerable children (children in care), or for ill,[26] frail or dependent adults (social care). This area is

---

21 See, for instance: Joan Tronto, *Moral Boundaries: A Political Argument for an Ethic of Care* (Routledge 1993); Jane Lewis, "Childcare Policies and the Politics of Choice" (2008) 79 *Political Q* 499; Mary Daly, "Care as a Good for Social Policy" (2002) 31 *Journal of Social Policy* 251; Mary Daly and Jane Lewis, "The Concept of Social Care and the Analysis of Contemporary Welfare States" (2000) 51 *British Journal of Sociology* 281; Naomi Gerstel, "The Third Shift: Gender and Care Work Outside the Home" (2000) 23 *Qualitative Sociology* 467; Birgit Pfau-Effinger, "Welfare State Policies and the Development of Care Arrangements" (2005) 7 *European Societies* 321; Birgit Pfau-Effinger and Birgit Geissler, *Care and Social Integration in European Societies* (Policy Press 2005); Selma Sevenhuijsen, "The Place of Care: The Relevance of the Feminist Ethic of Care for Social Policy" (2003) 4 *Feminist Theory* 179.
22 See footnote 15.
23 Gillian Douglas, "Marriage, Cohabitation and Parenthood: From Contract to Status?" in Sanford Katz, John Eekelaar and Mavis Maclean (eds), *Cross Currents: Family Law and Policy in the United States and England* (OUP 2000); Jonathan Herring, *Family Law* (8th ed, Pearson 2017); Jonathan Herring, *Caring and the Law* (Hart Publishing 2013) ch 6; Gillian Douglas, *Obligation and Commitment in Family Law* (Hart Publishing 2018).
24 Nicole Busby, "Labour Law, Family Law and Care; A Plea for Convergence" in Julie Wallbank and Jonathan Herring (eds), *Vulnerability Care and Family Law* (Routledge 2014b); Grace James, "Mothers and Fathers as Parents and Workers: Family-friendly Employment Policies in an Era of Shifting Identities" (2009) 31 *Journal of Social Welfare & Family Law* 271; Joan Williams, *Reshaping the Work-Family Debate* (Harvard University Press 2010); Eugenia Caracciolo di Torella and Annick Masselot, "Work and Family Life Balance in EU Law and Policy 40 Years On: Still Balancing, Still Struggling" (2013) 2 *European Gender Equality L Rev* 6; Eugenia Caracciolo di Torella and Annick Masselot, *Reconciling Work and Family Life in EU Law and* Policy (Palgrave Macmillan 2010).
25 See, *inter alia*, Jonathan Herring, "Where Are the Carers in Healthcare Law and Ethics?" (2007) 27 LS 51; Kirsty Keywood, "Gatekeepers, Proxies, Advocates? The Evolving Role of Carers under Mental Health and Mental Incapacity Law Reforms" (2003) 25 *Journal of Social Welfare & Family Law* 355.
26 André Den Exter and Tamara Hervey (eds), *European Union Health Law: Treaties and Legislation* (Maklu 2012); Johan Gronden, Erika Szyszczak, Ulla Neergaard, Markus Krajewski (eds), *Health Care and EU Law* (Springer 2011).

regulated by a mixture of social welfare, social security and/or health care law provisions.[27] The third area is more general, and involves analysing care as an overarching principle. A few examples can be pointed out: education policy,[28] the management of care in the context of business organisations[29] and the duty of care as envisaged in tort law.[30] These three areas highlight how broadly care can permeate the law: we must be aware, however, that the law's engagement with the caring relationship has been different in each of them. To explore all of these aspects would be over-ambitious. Thus, we have chosen to focus on the discrete area of the role of care and its socio-economic consequences faced by those carers involved in individual caring relationships in the specific context of EU employment law.[31] This will necessarily entail taking into account other areas of law. For example, the content of employment law is linked to and influenced by what happens in the family: family commitments, including unpaid care, will in fact inevitably influence the active participation of women in the employment market.[32] Equally, judges will inevitably consider working commitments of fathers when deciding upon their relationships with their children in the context of parental breakdown.[33]

Even within this narrow context, care remains difficult to define. To start, a basic distinction can be drawn between "caring about" and "caring for".[34] The former refers to a general attitude of the mind, an acknowledgement that there is a need for care but does not necessarily imply doing something or making sure that somebody's daily needs are met. By contrast, "caring for" implies the

---

27 Tamara Hervey and Jean McHale, *European Union Health Law: Themes and Implications* (CUP 2015).
28 Marie-Pierre Moreau and Murray Robertson, "'You Scratch My Back and I'll Scratch Yours'? Support to Academics Who Are Carers in Higher Education", (2019) 8(6) *Social Sciences*, 164.
29 For example: Gregory Simon and others, "Randomised Trial of Monitoring, Feedback, and Management of Care by Telephone to Improve Treatment of Depression in Primary Care" (2000) 320 *BMJ* 550; David Challis and others, "Care Management, Dementia Care and Specialist Mental Health Services: An Evaluation" (2002) 17 *Intl J Geriatric Psychiatry* 315; Stephen Shortell and Arnold Kaluzny, *Health Care Management: Organization, Design and Behavior* (Delmar Publishers 1994).
30 Jonathan Herring, *Caring and the Law* (Hart Publishing 2013) 242–247.
31 This is, of course, not to say that other carers do not deserve protection or are not in a vulnerable position but they have a set of different problems that go beyond the scope of this book.
32 Nicole Busby, "Labour Law, Family Law and Care: A Plea for Convergence" in Julie Wallbank and Jonathan Herring (eds), *Vulnerability Care and Family Law* (Routledge 2014) 181–198.
33 See for example Julia Tolmie and others, "Imposing Gender Neutral Standards in a Gendered World: Parenting Arrangements in Family Law Post Separation" (2010) 16 *Canta LR* 302.
34 Carol Smart, "The Legal and Moral Ordering of Child Custody" (1991) 18 *J L and Society* 485; Joan Tronto, *Moral Boundaries: A Political Argument for an Ethic of Care* (Routledge 1993); Jonathan Herring, *Caring and the Law* (Hart Publishing 2013).

taking responsibility for doing something to meet the needs in question.[35] Carol Smart looks at this dichotomy within the context of childcare: whilst the labour of "caring for" children's everyday needs has traditionally been a mother's prerogative, fathers are more involved in the abstract concern of "caring about".[36] She concludes that the law does not attach particular significance to the distinction, thus underplaying the role of care and caring for:

> [M]others, when they spoke about the work they did in caring for their children and the sacrifices they made, were hardly acknowledged. These actions were seen as being normal as breathing and thus worthy of as much acknowledgment as such taken for granted activities usually generate. But when fathers articulated their care about their children, even if they had really never cared for them, their utterances seemed to reverberate the courts with a deafening significance.[37]

In a similar vein, Annette Lareau[38] found that the fathers she interviewed did not generally have a detailed knowledge of their children's day-to-day lives because they did not do the intimate work of "caring for" their children that would have enabled them to acquire such knowledge, although they may have "cared about" their children very much. We agree with Jonathan Herring when he states that care "must be more than a feeling".[39] Accordingly, we differentiate between the two and are concerned with the practical implications of "caring for" rather than "caring about".

The next step is thus to identify what "caring for" entails. Many scholars have provided specific definitions which proceed from their various approaches and disciplines. The definition of care can be broad or narrow depending on the agenda pursued. For example, Joan Tronto and Berenice Fischer define care in broad terms, going beyond family and the domestic sphere, as:

> a species of activity that includes everything we do to maintain, continue and repair our 'world' so that we can live in it as well as possible. That world includes our bodies, ourselves and our environment.[40]

---

35 See also Selma Sevenhuijsen, "The Place of Care: The Relevance of the Feminist Ethic of Care for Social Policy" (2003) 4 *Feminist Theory* 179.
36 Carol Smart, "The Legal and Moral Ordering of Child Custody" (1991) 18 *J L and Society* 485.
37 Carol Smart, "Losing the Struggle from Another Voice: The Case for Family Law" (1995) 15 *Dal L J* 173.
38 Annette Lareau, "My Wife Can Tell Me Who I Know: Methodological and Conceptual Problems in Studying Fathers" (2000) 23 *Qualitative Sociology* 407, 408.
39 Jonathan Herring, *Caring and the Law* (Hart Publishing 2013) 15.
40 Berenice Fisher and Joan Tronto, "Toward a Feminist Theory of Caring" in Emily Abel and Margaret Nelson (eds), *Circles of Care: Work and Identity in Women's Lives* (SUNY Press 1990) 40.

This is further echoed by Carol Gilligan who emphasises that the activity of carers is to "tak[e] care of the world by sustaining the web of connection so that no one is left alone".[41]

By contrast, Mary Daly has argued that to care simply means to look after those who cannot take care of themselves.[42] This involves a broad range of often unpaid activities aimed at "meeting the physical and emotional requirements of dependent adults and children"[43] which are not as simple to categorise. Nancy Folbre sees care as the "paid or unpaid effort to meet the needs of dependant, including direct care-work that involves personal connection and emotional attachment to care recipients."[44] Similarly, Daly and Jane Lewis talk about "the activities and relations involved in meeting the physical and emotional requirements of dependent adults and children, and the normative economic and social frameworks within which these are assigned and carried out."[45]

Policy makers sometimes prefer to define carers rather than care because it allows for clearer delineation. The UK government, for instance, provides this narrow interpretation of the activities of carers that only include a certain group of persons:

> A carer spends a significant proportion of their life providing unpaid support to family or potentially friends. This could be caring for a relative, partner or friend who is ill, frail, disabled or has mental health or substance misuse problems.[46]

The markers of the caring relationship

If anything, these definitions highlight that care represents a "cluster"[47] of activities, practices, social process, values, dispositions or virtues, revealing "the complexity and diversity of the ethical possibilities [inherent in] care".[48] In the absence of a clear definition, over the years, legal commentators have suggested the use of

---

41 Carol Gilligan, *In a Different Voice: Psychological Theory and Women's Development* (Harvard University Press 1982) 62.
42 Mary Daly, "Care as a Good for Social Policy" (2002) 31 *Journal of Social Policy* 251.
43 Mary Daly and Jane Lewis, "The Concept of Social Care and the Analysis of Contemporary Welfare States" (2000) 51 *British Journal of Sociology* 281.
44 Nancy Folbre, "Reforming Care" in Janet Gornick and Marcia Meyers (eds), *Gender Equality, Transforming Family Divisions of Labor* (Verso 2009).
45 Mary Daly and Jane Lewis, "The Concept of Social Care and the Analysis of Contemporary Welfare States" (2000) 51 *British Journal of Sociology* 281, 285.
46 Department of Health, "Carers at the Heart of 21st Century Families and Communities: A Caring System on Your Side, a Life of Your Own" (Department of Health Stationary Office 2008) 18.
47 Virginia Held, *The Ethic of Care: Personal, Political, and Global* (OUP 2006) 36–40.
48 Peta Bowden, *Caring: Gender Sensitive Ethics* (Routledge 1997) 183.

"markers".[49] Drawing on this work, we emphasise four main markers. Although we are aware that these are not exhaustive, they will help to frame the parameter of the discussion and, in turn, to identify the features that determine a carer. Ultimately, we seek to "translate" them into fully fledged legal concepts.[50]

The first marker is the *constant ongoing responsibilities* inherent in care. Carework is often a boundless and endless job that might "not [be] contained within a specific timescale, but is virtually limitless, characterised by spontaneous, unexpected events or cries which could occur at any time".[51] On the one hand, the responsibilities involved in caring require an emotional commitment to give and receive, to acknowledge vulnerability in our human condition and dependence of others. On the other hand, there are physical responsibilities involved in caring: a form of labour that is not considered to require specialisation of skills. Of course, some care professions, such as doctors and consultants, are highly specialised and valued. In a competitive environment, specialisation is considered to be a guarantee of efficient work. However, we are concerned with the more basic everyday care-giving that is often viewed as unskilled "body work".[52] Changing nappies, feeding or washing another person does not require a high level of education or specialisation:[53] although this is work that must be done, it is perceived as work that anyone can do. As a result, it is not deemed to deserve (much) reward. It is not only the direct physical interaction with another person that constitutes care-work, but also a wider variety of activities. Care-work or care activities can, for instance, involve doing the grocery shopping for an elderly relative, doing the laundry for the family, managing financial issues or planning children's schedules.[54] Moreover, Herring points out that under certain circumstances, refraining from entering into direct interaction with another can constitute work, when for instance one allows the care recipient to become autonomous by letting them do the work.[55] Whatever the aspects of caring (physical or psychological), it is ongoing and entails commitment, self-sacrifice and endurance.[56]

---

49 See Joan Tronto, *Moral Boundaries: A Political Argument for an Ethic of Care* (Routledge 1993); Jonathan Herring, *Caring and the Law* (Hart Publishing 2013). Other authors have identified "values", see the work of Selma Sevenhuijsen.
50 See the discussion further in Chapter 5.
51 Susan Pickard and Caroline Glendinning, "Comparing and Contrasting the Role of Family Carers and Nurses in the Domestic Health Care of Frail Older People" (2002) 10 *Health and Social Care in the Community* 144.
52 See the work of Julia Twigg, "Carework as a Form of Body Work" (2000) 20 Ageing and Society 389 and Julia Twigg, *The Body in Health and Social Care* (Palgrave McMillian 2006).
53 Amy Mullin, "Parents and Children: An Alternative to Selfless and Unconditional Love" (2006) 21 *Hypatia* 181.
54 Michael Nolan, Gordon Grant and John Keady, *Understanding Family Care: A Multidimensional Model of Caring and Coping* (Open University Press 1996).
55 Jonathan Herring, *Caring and the Law* (Hart Publishing 2013) 19.
56 Carol Smart, *Personal Life: New Directions in Sociological Thinking* (Polity Press 2007) 66–67.

The second marker is the actual or perceived *absence of choice*. The obligations and responsibilities inherent in the caring relationship are non-negotiable: in reality caring is seldom a choice. If and when it is perceived as a choice, this is heavily influenced by cultural, emotional and personal experiences. For example, it has been argued that having children and thus, to care is the result of life choices.[57] We disagree with this position: whilst it might be possible to choose how to care, whether to delegate it, or whether to prioritise it over work,[58] it is not possible to choose whether to care or not. As Miriam Glucksmann starkly points out, "if babies are not looked after they will die, if food is not prepared people will starve."[59]

The third marker refers to the *financial, physical and emotional costs* involved in caring, especially when it is informal.[60] As care takes place in the context of a relationship,[61] both parties participate in an exchange. Although this transaction has value in itself,[62] it is also costly, both financially and emotionally. The fact that carers suffer disadvantages and discrimination in the labour market and in society in general is well documented.[63] Over a decade ago Herring declared that, "carers get a raw deal".[64] More recently, Charlotte O'Brien has talked about a

---

57 Catherine Hakim, "Lifestyle Preferences as Determinants of Women's Differentiated Labor Market Careers" (2002) 29 *Work and Occupations* 428; Philip Morgan and Rosalind Berkowitz King, "Why Have Children in the 21st Century? Biological Predisposition, Social Coercion, Rational Choice" (2001) 17 *European Journal of Population/Revue Européenne de Démographie* 3.
58 For example parents, in particular mothers, might choose to care for their children (but also for other dependants) and forfeit or put on hold their career regardless of the economic outcome of their decision simply because they value the caring relationship with their children. Choosing to care should be a legitimate option.
59 Miriam Glucksmann, "Why 'Work'? Gender and the 'Total Social Organisation of Labour'" (1995) 2 *Gender, Work and Organisation* 63, 70.
60 See for example Carers UK, "Carers at a Breaking Point" (2014); Beverley Clough, "What about Us? A Case for Legal Recognition of Interdependence in Informal Care Relationships" (2014) 36 *Journal of Social Welfare & Family Law* 129.
61 Sara Ruddick, "Care as Labor and Relationship" in Joram Haber and Mark Haflon (eds), *Norms and Values: Essays on the Work of Virginia Held* (Rowman & Littlefield 1998); Diemut Bubeck, *Care, Gender and Justice* (Clarendon Press 1995); Maurice Hamington, *Embodied Care: Jane Addams, Maurice Merleau-Ponty and Feminist Ethics* (University of Illinois Press 2004).
62 Mary Daly and Jane Lewis, "The Concept of Social Care and the Analysis of Contemporary Welfare States" (2000) 51 *British Journal of Sociology* 281.
63 Department of Health (UK), "Caring about Carers: A National Strategy for Carers" (1999); Department of Health (UK), "Carers at the Heart of 21st Century Families and Communities: A Caring System on Your Side, a Life of Your Own" (2008); Veerle Miranda, "Cooking, Caring and Volunteering: Unpaid Work around the World" (OECD Social, Employment and Migration Working Papers No. 116, OECD Publishing, 2011).
64 Jonathan Herring, "Caring" (2007) 89 *Law and Justice – Christian Law Review* 89.

"care penalty".[65] Carers are likely to suffer in terms of well-being, health and social exclusion, regardless of where the care is performed.[66] When it is considered within the confines of the private sphere of the family or the emotion, care is not valued in traditional accounting methods. When it is considered as paid labour, care is typically undervalued and inadequately compensated.

The final mark is that, more often than not, care is perceived as a "labour of love",[67] which involves an *emotionally sensitive personal connection* between the carer and the person who is cared for.[68] Indeed, usually, albeit not always, we care in the context of an individual relationship for somebody who is close to us. Therefore, it has been suggested that the detrimental impact on the ability to work is "counterbalanced by the rewards and satisfaction of being able to provide care for a close relative".[69] This is disputable, even if the emotional link in many cases is present.

As a consequence of these markers, the caring relationship is characterised by an inherent *vulnerability*. This is a concept that, despite being notoriously vague,[70] is steadily gaining momentum in many areas of law and is of particular importance to help us appreciate the very essence of the caring relationship.[71] To provide a definition is difficult because vulnerability can be conceptualised in two different, almost opposite, ways. At one end of the spectrum it can be a specific feature of certain subjects that make them worthy of special protection and consideration.[72] This can be because of harm, injury or simply misfortune, but vulnerability can also result from an event caused by a human act. At the other end, vulnerability is seen in a broader way: "inevitable" and "inherent in the human condition".[73] This

---

65 Charlotte O'Brien, "Confronting the Care Penalty: The Cause for Extending Reasonable Adjustment Rights along the Disability/Care Continuum" (2012) 34(1) *Journal of Social Welfare & Family Law* 5.
66 Nicole Busby, "Labour Law, Family Law and Care: A Plea for Convergence" in Julie Wallbank and Jonathan Herring (eds), *Vulnerability Care and Family Law* (Routledge 2014).
67 Janet Finch and Dulcie Groves (eds), *A Labour of Love* (Routledge 1983).
68 Nancy Folbre, "Reforming Care" in Janet Gornick and Marcia Meyers (eds), *Gender Equality, Transforming Family Divisions of Labor* (Verso 2009) 111–112.
69 Caroline Glendinning and others, "Care Provision within Families and its Socio-Economic Impact on Care Providers across the European Union" Social Policy Research Unit, University of York, Working Paper No. EU 2342 (May 2009).
70 Jonathan Herring, *Vulnerable Adults and the Law* (OUP 2016), 6 discussing Barbara Fawcett, "Vulnerability: Questioning the Certainties in Social Work and Health" (2009) 52 *Intl Social Work* 473; Samia Hurst "Vulnerability in Research and Health Care: Describing the Elephant in the Room" (2004) 7 *Medicine, Healthcare and Philosophy* 191.
71 Julie Wallbank and Jonathan Herring (eds), *Vulnerability Care and Family Law* (Routledge 2014).
72 E.g. see Lisa Rodgers, "Labour Law and Vulnerability" in Daniel Bedford and Jonathan Herring (eds), *Embracing Vulnerability: The Implications and Challenges for Law* (Routledge 2019).
73 Martha Fineman, "The Vulnerable Subject: Anchoring Equality in the Human Conditions" (2008) 20 *Yale J L & Feminism* 1.

is what Martha Fineman refers to as "universal vulnerability". She convincingly argues that our vulnerability derives from "[o]ur bodily materiality" and thus:

> it is both universal and constant. [It] is apparent at the beginning of life when we are totally dependent on others for survival [but it also] accompanies us throughout life, as we age, become ill, disable or need care from others and, finally, die.[74]

Furthermore, being vulnerable does not always have to be in absolute terms: sometimes otherwise able adults are in a position of vulnerability.[75]

Although these approaches have been criticised as "too broad and too narrow",[76] they are equally important because they can both be related to the caring relationship: as care provider or as care recipient. Indeed, "we readily class those who need care from others as vulnerable, without seeing the vulnerability that caring creates for the carers".[77]

In this book we employ the concept of universal vulnerability: we argue that vulnerability should not be seen as a failure to attain autonomy but rather as an inevitable aspect of life[78] and it is imperative to identify what the law can do to protect it.

Childcare vs. other types of care

Not all types of caring relationships are the same, and equally there is no such thing as a single type of care. Traditionally, a distinction can be made between, on the one hand, caring activities such as cleaning, cooking, grocery shopping, laundry and DIY and, on the other hand, caring for individuals. Caring for individuals can, in turn, be further divided into two subgroups: caring for children and caring for dependent adults. For many people, the care provided to children is considered

---

75 See, for example, Alison Diduck, "Autonomy and Vulnerability in Family Law: The Missing Link" in Julie Wallbank and Jonathan Herring (eds), *Vulnerabilities, Care and Family Law* (Routledge 2013). In the recent case of *Tarola*, for example, it was acknowledged that under certain circumstances, a worker may be in a position of vulnerability; see the opinion of AG Szpunar in Case C-483/17 *Neculai Tarola* v *Minister for Social Protection*. ECLI:EU:C:2018:919.
74 Martha Fineman, *The Autonomy Myth* (New Press 2004); Martha Fineman, "Responsibility, Family and the Limits of Equality: An American Perspective" in Craig Lind, Heather Keating and Jo Bridgeman (eds), *Taking Responsibility, Law and the Changing Family* (Ashgate 2011) 46. See also the discussion in Jonathan Herring, *Caring and the Law* (Hart Publishing 2013).
76 Samia Hurst, "Vulnerability in Research and Health Care: Describing the Elephant in the Room" (2004) 7 *Medicine, Healthcare and Philosophy* 191, 192.
77 Bill Hughes and others, "Love's Labour's Lost? Feminism, the Disabled People's Movement and the Ethic of Care" (2005) 39 *Sociology* 259, 264.
78 See also Susan Dodds, "Depending on Care: Recognition of Vulnerability and the Social Contribution of Care Provisions" (2007) 21 *Bioethics* 500.

12 Setting the scene

to be more gratifying than other forms of care.[79] Most people value the time they spend with their children, which is not always the case for other domestic tasks or even when caring for dependant adults. When addressing the care of individuals, EU legislation and policy as well as the Member States have used this distinction. We also use this distinction as the starting point for our analysis. Childcare is perhaps more "conventional" – it is the care involved in looking after healthy young children. Caring for children is conventional in two respects. First, childcare is easier to understand and thus to regulate, because it is perceived as a normal feature of life. Second, it is accepted as an investment for future generations.[80]

Accordingly, childcare has been presented as a "special case"[81] in which children are "public goods",[82] which are seen as an investment that will benefit society.[83] In the same vein, it has been construed as being economically productive because it enhances society's future human capital and ensures the workforce of the next generation.[84] Care for young children is therefore more easily "visible" and is increasingly considered to be part of the market. This might explain why childcare is a (relative) priority in policy and legislative intervention in comparison to other areas of care[85] and why sometimes it is funded over other types of care.[86]

Not only children need care; there are other forms of care, such as that for frailer adults or disabled children. In this case, care might not be seen as an investment or as part of the market: does this make the caring relationship less worthy? Whilst this book accepts that there is value in investing in future generations for the benefit of the entire society, it firmly maintains that human beings are more than just a means of economic investment and that we should value care *per se*. The principle of human dignity[87] has been used to highlight

---

79 Marta Dominguez Folgueras, "L'inégal Partage des Responsabilités Familiales et Domestiques est Toujours d'Actualité" (2014) 2 *Regards Croisés sur l'Economie* 183.
80 European Commission Recommendation 2013/112/EU of 20 February 2013, Investing in children: breaking the cycle of disadvantage, O.J. [2013] L59/5.
81 Janet Gornick and Marcia Meyers, "Institutions that Support Gender Equality in Parenthood and Employment" in Janet Gornick and Marcia Meyers (eds), *Gender Equality, Transforming Family Divisions of Labor* (Verso 2010).
82 See for example, Nancy Folbre, "Reforming Care" in Janet Gornick and Marcia Meyers (eds), *Gender Equality, Transforming Family Divisions of Labor* (Verso 2009) 120.
83 However, see Isabella Moebius and Erika Szyszczack, "Of Raising Pigs and Children" (1998) 18 *YEL* 125.
84 Organisation for Economic Co-operation and Development (OECD), "Starting Strong: Childhood Education and Carer" (2001) and more recently European Commission Recommendation 2013/112/EU of 20 February 2013, Investing in children: breaking the cycle of disadvantage, O.J. [2013] L59/5.
85 But see the discussion in Chapter 2.
86 Communication from the Commission to the European Parliament, the Council, the European Economic and Social Committee and the Committee of the Regions, "Towards Social Investment for Growth and Cohesion – Including Implementing the European Social Fund 2014–2020", COM(2013) 83.
87 See the discussion further in Chapter 1.

and protect the needs of vulnerable people, be they children and/or adults, cared for and/or carers.[88]

In this book, we argue for a holistic concept of care. Whatever the different types of care or the reasons individuals have for caring, individuals share commitment and responsibilities. Thus, conceptually, to ensure consistency, a legislative framework on care should be underpinned by the same principles, regardless of who is cared for. However, the response of the law must take into consideration the fact that childcare and LTC have specific features which affect working carers in different ways, and therefore a unique generic framework accommodating childcare and LTC is both unrealistic and unfair.

The demographic of care

Care as a gendered activity

In the same way as there is no single type of caring relationship or care, there is no single type of carer. Carers are a heterogeneous cohort: they come from all walks of life, can be of any age, and can be carers for different reasons. They might experience different disadvantages specific to their personal circumstances, raising issues of intersectional discrimination.[89] However, they often share a characteristic, namely their gender. There is a wealth of evidence showing that, in the main, care remains a gendered activity in both the domestic[90] and public sphere.[91] Women

---

88 See Catherine Dupré, "Article 1: Dignity" in Steve Peers, Tammara Harvey, Jeff Kenner and Angela Ward (eds), *The EU Charter of Fundamental Rights – A Commentary* (Hart Publishing 2014); see further discussion in this book, in particular in Chapter 3.

89 Jess Bullock and Annick Masselot, "Multiple Discrimination and Intersectional Disadvantages Challenges and Opportunities in the EU Legal Framework" (2013) 19 *Columbia J European L* 55; Annick Masselot and Jess Bullock, "Intersectional Aspirations in the EU Anti-Discrimination Legal Framework" (2012–2013) *Australian and New Zealand J European Studies* 3; Dagmar Schiek and Victoria Chege, *European Union Non-Discrimination Law. Comparative Perspectives on Multidimensional Equality Law* (Routledge Cavendish 2009); Dagmar Schiek and Anna Lawson (eds), *European Union Non-Discrimination Law and Intersectionality: Investigating the Triangle of Racial, Gender and Disability Discrimination* (Ashgate Publishing 2013).

90 Rosemary Crompton and Clare Lyonette, "Who Does the Housework? The Division of Labour within the House" in Alison Park, John Curtice, Katarina Thomson, Miranda Philipps, Mark Johnson and Elizabeth Clery (eds), *British Social Attitudes: The 24th Report* (Sage 2008); Julie Wallbank and Jonathan Herring, "Introduction: Vulnerabilities, Care and Family Law" in Julie Wallbank and Jonathan Herring (eds), *Vulnerability Care and Family Law* (Routledge 2014) 12–13; Francine Deutsch, *Halving It All: How Equally Shared Parenting Works* (Harvard University Press 1999); Theodore Greenstein, "Economic Dependence, Gender, and the Division of Labor in the Home: A Replication and Extension" (2000) 62 *J Marriage and Family* 322.

91 Lisa Waddington, "Carers, Gender and Employment Discrimination: What Does EU Law offer Europe's Carers" in Marie-Ange Moreau (ed), *Before and After the Economic Crisis: What Implications for the "European Social Model"?* (Edward Elgar 2011); Fiona Carmichael and Susan Charles, "The Opportunity Costs of Informal Care: Does Gender

are traditionally more likely to provide physical, emotional and long-term care.[92] Surveys taken over the past 50 years have reported accurately on the proportion of time that individuals spend caring according to their gender.[93] They reveal that the fact that women have massively entered the labour market in the past decades has only minimally impacted on the sharing of domestic and caring responsibilities between men and women: whilst women have had to reduce the time spent providing care, men have only moderately increased theirs.[94] Although there are variations across countries, generations and the civil status of individuals,[95] by and large, care and domestic tasks remain female activities. In 2010, 80% of the parents who felt they had to reduce their working time because of childcare responsibilities were women.[96] In 2014, 25% of women with a child under the age of three, and 26% of women with a child between the age of three and the mandatory

Matter?" (2003) 22 *J Health Economics* 781. See also Ricardo Rodrigues, Manfred Huber, and Giovanni Lamura (eds), *Facts and Figures on Healthy Ageing and Long-term Care: Europe and North America* (European Centre for Social Welfare Policy and Research 2012), discussed in the European Commission Staff Working Document, "Long-Term Care in Ageing Societies – Challenges and Policy Options" SWD (2013) 41 final, 20 February 2013, Rosemary Crompton and Clare Lyonette, "Who Does the Housework? The Division of Labour within the House" in Alison Park, John Curtice, Katarina Thomson, Miranda Philipps, Mark Johnson and Elizabeth Clery (eds), *British Social Attitudes: the 24th Report* (Sage 2008) 53–81.

92 Eurofound, "Striking the Balance: Reconciling Work and Life in the EU" (Publications Office of the European Union 2018) and Organisation for Economic Co-operation and Development, "Balancing Paid Work, Unpaid Work and Leisure" (2018). See also Lisa Waddington, "Carers, Gender and Employment Discrimination: What Does EU Law offer Europe's Carers" in Marie-Ange Moreau (ed), *Before and After the Economic Crisis: What Implications for the "European Social Model"?* (Edward Elgar 2011), Fiona Carmichael and Susan Charles, "The Opportunity Costs of Informal Care: Does Gender Matter?" (2003) 22 *J Health Economics* 781, Veerle Miranda, "Unpaid Work of Older Adults in OECD Countries" (Social Situation Observatory, 29 November 2011b); Veerle Miranda, "Cooking, Caring and Volunteering: Unpaid Work around the World" (OECD Social, Employment and Migration Working Papers No. 116, OECD Publishing, 2011) 1.

93 Marta Dominguez Folgueras, "L'inégal Partage des Responsabilités Familiales et Domestiques est Toujours d'Actualité" (2014) 2 *Regards Croisés sur l'Economie* 183.

94 Veerle Miranda, "Cooking, Caring and Volunteering: Unpaid Work around the World" (OECD Social, Employment and Migration Working Papers No. 116, OECD Publishing, 2011a); Marta Dominguez Folgueras, "L'inégal Partage des Responsabilités Familiales et Domestiques est Toujours d'Actualité" (2014) 2 *Regards Croisés sur l'Economie* 183. In addition, convergence appears to be slowing down: Francine Blau and Lawrence Kahn, "The Gender Pay Gap: Have Women Gone as Far as They Can?" (2007) 21 *Academy of Management Perspectives* 7; Kai-Uwe Müller, Michael Neuman and Katharina Wrohlich, "The Family Working-Time Model: Towards More Gender Equality in Work and Care" (2018) 28 *Journal of European Social Policy* 471.

95 Scott Coltrane, "Research on Household Labour: Modelling and Measuring the Social Embeddedness of Routine Family Work" (2000) 62 *J Marriage & Family* 1208.

96 European Commission, "2013 Report on the Application of the EU Charter of Fundamental Rights", COM(2014) 224 final.

school age, were not working or were working part-time. These women reported that they could not take up full-time employment because childcare services were either unavailable or unaffordable.[97] Women were also more likely than men to assume the role of informal carers for a wide range of individuals.[98] In 2015, 37.5% of women cared for their children, grandchildren, elderly relatives or people with disabilities.[99] As Fineman remarks:

> [i]n the pattern of long-standing traditions, caretaking continues to be delegated to women – assigned as the responsibility of the person occupying the gendered role of wife, or mother, or grandmother, or daughter-in-law or sister.[100]

Conversely, men usually care for fewer hours per week and undertake less demanding tasks. This is not to say that men are completely absent from the discourse. However, when involved, they are more likely to care for frailer spouses or partners. In this case, although the picture remains on the whole gendered, research commissioned by the European Commission in 2013 found that men account for over 39% of the carers in 13 countries included in the datasets and their contribution is on the rise.[101]

This trend is likely to increase in the near future as societal changes have and will continue to impact on traditional arrangements of care. For example, the increasing fluidity of family formation and new forms of families, including same-sex couples, are bound to produce different forms of gender roles associated with care; the decline of the male breadwinner model[102] as well as an elevated divorce rate

---

97 Melinda Mills and others, "Use of Childcare Services in the EU Member States and Progress Towards the Barcelona Targets" (Short Statistical Report 1), (European Union 2014) 17, 19.
98 European Commission Staff Working Document, "Analytical document accompanying the consultation document second-stage consultation of the social partners at European level under Article 154 TFEU on possible action addressing the challenges of work-life balance faced by working parents and caregivers" 12 July 2016, SWD (2016) 145 final.
99 European Institute for Gender Equality (EIGE), "Gender Equality Index 2017: Measuring gender equality in the European Union 2005–2015" (2017) 39.
100 Martha Fineman, *The Autonomy Myth* (New Press 2004).
101 Francesca Bettio and Alina Verashchagina, "Long-Term Care for the Elderly: Provisions and Providers in 33 Countries" (Publication Office of the European Union 2013). In addition, the difference in life expectancy between men women means that, statistically, men necessarily benefit more often from the care of their spouse than the other way around. See also European Commission, "Strategic Engagement for Gender Equality 2016–2019" (European Union 2015) https://ec.europa.eu/anti-trafficking/sites/antitrafficking/files/strategic_engagement_for_gender_equality_en.pdf. Accessed 10 January 2019.
102 Rosemary Crompton, Suzan Lewis and Clare Lyonette, "Introduction: The Unravelling of the Male Breadwinner Model – And Some of Its Consequences" in Rosemary Crompton, Suzan Lewis, Clare Lyonette (eds), *Women, Men, Work and Family in Europe* (Palgrave Macmillan 2007).

16 *Setting the scene*

means that a growing number of fathers are increasingly in the position of having to combine childcare and work responsibilities. At the same time, an enthusiastic and vocal significant minority of fathers are complaining about the lack of time they have with their family.[103] Thus, the law should strive to acknowledge and encourage men's role as carers in both childcare and LTC. Men need to be adequately recognised in order to avoid being marginalised when they become carers.[104] Men's engagement in care is also likely to contribute to fully enabling women to make genuine choices.[105]

With that said, for the time being, women disproportionately continue to do most of the informal and unpaid care. Thus, it is women who are, in the vast majority, overwhelmed by the dual burden of care and work and suffer more significantly with the impact on their career and earnings.[106] The "second shift",[107] and increasingly the "third shift",[108] is unsustainable on many levels. The European Commission has further highlighted that "[w]omen's activity rate is still 16.4% below that of men, reflecting persistent gender divisions in household responsibilities".[109] Accordingly, women are less likely to participate in paid employment compared to men because of their care responsibilities and, in turn, are more prone to end up living in poverty.[110] When they work, women are eight times more likely

103 Eugenia Caracciolo di Torella, "Brave New Fathers for a Brave New World? Fathers as Caregivers in an Evolving European Union" (2014) 20 *European Law Journal* 88; see also Esther Dermott, *Intimate Fatherhood: A Sociological Analysis* (Routledge 2014) 1.
104 Kirsty Slack and Moira Fraser, "Husband, Partner, Dad, Son, Carer? A Survey of the Experiences and Needs of Male Carers" (Carers Trust 2014).
105 Jane Lewis and Mary Campbell, "UK Work/Family Balance Policies and Gender Equality, 1997–2005" (2007) 14 *Social Politics: Intl Studies in Gender, State & Society* 4.
106 See Giselle Cory and Alfie Stirling, *Pay and Parenthood: An Analysis of Wage Inequality between Mums and Dads* (Touchstone Extra 2016). It is depressing to see how little has changed over the years, see Tamara Hervey and Jo Shaw, "Women, Work and Care: Women's Dual Role and Double Burden in EC Sex Equality Law" (1998) 8 *Journal of European Social Policy* 43.
107 Arlie Hochschild and Anne Machung, *The Second Shift: Working Parents and the Revolution at Home* (Viking Penguin 1989).
108 The expression "third shift" sometime refers to care-giving outside the home either informally to relatives and friends or more formally to neighbours and strangers within volunteer organisations: Naomi Gerstel, "The Third Shift: Gender and Care Work Outside the Home" (2000) 23 *Qualitative Sociology* 467.
109 Communication from the Commission to the European Parliament, the Council, the European Economic and Social Committee and the Committee of the Regions, "Towards Social Investment for Growth and Cohesion – including implementing the European Social Fund 2014–2020", COM(2013) 83, 7.
110 The Commission estimate that, 12 million more women than men in the EU are living in poverty. "Communication from the Commission to the European Parliament, the Council, the European Economic and Social Committee and the Committee of the Regions, 'Towards Social Investment for Growth and Cohesion – including implementing the European Social Fund 2014–2020", COM(2013) 83, 7–8.

to work part-time than men.[111] It is therefore not surprising that care-giving has been identified as the main obstacle to achieving gender equality.[112] Furthermore, carers also face negative perceptions and stereotypes. Employers have been known to refuse employment not only because of existing caring responsibilities, but also on the basis of the perception that a candidate might in the future undertake such responsibilities.[113] Indeed, statistical discrimination, the economic theory of gender inequalities based on stereotypes, is well documented.[114] As a result, it is not uncommon for young women to be refused employment (especially in the private sector),[115] for instance, based on the assumption that they are likely to become mothers and that with new caring responsibilities, they will leave their job or be less committed to their professional career.[116] In other words, there is a perception that young women need less investment in their careers than young men because childbearing, almost inevitably, will drive them out of the labour force.

Do women choose to care?

Much has been written to explain why women are disproportionally providing care. One of the main reasons put forward is that traditionally care has been linked to female emotions and sensibilities. As a result, it has been considered to be a natural part of women's life; an "extension" of their reproductive ability.[117] Another explanation is that women's "special ability" to care might well result from the

---

111 European Network of Equality Bodies (Equinet), "In Focus Brief, Work-Life Balance" (May 2018).
112 Susanne Burri, "Reconciliation of Work and Private Life in EU Law: State of Affairs" (2010) 11 *ERA Forum* 111; Tamara Hervey and Jo Shaw, "Women, Work and Care: Women's Dual Role and Double Burden in EC Sex Equality Law" (1998) 8 *Journal of European Social Policy* 43.
113 Eugenia Caracciolo di Torella and Annick Masselot, "Work and Family Life Balance in EU Law and Policy 40 Years On: Still Balancing, Still Struggling" (2013) 2 *European Gender Equality L Rev* 6; Winnie Chan, "Mothers, Equality and Labour Market Opportunities" (2013) 42 *Industrial Law Journal* 224.
114 William Bielby and James Baron, "Men and Women at Work: Sex Segregation and Statistical Discrimination" (1986) 91 *Am J Sociology* 759; Bev Dahlby, *Adverse Selection and Statistical Discrimination* (Springer 1992); Annick Masselot and others, "Thematic Report of the European Network of Legal Experts in the Field of Gender Equality 'Fighting Discrimination on the Grounds of Pregnancy, Maternity and Parenthood – The Application of EU and National Law in Practice in 33 European Countries'" (European Commission 2012); Annick Masselot, "Family leave: enforcement of the protection against dismissal and unfavourable treatment" (European Commission 2018).
115 Hadas Mandel and Moshe Semyonov, "A Welfare State Paradox: State Interventions and Women's Employment Opportunities in 22 Countries" (2006) 111 *Am J Soc* 1910.
116 Annick Masselot and others, "Thematic Report of the European Network of Legal Experts in the Field of Gender Equality 'Fighting Discrimination on the Grounds of Pregnancy, Maternity and Parenthood – The Application of EU and National Law in Practice in 33 European Countries'" (European Commission 2012).
117 See also the discussion on the ethic of care and the work of Gilligan in Chapter 1.

18 *Setting the scene*

fact that traditionally they have found themselves in the position of *having* to care. Arguably, care-work is passed on from one (female) generation to another without being questioned.[118] Some children (often girls) are being groomed to do care activities, whereas other children (often boys) become accustomed to relying on others. The work of Pascale Molinier in the field of psychodynamics shows that it is the experience that transforms the subject, hence "one is not born carer but rather one becomes one".[119] In other words, the "ability" to care often results from experiences and the environment we live in.[120] In turn, women's reputation as carers impacts on their ability to choose otherwise: "they are less likely to have 'legitimate excuses' not to care".[121] Following on from this, it has become all too easy to argue that women naturally "choose" this "labour of love",[122] whether in an informal context or in the paid sector. Any penalties associated with caring, accordingly are considered to result from (the illusion of) life choices,[123] and have too often gone unchallenged. The gendered nature of these "choices" has also been used as an argument to undervalue its production. Care is an activity which has predominantly been regarded as the work done by "slaves, servants and women";[124] it has always been undervalued and has consistently not been counted in classical economic analysis[125] despite the fact that it is a necessary activity of any society.

Choices and opportunities are central to gender equality: the ability for parents to make real choices regarding care and paid work can only exist if all the legal provisions relating to reconciliation between work and family life are adequately and equally developed.[126] If, as is currently the case in the EU legal system, provision regarding time and leave are more developed than childcare

---

118 Gillian Douglas, *Obligation and Commitment in Family Law* (Hart Publishing 2018).
119 Pascale Molinier, *L'Enigme de la Femme Active* (Payot 2003). This is echoed by Simone de Beauvoir's saying: "On ne naît pas femme: on le devient" (One is not born, but rather becomes, a woman), Simone de Beauvoir, *Le deuxième sexe* (Gallimard 1949) 285–286.
120 Pascale Molinier, Sandra Laugier and Patricia Paperman, "Introduction: Qu'est-ce que le Care?" in Pascale Molinier, Sandra Laugier and Patricia Paperman (eds), *Qu'est-ce que le Care? Souci des autres, sensibilité, résponsibilité* (Payot et Rivages 2009) 15.
121 Jane Lewis and Susanna Giullari, "The Adult Worker Model Family, Gender Equality and Care: the Search for New Policy Principles and the Possibilities and Problems of a Capabilities Approach" (2005) 34 *Economy and Society* 76.
122 Janet Finch and Dulcie Groves (eds), *A Labour of Love* (Routledge 1983).
123 Catherine Hakim, "Lifestyle Preferences as Determinants of Women's Differentiated Labor Market Careers, (2002) 29 *Work and Occupations* 428.
124 Joan Tronto, *Moral Boundaries: A Political Argument for an Ethic of Care* (Routledge 1993) 21.
125 Catherine Hoskyns, "Linking Gender and International Trade Policy: Is Interaction Possible?" (Centre for the Study of Globalisation and Regionalisation, Working Paper 217/07, February 2007); Marilyn Waring, *Counting for Nothing: What Men Value and What Women are Worth* (Allen and Unwin 1988).
126 Eugenia Caracciolo di Torella and Annick Masselot, *Reconciling Work and Family Life in EU Law and Policy* (Palgrave Macmillan 2010).

policy, it restricts parents' choice as to how they can care for their children. This ultimately means that mothers are more likely to take up part-time work. Consequently, this hinders the principle of gender equality. With that said, the type of care should be freely chosen. Out-of-home childcare facilities, for example, should be intended as an available option for parents to use, and not as an obligation: mothers (and parents in general) should be able to use childcare *should they choose to*. This position is supported by the ethic of care,[127] which reminds us that care should be valued and cannot be regarded as an undesirable burden. Indeed, many parents, especially mothers, choose to care for their children and other family members whilst forfeiting or putting on hold their career, regardless of the economic outcome of their decision, simply because they value the caring relationship with their children and others. Choosing to care should not only be valued, it should also be a legitimate option for individuals. This is a choice that cannot solely be dictated by economic rational. Caring relationships are essential to human life and represent a central aspect of citizenship. They are influenced by cultural, emotional and personal experiences. As a promoter of "the well-being of its peoples",[128] the EU has an obligation to lead the development of a care strategy which both reflects the imperative of gender equality and supports caring relationships. Such support would need to ensure a fair sharing of the disadvantages that care-work can bring[129] and enable individuals to fulfil their caring responsibilities.[130] In sum, the ability to make choices is a freedom which allows individuals to realise their full potential.

Should the EU care about care?

Regardless of how difficult and controversial it might be to define the caring relationship and to fit it into a normative framework, the impact of care on individuals, and generally on society, is becoming too widespread to remain ignored. Care has become a major item on the agenda of most industrialised countries due to pressing socio-economic issues related to the ageing population, the decrease in fertility rates, the fight against child poverty and the management of an increasingly diverse workforce in a 24/7 global and progressively digitised economy. In other words, we are experiencing a care-crisis that needs urgent attention.

At the time of writing, however, specific legislative intervention has only started to emerge. In the main, the EU still does not have the necessary competences to regulate care: it can only address the concept of work understood as a "genuine economic activity".[131] In contrast, care lies outside the traditional market-based,

---

127 See further our discussion in Chapter 1.
128 Article 2 TEU.
129 Jonathan Herring, *Caring and the Law* (Hart Publishing 2013).
130 Fiona Williams, "The Presence of Feminism in the Future of Welfare" (2002) 31 *Economy and Society* 502.
131 Case 53/81 *D.M. Levin v Staatssecretaris van Justitie*. ECLI:EU:C:1982:105.

20 Setting the scene

commodifiable EU notion of work.[132] This was recently reiterated by the CJEU in *Saint Prix* where it did not hesitate to confirm that the status of "worker under Article 45 TFEU (...) [does] not necessarily depend on the actual or contingent existence of an employment relationship".[133] Yet by extending the relevant protection to a migrant worker who had to give up work because of pregnancy, and by focusing exclusively on *the absence of women from employment*, the Court avoided a discussion of unpaid care. We argue that as care and work are interrelated, the EU must develop a framework and lead the advancement of the rights of carers. There are at least three reasons supporting our position, which are explored further in the next sections.

(i) Care cannot be confined to domestic borders

First, the EU should intervene because it is becoming increasingly apparent that care cannot be addressed solely within national borders. As a service, it can be provided freely across the internal market. Thus, the demand for and the offer of care affect the free movement provisions within the EU. Whilst care *per se* is not regulated in the same way as paid work, the protection of carers can be relevant to the free movement of workers across the EU. If the EU does not intervene, the situation might arise where carers are protected in one Member State but not in another because they are not regarded as workers. Ultimately, this could hinder the application of the free movement provisions. The intervention of the EU legislator would ensure some level of harmonisation across Europe. Furthermore, the debate surrounding care has increasingly been framed in the EU within the concept of citizenship rights and welfare-state obligations.[134] In addition, care is rapidly changing into services accessible on the global market. As a regulator of the internal market, at the very least concerned with the free movement of persons of EU citizenship and a global actor, the EU is well placed to address care.

---

132 Case 344/87 *I. Bettray Staatssecretaris van Justitie*. ECLI:EU:C:1989:226; Case C-413/01 *Franca Ninni-Orasche v Bundesminister für Wissenschaft, Verkehr und Kunst*. ECLI:EU:C:2003:600; Case C-14/09 *Hava Genc v Land Berlin*. ECLI:EU:C:2010:57. As confirmed by the CJEU in Case 44/88 *J. E. G. Achterberg-te Riele and others v Sociale Verzekeringsbank*. ECLI:EU:C:1989:261; Case C-31/90 *Johnson v Chief Adjudication Officer*. ECLI:EU:C:1991:311; Case C-325/09 *Secretary of State for Work and Pensions v Dias*. ECLI:EU:C:2011:498. For a comment see for example Elisabeth Vigerust, *Arbeid, barn og likestilling* (Tano Ashehoug 1998); Isabella Moebius and Erika Szyszczack, "Of Raising Pigs and Children" (1998) 18 *YEL* 125; Nicole Busby, "Unpaid Care-Giving and Paid Work within a Right Framework" in Nicole Busby and Grace James (eds), *Families, Care-Giving and Paid Work* (Edward Elgar 2011).
133 Case C-507/12 *Jessy Saint Prix v Secretary of State for Work and Pensions*. ECLI:EU:C:2014:2007, para 40.
134 Trudie Knijn and Monique Kremer, "Gender and the Caring Dimension of Welfare State: Towards Inclusive Citizenship" (1997) 4 *Social Politics* 328.

Furthermore, the care-crisis has contributed to migratory movements within the EU and globally, which have led some to characterise care a "global merchandise",[135] a commodified service which can be marketed. The migration of women, in particular, from developing countries such as the Philippines or Indonesia into richer countries for domestic work, and the migration of EU citizens from poorer Member States to richer ones,[136] clearly illustrate this phenomenon.[137] Indeed, there are examples where care transcends domestic boundaries and involves EU law.[138] This is exemplified in situations in which third country nationals come into the EU as spouses and care becomes the only link that they have with the EU.[139]

The globalisation and the commodification of care, moreover, contributes to worsening the care-crisis. A number of low-income countries experience their own form of care-crisis as they lose their carers who migrate to take up jobs in wealthy Western countries, which are encouraging care/healthcare-work immigration through various laws and policies.[140] In turn, this leads not only to a care deficit but also to an accelerated brain-drain in low-income countries. As the demographics of wealthier countries are ageing and women continue to massively take part in the labour market, the demand for care increases proportionately. This means that the demand for carers from poorer regions of the world is growing. The recipient countries in the wealthy West not only contribute to create patterns of care-drain of low-income countries but entrench care-workers into precarious work-patterns.

---

135 Joan Tronto, "*Care* démocratique et démocratie du *care*" in Pascale Molinier, Sandra Laugier and Patricia Paperman (eds), *Qu'est-ce que le Care? Souci des autres, sensibilité, résponsibilité* (Payot et Rivages 2009) 44.
136 Francesca Bettio, Annamaria Simonazzi, and Paola Villa, "Change in Care Regimes and Female Migration: The 'Care Drain' in the Mediterranean" (2006) 16 *Journal of European Social Policy* 271; Helma Lutz and Ewa Palenga-Möllenbeck, "Care Workers, Care Drain, and Care Chains: Reflections on Care, Migration, and Citizenship" (2012) 19 *Social Politics: Intl Studies in Gender, State & Society* 15.
137 Evelyn Nakano Glenn, "From Servitude to Service Work: Historical Continuities in the Racial Division of Paid Reproductive Labor" (1992) *Signs: J Women in Culture and Society* 1; Selma Sevenhuijsen, *Citizenship and the Ethics of Care: Feminist Considerations on Justice, Morality, and Politics* (Psychology Press 1998); Martha Doyle and Virpi Timonen, "The Different Faces of Care Work: Understanding the Experiences of the Multi-cultural Care Workforce" (2009) 29 *Ageing and Society* 337.
138 In Italy, for example, it is estimated that three quarters of all carers are (often undeclared) migrant, see Mirko Di Rosa and others, "The Impact of Migrant Work in the Elder Care Sector: Recent Trends and Empirical Evidence in Italy" (2012) 15 *European Journal of Social Care* 9. More generally see Organisation for Economic Co-operation and Development, "Health at a Glance 2013: OECD Indicators, (2013).
139 For example see Case C-413/99 *Baumbast and R. v Secretary of State for the Home Department*. ECLI:EU:C:2002:493 and Case C-60/00 *Mary Carpenter v Secretary of State for the Home Department*. ECLI:EU:C:2002:434.
140 Lucas Kaelin, "Care Drain: The Political Making of Health Worker Migration" (2011) 32 *J Public Health Policy* 489.

Indeed, the status of these "servants of globalisation"[141] places them in great legal, economic and socially vulnerable positions.

The consequences of the care-crisis are therefore far from limited to professional wealthy women and their ability to reconcile work and family obligations. The impacts of the care-crisis extend to women who migrate far away from their own family, leaving their children and other care dependants without adequate care for long periods of time. The impact of the care-crisis on these migrating families changes their local structure of care and these challenges are not always recognised in terms of care.[142] It is nevertheless a global crisis which impacts and cuts across gender, class and race relations. It is argued that the EU would be best placed to lead a care strategy which could impact positively on migrant and poor care-workers. At the same time, the EU recognises fundamental values such as gender, race and class equality, which could provide a guide to the development of such a global strategy.

(ii) The business case

Second, there is a clear business case that justifies EU engagement in this area: care is instrumental to the achievement of important EU economic goals. To start with, care underpins the functioning of the economy (internal market) and is instrumental to the employment policy. Employment targets cannot be achieved without strong gender equality policies in place. In other words, the 75% employment target of the Lisbon agenda cannot be achieved without the realignment of the uneven distribution of domestic work between men and women. Such a strategy directly impacts on the achievement of gender equality, which is "one of the central missions and activities of the Union".[143] From the economic perspective, there is a clear link between care and the realisation of the objectives of the internal market. Women's participation in paid work represents a structural change encouraged by the EU. Indeed, in 1997, the European Employment Strategy (EES) established that employment rates needed to increase to fit in with the EU's Growth Strategy. Under this policy, women have been targeted as the largest group to be "activated" into the labour market, thus providing the EU with legitimate, albeit indirect competence in the area of care. In addition, the economic perspective is not necessarily contradictory to some feminist views, which value women's economic emancipation through education and work.[144]

---

141 Rhacel Parreñas, *Servants of Globalization: Women, Migration and Domestic Work* (Stanford University Press 2001).
142 Rhacel Parreñas, "The Care Crisis in the Philippines: Children and Transnational Families in the New Global Economy" in Barbara Ehrenreich and Arlie Hochschild (eds), *Global Woman: Nannies, Maids, and Sex Workers in the New Economy* (Macmillan 2003).
143 Mark Bell, "The Principle of Equal Treatment: Widening and Deepening" in Paul Craig and Gráinne de Búrca (eds), *The Evolution of EU Law* (OUP 2012).
144 See Chapter 1.

Care, moreover, raises issues of unfair treatment and discrimination in the labour market. The EU, in this context, has proven to be an unlikely positive force in terms of fighting discrimination and promoting equality. Finally, the economic value of care for individual states cannot be underestimated: for example, in the UK research showed that the value of unpaid care is around GBP 123 billion per year.[145] Employment is valued as a source of wealth and growth but also as a protection against risks. Active engagement in paid employment assists in avoiding the long-term consequences of the so-called "old social risks",[146] such as unemployment and long-term poverty,[147] as well as the "new social risks",[148] most notably inadequate social security coverage.[149] Individuals who do not participate in paid work are unable to contribute to occupational pension funds, which is currently essential to sustain an ageing society.[150] Employment is a priority for the EU, as illustrated by the target of a 75% employment rate in the Europe 2020 strategy.[151] It is easy to see how care impacts on these targets. People with heavy caring responsibilities are less likely than people with less or no care responsibilities to be in (full-time) employment.

Seen in this light, the economic rationale is straightforward and shows that the EU needs to develop suitable strategies, as a matter of urgency, to allow individuals to care for their dependents and at the same time to enable them to participate in paid employment. It is somewhat puzzling that the link between the two has not yet been clearly made: a right to care would provide individuals with *time to work*.[152]

---

145 Lisa Bukner and Sue Yeandle, "Valuing Carers the Rising Value of Carers Support – Calculating the Value of Unpaid Care" (Carers UK 2015). See also a previous study Lisa Bukner and Sue Yeandle, "Valuing Carers – Calculating the Value of Carers, Support" (CIRCLE, University of Leeds 2011).
146 Abigail Gregory, Sue Milner and Jan Windebank, "Work-life Balance in Times of Economic Crisis and Austerity" (2013) 33 *Intl Journal of Sociology and Social Policy* 528.
147 See the work of Nicole Busby, "Only a Matter of Time" (2001) 64 *MLR* 489.
148 Giuliano Bonoli, "The Politics of the New Social Policies: Providing Coverage against New Social Risks in Mature Welfare States" (2005) 33 *Policy and Politics* 431, 433ff; Gøsta Esping-Andersen, "A Child-Centred Social Investment Strategy" in Gøsta Esping-Andersen (ed), *Why We Need a New Welfare State* (OUP 2002); Peter Taylor-Gooby, "New Risks and Social Changes" in Peter Taylor-Gooby (ed), *New Risks, New Welfare; The Transformation of the European Welfare State* (OUP 2004); Jane Jenson, "Social Investment for New Social Risks: Consequences of the LEGO Paradigm for Children" in Jane Lewis (ed), *Children in Context: Changing Families and Welfare States* (Edward Elgar Publishing 2006).
149 Janet Gormick and Marcia Meyers, *Families that Work: Policy for Reconciling Parenthood and Employment* (Russell Sage Publication 2005); Chiara Saraceno, "Childcare Needs and Childcare Policies: A Multidimensional Issue" (2011) 59 *Current Sociology* 78.
150 Paul Callister and Judith Galtry, "'Baby Bonus' or Paid Parental Leave – Which One Is Better?" (2009) 34 *Social Policy Journal of New Zealand* 1.
151 Communication from the Commission, "Europe 2020 – A Strategy for Smart, Sustainable and Inclusive Growth", COM(2010) 2020 final.
152 Jane Lewis, "Childcare Policies and the Politics of Choice" (2008) 79 *Political Q* 499.

(iii) The moral case

Third, the very value of care goes beyond its economic currency. To emphasise the productivity element of care risks leading care to lose its value: "[c]are is the development of a relationship, not the production of a product that is separable from the person delivering it".[153] The economic argument cannot be "decoupled" from a moral claim that values informal carers for what they are actually doing, for their contribution to society rather than focusing on their reduced potential in the employment market.[154] This moral argument is, in turn, based on the ethic of care that uses as a starting point the fact that we are all in mutually interdependent relationships and, as individuals, we can only exist because of these very caring relationships.[155] Care is important because it is the foundation of society. It is a most basic human need:[156] young children and frailer adults cannot survive without care.[157] It is essential to the welfare of society as well as that of individuals. As Mary Daly claims, it is a form of social capital[158] that should be embedded in a variety of social fields.[159] At the very least, care should be constructed as a moral obligation to provide for people who cannot support themselves. If caring for children can be seen as an investment, it is simply not acceptable to exclusively view people in need of care as "economic resources" or "potential investments". Care should be considered to be intrinsic to the normal cycle of life. All individuals at some stage(s) in life need care. Finally, as care is reciprocal,[160] providing specific legal rights for carers ultimately also confers better protection for those for whom they care.[161] The caring relationship cannot be exclusively viewed as a transactional connection.

The development of a care strategy from a moral perspective fits well with the EU objectives as listed in the Treaty of Lisbon, which include *inter alia* the promotion of solidarity between generations, protection of human dignity and

---

153 Susan Himmelweit, "Rethinking Care, Gender Inequality and Policies" (United Nations, Division for the Advancement of Women, EGM/ESOR/2008/EP.7, 25 September 2008).
154 Grace James, "Mothers and Fathers as Parents and Workers: Family-Friendly Employment Policies in an Era of Shifting Identities" (2009) 31 *Journal of Social Welfare & Family Law* 271.
155 The leading work in this area is Carol Gilligan, *In a Different Voice: Psychological Theory and Women's Development* (Harvard University Press 1982).
156 Kathleen Lynch, "Affective Equality: Who Cares?" (2009) 52 *Development* 410.
157 Eva Feder Kittay, *Love's Labour: Essay on Women, Equality and Dependency* (Routledge 1999).
158 Mary Daly, "Caring in the Third Way: the Relationship between Obligation, Responsibility and Care in Third Way Discourse" (2000) 20 *Critical Social Policy* 5.
159 Selma Sevenhuijsen, "Care as a Good for Social Policy" (2002) 31 *Journal of Social Policy* 251.
160 Deborah Stone, "For Love Nor Money: The Commodification of Care" in Martha Ertman and Joan Williams (eds), *Rethinking Commodification: Cases and Readings in Law and Culture* (NYU Press 2005) 273; Joan Tronto, *Moral Boundaries: A Political Argument for an Ethic of Care* (Routledge 1993). See further Chapter 1.
161 Rachel Horton, "Caring for Adults in the EU: Work-life Balance and Challenge for EU Law" (2015) 37 *Journal of Social Welfare & Family Law* 356.

protection of the rights of the child. Furthermore, the EU's obligation to promote "the well-being of its peoples"[162] means that a common development of a care strategy will need to reflect both gender equality values and support caring relationships. Ultimately, in developing a care strategy, it is the moral argument that should lead the legal response.

Structure of the book

In order to arrive at proposals for a policy and normative framework to offer stronger protection to carers, this book is organised into five chapters. Chapter 1 (Conceptualising Care) explores the conceptual underpinning of care. At the time of writing, any attempt to provide a normative framework for care has been framed in terms of rights as traditionally understood. This chapter argues that such an approach is unsatisfactory: the language of rights fails to capture the very essence and the complexity of the caring relationship, at the very least because it is still firmly rooted in the public/private dichotomy. Indeed, the conceptualisation of care as part of the private sphere makes it invisible. Such a construct offers only limited and inadequate opportunities for normative regulation. As a result, the current legal framework at worst ignores the caring relationship and at best is ill-equipped to address it. Yet rights are crucial to confer the caring relationship visibility and legal standing. To move forward, this chapter suggests that the relevant rights should be interpreted through the lens of the ethic of care that has the potential to give "texture" to the relevant rights.

Against this background, the following chapters consider the caring relationship as it has been addressed at EU level. These are organised according the traditional dichotomy adopted around childcare and other forms of care. Chapter 2 (The emergency EU childcare strategy) focuses on the care of young healthy children, namely childcare. Despite the fact that this is relatively uncontroversial terrain and that over the years a childcare strategy has emerged, the regulation of this area remains patchy. Yet childcare is considerably better developed and regulated than other types of care. These are addressed in Chapter 3 (The EU and long-term care), which, starting from the premise that the caring relationship does not end with children, turns to the challenges of other types of caring relationships, namely the care of disabled children and adults, elderly and frailer members of society. It refers to this type of care as long-term care to emphasise the fact that its consequences are durable. In this area, progress has been very slow: although there are policy documents, there is virtually no binding legislation. The only credible attempt is the recently adopted Work-Life Balance Directive;[163] yet its impact is still unclear. The discussion in Chapters 2 and 3 highlights

---

162 Article 2 TEU.
163 Directive (EU) 2019/1158 of the European Parliament and of the Council of 20 June 2019 on work-life balance for parents and carers and repealing Council Directive 2010/18/EU, O.J. [2019] L188/79.

that the EU has a limited scope within which it can manoeuvre to regulate *care*, which is mainly due to the lack of clear EU competences. Furthermore, it is arguably debatable whether the EU should have the right to "interfere" in the Member States' prerogative over how to regulate and arrange care. The EU should not ignore the burden on *carers*, however. The position of carers is addressed in Chapter 4 (The EU and Carers) where we argue that the EU legislator and policy makers are in a good position to intervene. In this area, although the EU has no express competences, there is a set of provisions that can be used to create a sound normative framework, namely the general non-discrimination provisions and the specific reconciliation measures. This Chapter looks at both their potential and limitations. Against this backdrop, Chapter 5 (Reframing the debate) suggests an alternative framework that addresses the position of carers, of children and adults alike, within the EU where rights are underpinned and interpreted in light of the EU general principles. Drawing on the theoretical framework developed in Chapter 1, we argue that such principles lay the foundations of the "EU ethic of care". Indeed, the Directive on Work-Life Balance is a demonstration that, amidst difficulties, an alternative framework can be developed. This chapter proposes to build on the (potential) success of this directive in order to develop a clear set of specific rights for carers. In light of this discussion, we conclude that the EU should take the lead in developing a strong framework to protect carers. In turn, this would benefit those who are cared for and, ultimately, will acknowledge and promote the value of the caring relationship.

1 Conceptualising care

Introduction

Care is not only an inevitable part of life;[1] it is essential to the development and upkeep of society. The law should protect care because this is, in itself, enough to trigger specific rights. Rights indeed exist "[in a moral theory or legal system] whenever the protection or advancement of some interest ... is recognised ... as a reason for imposing duties or obligations on others".[2] However, for several reasons further explored in the course of this book, the law of the European Union (EU) still struggles to fully address the caring relationship, both in terms of policy and legislation. Although EU law might provide *some* rights for *certain* employees with *specific* caring responsibilities,[3] such rights, at the moment, are not formulated as a cohesive strategy, nor are they underpinned by a comprehensive theoretical framework. To develop a set of rights in this area is important, as it will enhance the visibility of care as well as empower and protect carers. At the same time, however, rights cannot adequately capture the caring relationship. Rights are traditionally structured around individualistic notions of rationality, personal autonomy[4] and the free market where "what is most essential ... is the individual's capacity to choose his or her own roles and identities, and to rethink those choices."[5] Presently, in this reality, what is relevant is the "well-dressed businessman with his right to autonomy"[6] and freedom to choose to enter a contract. By contrast, the 'exhausted mother ... with little autonomy [or] freedom'[7] remains outside the law. Thus, a system based purely on rights, or rather on rights as they are currently structured, fails to accommodate today's social reality where care is a prominent feature of everybody's lives – whether exhausted mothers or

---

1 Mary Daly, "Care as Good for Social Policy" (2002) 21 *Journal of Social Policy* 251. See the discussion in "Setting the Scene: 'Everyone cares. Everyone is Cared for'".
2 Jeremy Waldron, *Theories of Rights* (OUP 1984).
3 See further the discussion in Chapter 4.
4 Joseph Raz, *The Morality of Freedom* (OUP 1986).
5 Helen Reece, *Divorcing Responsibilities* (Hart Publishing 2003) 13.
6 Jonathan Herring, *Caring and the Law* (Hart Publishing 2013) 1.
7 Ibid.

well-dressed businessmen. In sum, we are faced with a paradox: whilst a rights-based approach would offer a concrete way to make care more visible and protect carers from discrimination, rights are inadequate as they fail to grapple with the very essence of care.

This chapter reviews the current theoretical approach that underpins the EU normative framework in this area. It seeks an alternative "way of 'doing' law and justice",[8] in order to develop a legal system that acknowledges, promotes and protects the caring relationship and carers because ultimately the law should "exist for people [and] for the sake of people".[9] For this purpose, this chapter is organised into two sections. The first section (Rights and care) looks at the traditional legal approach used to frame this area, namely rights. This section identifies the difficulties inherent in using rights to address care, not least the fact that rights are firmly entrenched in the public/private sphere dichotomy. These difficulties, which become even more evident at EU level, are clearly identified and critiqued through the feminist debate. The second section (Beyond the equality/difference debate: an alternative perspective on rights) explores how the difficulties inherent in rights could be mitigated using the dual carer/earner model.[10] We argue that, in order to be effective, this model needs to be interpreted in light of the capability approach. Originally devised by Amartya Sen[11] and further developed by Martha Nussbaum,[12] the capability approach is particularly apt in this area because it offers the theoretical space to understand the divide between what individual carers aspire to and "their opportunities to be and do".[13] Yet, although valuable, this approach has some drawbacks. In particular, it still presupposes an element of choice, often lacking in the caring relationship.[14] Against this background, this section moves further to identify concepts that could help the development of a specific rights-based strategy in this area. Drawing on Carol Gilligan's work, it explores the potential of the ethic of care to act as a "lens" to interpret the relevant rights.

---

8 Nuno Ferreira, "The Human Face of the European Union. Are EU Law and Policy Humane Enough? An Introduction" in Nuno Ferreira and Dora Kostakopoulou (eds), *The Human Face of the European Union: Are EU Law and Policy Humane Enough?* (CUP 2016).
9 Ibid.
10 This is also called the "adult carer model".
11 Amartya Sen, *Inequality Re-examined* (Harvard University Press 1992). See also further discussion in Chapter 1.
12 Martha Nussbaum, *Sex and Social Justice* (OUP 1999); Martha Nussbaum, "Human Capabilities, Female Human Beings" in Martha Nussbaum and Jonathan Glover (eds), *Women, Culture and Development: A Study of Human Capabilities* (OUP 1995); Martha Nussbaum, *Women and Human Development: The Capabilities Approach*, vol 3 (CUP 2001); Martha Nussbaum, "Capabilities and Social Justice" (2002) 4 *Intl Studies Rev* 123.
13 Barbara Hobson (ed), *Worklife Balance. The Agency and Capabilities Gap* (OUP 2014).
14 See the discussion in "Setting the Scene: 'Everyone Cares. Everyone is Cared for'".

Rights and care

It is commonplace to say that the law speaks "the language of rights".[15] The starting point will thus be to define what a right is and to establish how a rights-based approach has been used in the context of the caring relationship.

Rights are important because "they recognise the respect their bearers are entitled to. To accord a right is to respect dignity: conversely, to deny rights is to cast doubt on humanity and integrity". Rights are an affirmation of the Kantian basic principle that "we are ends in ourselves, and not means to the ends of others".[16] Thus, in essence, rights confer a specific claim onto somebody; they have the power to transform issues that would normally be addressed within the context of welfare and justice into precise entitlements.[17] Furthermore, rights can impose duties that, in turn, the law can enforce. In other words, rights can provide the tools to create a framework where the caring relationship can flourish.[18] They can be general, namely when they are addressed to any person, such as, for example, the right to life, or specific, when they are linked to one or a group of individuals.[19] In the context of this book, whilst the generic right is the right to care, the specific rights are those that address the needs of individual carers. Thus, the benefits of rights cannot be underestimated. Their potential ability "to provide protection to the individual against state intervention has been illustrated repeatedly in liberal legal theory and can barely be disputed".[20]

Not all rights have the same status: they can be either legal or moral.[21] Although in practice the two often coincide, this might not always be the case. Legal and moral rights are not necessarily connected, and the protection that they are offered will differ accordingly. A legal right attracts the protection of the legal system; by contrast, this will not be the case for a moral right. Shazia Choudry and Jonathan Herring give the example of a child who has a moral right to be loved by his or her parents. Importantly, this right cannot be protected and enforced by legislation.[22] A right to care is certainly (at least) a moral right. But can it also be a legal right?

A difficulty in using the traditional understanding of legal rights in the context of care is that they are very much based on the concept of personal autonomy. This

---

15 Ronald Dworkin, *Taking Rights Seriously* (Harvard University Press 1978); Jeremy Waldron, *Theories of Rights* (OUP 1984); Herbert Hart, *Legal Rights* (OUP 1982).
16 As discussed in Michael Freeman, "The Human Rights of Children" (2010) 63 *CLP* 1.
17 Shazia Choudhry, Jonathan Herring and Julie Wallbank, "Welfare, Rights, Care and Gender in Family Law" in Julie Wallbank, Shazia Choudhry and Jonathan Herinng (eds), *Rights, Gender and Family Law* (Routledge 2010).
18 Jonathan Herring, "Compassion, Ethic of Care and Legal Rights" (2017) 13 *Int JL Context* 158.
19 Herbert Hart, "Bentham on Legal Rights" in Alfred Simpson (ed), *Oxford Essays in Jurisprudence* (OUP 1973).
20 Vanessa Munro, *Law and Politics and the Perimeter: Re-evaluating Key Debates in Feminist Theory* (Hart Publishing 2007) 74.
21 Joseph Raz, "Legal Rights" (1984) 4 *Journal of Legal Studies* 1.
22 Shazia Choudhry and Jonathan Herring, *European Human Rights and Family Law* (Hart Publishing 2010) 99.

implies that people have the freedom to make decisions as to how they want to live their life,[23] or as Joseph Raz puts it, they "can make their own lives".[24] Thus, personal autonomy implies the ability to make choices that the recipient is then able/free to exercise or not.[25] Fineman further observes that autonomy is interconnected with a range of other important values such as (moral) independence, pluralism and liberty.[26] Personal autonomy has, therefore, a role to play in the construction of rights and cannot be dismissed. However, autonomy does not sit easily with caring relationships where, more often than not, the choice element is lacking.[27] In this case a more appropriate framework would be that of relational autonomy that persons are "socially embedded ... and formed within the context of social relationships and shaped by a complex of intersecting social determinants, such as race, class, gender and ethnicity."[28]

Furthermore, rights are deeply entrenched in the public/private dichotomy. Legal rights are, in the main, visible and tangible entities that tend to belong to the public sphere, which refers to "the values of the marketplace, work, the male domain or that sphere of activity which is regulated by law."[29] By contrast, caring is often informal and takes place within ordinary family, friendship and/or neighbour/community relationships and, as such, care is traditionally perceived to be outside the law. Thus, care remains unregulated, invisible, unaccounted for, unpaid or poorly paid.[30] Indeed, care is placed in the private sphere which "denote[s] civil society, the values of family, intimacy, the personal life, home, women's domain or behaviour unregulated by law."[31] Locating caring relationships outside the public sphere has led to the perception that care is a peripheral activity that people do in their own time. This has been challenged on numerous occasions by feminist scholars who have argued that what happens in the private sphere, far from being akin to a leisure activity, supports, and is the precondition of, what takes place in the public sphere.[32] Simply put, "without the contribution

---

23 Ronald Dworkin, *Life's Dominion* (OUP 1993).
24 Joseph Raz, *The Morality of Freedom* (OUP 1986) 369.
25 Herbert Hart, "Bentham on Legal Rights" in Alfred Simpson (ed), *Oxford Essays in Jurisprudence* (OUP 1973).
26 Martha Fineman, *The Autonomy Myth* (New Press 2004) ch 1.
27 See the discussion in the "Setting the Scene. 'Everyone Cares. Everyone is Cared for'".
28 Catriona Mackenzie and Natalie Stoljar (eds), *Relational Autonomy: Feminist Perspectives on Autonomy, Agency, and the Social Self* (OUP 2000). See also Jonathan Herring, *Relational Autonomy and Family Law* (Springer 2014). See further discussion on the ethic of care in this Chapter.
29 Katherine O'Donovan, *Sexual Division in Law* (Weidenfeld and Nicholson 1984).
30 Joan Tronto, "The Value of Care" (*Boston Review*, 6 February 2002) http://bostonreview.net/BR27.1/tronto.html. Accessed 25 July 2019.
31 Katherine O'Donovan, *Sexual Division in Law* (Weidenfeld and Nicholson 1984).
32 Sandra Fredman, *Women and the Law* (OUP 1998). See also Susan Moller-Okin, *Justice, Gender and the Family* (Basic Books 1998) and Frances Olsen, "The Family and the Market: a Study on Ideology and Market Reform" (1993) 96 *Harv L Rev* 1497.

of unpaid care, markets would not grow, economies would not prosper and capitalism would not be possible".[33]

It would be tempting, yet simplistic, to conclude that care is low status and unregulated simply because it belongs to the private sphere.[34] In reality, the situation is more complex than that. In this context, care highlights the irrelevance of the public/private sphere dichotomy for two main reasons. First, when done in the context of the public sphere, care is perceived as an extension of the private sphere: it continues to be regarded as a form of badly paid and low status employment. The low status of care is linked to its lack of recognition, regardless of its belonging to the private or public sphere. Second, in many cases, care cannot be pigeonholed into one sphere (the private one) or the other (the public one), rather, it is often used in combination, and this blurs the boundaries between the two spheres.

Rights, care and the EU: uneasy bedfellows?

The complexities in addressing care within a traditional rights framework become even more evident when looking at the EU context.

EU law and policy have traditionally been based on the tension between social rights and economic imperatives and this can be problematic when addressing the care discourse.[35] This tension is not a new phenomenon and has been an ongoing preoccupation of most economist and liberal market thinkers. There are instances when some rights (namely, economic rights) might be regarded as more relevant than others (these being social rights, such as those aimed at promoting the well-being of people). This tension was acknowledged in cases such as *Defrenne (n.3)*[36] and *Deutsche Post/Sievers*[37] where the Court of Justice of the European Union (CJEU or the Court) emphasised that the economic aims are secondary to the social aims. Nevertheless, the tension exists and is rooted in the public/private dichotomy that becomes increasingly apparent in the caring relationships. In turn, this explains why care continues to be under-regulated at EU level. Not surprisingly, this tension becomes particularly acute in times of crisis. This was clear after the 2008 financial crisis when many governments

---

33 Nicole Busby, "Unpaid Care-Giving and Paid Work within a Right Framework" in Nicole Busby and Grace James (eds), *Families, Care-Giving and Paid Work* (Edward Elgar 2011) 203.
34 Eugenia Caracciolo di Torella, "Shaping and Re-shaping the Caring Relationship in European Law; A Catalogue of Rights for Informal Carers?" (2016) 28 *Child and Family LQ* 261.
35 Jenny Julén Votinius, "Parenthood Meets Market-Functionalism: Parental Rights in the Labour Market and the Importance of Gender Dimension" in Ann Numhausen-Henning and Mia Rönnmar (eds), *Normative Patterns and Legal Developments in the Social Dimension of the EU* (Hart Publishing 2013).
36 Case 149/77 *Gabrielle Defrenne v Société Anonyme Belge de Navigation Aérienne Sabena* (n.3). ECLI:EU:C:1978:130.
37 Case C-270/97 *Deutsche Post AG v Elisabeth Sievers*. ECLI:EU:C:2000:76.

across Europe adopted stringent austerity measures that deeply affected welfare policies.[38] Services in general, and in particular those aiming at supporting working parents and carers, have been (and in certain cases still are) cut back, postponed or abandoned due to economic reasons.[39] Although a European Economic Area (EEA) and not an EU Member State, Iceland is an example of the climate in Europe. Despite the existence of clear legal provisions,[40] the Supreme Court held that a bank was acting in its lawful capacity in dismissing a man who was taking paternity leave on the grounds of the economic difficulties following the 2008 financial collapse.[41]

Furthermore, the *sui generis*[42] nature of EU law is not best placed to address the care relationship. The EU is more than an international organisation but less than a state, and competences between the EU and the Member States are not always clearly delimited. In the case of care, this situation translates into the lack of EU explicit competences. Who should look after children and frailer members of society is very much perceived as the domain of domestic policies, rather than a matter for supranational intervention. Domestic policies are influenced and shaped by different perspectives and priorities, be those dictated by culture (expectation of the role of the family), working patterns (in particular amongst women), societal attitudes to care, religion and resources available.[43] Accordingly, national

---

38 Maria Karamessini and Jill Rubery (ed), *Women and Austerity: The Economic Crisis and the Future for Gender Equality* (Routledge 2014); European Women's Lobby, *The Price of Austerity – The Impact of Gender Equality in Europe* (Brussels 2012). See also Roberta Guerrina, "Socio-Economic Challenges to Work-Life Balance at Times of Crisis" (2015) 37 *J Social Welfare & Family L* 368.

39 Abigail Gregory, Sue Milner and Jan Windebank, "Guest Editorial: Work-Life Balance in Times of Economic Crisis and Austerity" (2013) 33 *Intl Journal of Sociology and Social Policy* 528; Francesca Bettio and others, "The Impact of the Economic Crisis on the Situation of Women and Men and on Gender Equality Policies" (Directorate-General for Justice, European Commission, 2012).

40 Article 30 Icelandic Act No. 95/2000 states that "[i]t is not permitted to dismiss an employee due to the fact that she/he has given notice of intended maternity/paternity leave or parental leave under Articles 9 or 26 or during her/his maternity/paternity leave or parental leave, without reasonable cause, and in such a case, the dismissal shall be accompanied by written arguments. The same rule shall apply to pregnant women, and women who have recently given birth".

41 Supreme Court judgment No. 11/2010.

42 Case 26/62 *Van Gend en Loos v Nederlandse Administratie der Belastingen*. ECLI: EU:C:1963:1.

43 Caroline Glendinning and others, "Care Provision within Families and its Socio-Economic Impact on Care Providers across the European Union" (Social Policy Research Unit University of York, Working Paper No. EU 2342, May 2009). See also, Tine Rostgaard, "Caring for Children and Older People in Europe – A Comparison of European Policies and Practice" (2002) 32 *Policy Studies* 51. Furthermore, the differences are emphasised by the fact that comparative information is currently patchy and does not provide a clear picture of the situation, see Social Protection Committee and the European Commission, "Adequate Social Protection for Long-term Care Needs in an Aging Society" (Publications Office of the European Union, 18 June 2014).

governments have allocated budgets that vary considerably.[44] Some governments have taken the policy decision to support carers of young children mainly through cash benefits,[45] while others, such as France[46] and Sweden,[47] invest heavily in formal public care arrangements. By contrast, in the UK, childcare provisions are very much market-oriented, and the choice to expand the public sector in this sense has been described as a Brave New Word scenario, with "rows of mothers at work and rows of tiny children in uniform state-run nurseries – a real nanny state".[48] The situation is no better for adult care. A joint report prepared by the Social Protection Committee and the Commission acknowledged that "there are more pronounced differences between Member States in the way long-term care is provided than in any other aspect of social protection."[49] The lack of uniformity in the treatment of care across European countries reflects and, at the same time, determines the lack of a cohesive EU position. In turn, this is exacerbated by the lack of a clear legal base for the EU to support the development of specific rights in this area.

A feminist analysis of care: the sameness/difference debate

The application of the traditional construction of rights to care raises issues of gender equality at both domestic and EU level. Thus, a feminist analysis is helpful to assist our understanding of this issue. Feminism "ask[s] questions about the lives of women"[50] and the lives of women are traditionally entangled with care. Whilst the concept of gender equality is a key element in unlocking the difficulties surrounding care, at the same time, it encapsulates the enduring "feminist

---

44 A study from 2007 shows that national governments have allocated different budgets for families and children, which vary from 0.7% to 3.9% of GDP see Communication from the Commission, "Promoting Solidarity between the Generations", COM(2007) 244 final. See also Francesca Bettio and Janneke Plantenga, "Comparing Care Regimes in Europe" (2004) 10 *Feminist Economics* 85.
45 Chiara Saraceno and Wolfgang Keck, "Can We Identify Intergenerational Policy Regimes in Europe?" (2010) 12 *European Societies* 675.
46 Marie-Thérèse Letablier and Marie-Thérèse Lanquetin, *Concilier Travail et Famille en France: Approches Socio-Juridiques* (Centre d'études de l'emploi 2005).
47 Ulla Björnberg, "Ideology and Choice Between Work and Care: Swedish Family Policy for Working Parents" (2002) 22 *Critical Social Policy* 33.
48 George Osborne, "Women at Work and Childcare" (speech, 27 February 2006) http://toryspeeches.files.wordpress.com/2013/11/osborne-women-at-work-and-childcare.pdf. Accessed 25 July 2019, quoted by Matthew Tempest, "Tories Reach Out to Young Mothers" *The Guardian* (London, 27 February 2006) www.theguardian.com/politics/2006/feb/27/conservatives.gender. Accessed 25 July 2019.
49 Social Protection Committee and the European Commission, "Adequate Social Protection for Long-Term Care Needs in an Aging Society" (Publications Office of the European Union, 18 June 2014) 8.
50 Alison Diduck and Katherine O'Donnovan, "Feminism and Families: Plus ça Change?" in Alison Diduck and Katherine O'Donnovan (eds), *Feminist Perspectives on Family Law* (Routledge-Cavendish 2006).

paradox" regarding *how* gender equality can be achieved. But before going any further, we need to acknowledge that there is not a single type of feminism and women are a diffused constituency: not all women lead similar lives and not all feminists agree on an identical vision of the world. The diversity of these voices is further affected by a multitude of factors such as class, race and culture. Although this is not the focus of this book, we must be aware that care is managed in different ways depending on the socio-economic and cultural backgrounds of those concerned. Indeed, despite the fact that care is often framed as a "new crisis" which affects middle class families, this crisis is neither new nor exclusively affecting the middle class: in reality working class families – and/or families from ethnic minority backgrounds – have always faced this crisis, to which they have responded in different ways. Working class women have always combined the care of their children and other dependants with paid work, which has typically been precarious, poorly paid and seldom covered by employment or work-family law.[51] Professional and often white women are more likely to be able to afford to pay for outsourcing some care-work, which is likely to be performed by individuals from lower socio-economic backgrounds and/or migrant workers.[52]

Against this backdrop, the feminist debate is essentially conceptualised around two opposing frameworks: equality as sameness and equality as difference.[53] Ultimately the choice of framework leads to questioning whether, when it comes to care, the law should be instrumental in the search for equality or whether, on the contrary, it should recognise and celebrate differences between genders.

The equality as sameness model supported by employment feminism, or liberal feminism, sees women as equally capable as men of participating in the labour market,[54] and therefore concentrates its effort on abolishing the barriers that prevent women from full participation in the market. It supports paid work opportunity through the removal of structures that can hinder access and participation to the labour market as a way to promote women's emancipation. This model maintains that female involvement in the labour market provides women with financial, social and intellectual independence. If there is

---

51 Leah Bassel and Akwugo Emejulu, *Minority Women and Austerity: Survival and Resistance in France and Britain* (Policy Press 2017).
52 Leah Bassel and Akwugo Emejulu, "Caring subjects: Migrant Women and the Third Sector in England and Scotland" (2018) 41 *Ethnic and Racial Studies* 36.
53 Julia Sohrab, "Avoiding the 'Exquisite Trap': A Critical Look at the Equal Treatment/Special Treatment Debate in Law" (1993) 1 *Feminist Legal Studies* 141.
54 Nicole Busby, *A Right to Care?: Unpaid Care Work in European Employment Law* (OUP 2011); Judith Evans, *Feminist Theory Today: An Introduction to Second-Wave Feminism* (Sage 1995); Vanessa Munro, *Law and Politics and the Perimeter: Re-evaluating Key Debates in Feminist Theory* (Hart Publishing 2007); Vicki Schultz, "Life's Work" (2000) 100 *Colum L Rev* 1881; Rebecca Ray, Janet Gornick and John Schmitt, "Who Cares? Assessing Generosity and Gender Equality in Parental Leave Policy Designs in 21 Countries" (2010) 20 *Journal of European Social Policy* 196, 197.

agreement on the general goal, the main debate in this context relates to the best method of achieving gender equality, whether by using formal or substantive equality.[55] On the one hand, formal equality addresses the access to basic rights for all regardless of gender; on the other hand, substantial equality promotes changes in the socio-economic and historical structural inequalities through, in particular, the dismantlement of the public/private divide[56] and the implementation of positive (and sometimes affirmative) actions.[57] For example, in this context specific legal provisions relating to pregnancy and maternity are part and parcel of substantive equality.[58]

The equality as sameness debate fails to consider who will contribute to the general care which women have been providing for free (yet at their personal cost) for so long. It also highlights the fact that this approach risks ignoring the reality of women's lives and requires them to comply with the ideal of the "male norm" of work, which includes high levels of flexibility and availability, long hours at work and primary commitment to the job.[59] More recently the pressure of globalisation has led to the male ideal as embodied in the male breadwinner model to be fast replaced by the, arguably fictitious, model of the "unencumbered worker".[60] This unencumbered worker with neither attachment nor responsibilities, in particular caring responsibilities, is based on an abstract procedural and judicial model of human relationship that has been criticised for lacking solidarity and depth of identity.[61] Following this model, workers are fully available for work 24/7, and there is a blurring of the workplace with the home and constant electronic access.[62] Here, women, who in reality provide most of the care, face a dilemma between conforming to the workplace expectation and their unpaid care commitment,

---

55 Julia Sohrab, "Avoiding the 'Exquisite Trap': A Critical Look at the Equal Treatment/Special Treatment Debate in Law" (1993) 1 *Feminist Legal Studies* 141.
56 Susan Boyd (ed), *Challenging the Public/Private Divide: Feminism, Law and Public Policy* (Toronto University Press 1997); Margaret Thornton (ed), *Public and Private: Feminists Legal Debates* (OUP 1995).
57 See Annick Masselot and Anthony Maymont, "Gendering Economic and Financial Governance through Positive Action Measures: Compatibility of the French Real Equality Measure under the European Union Framework" (2015) 22 *MJ* 57.
58 Case C-136/95 *Caisse nationale d'assurance vieillesse des travailleurs salariés (CNAVTS) v Evelyne Thibault*. ECLI:EU:C:1998:178, para 26.
59 Joan Williams, *Unbending Gender: Why Family and Work Conflict and What to Do about It* (OUP 2000).
60 See Sandra Berns, *Women going Backwards: Law and Change in a Family-Unfriendly Society* (Ashgate 2002); Joan Williams, *Unbending Gender: Why Family and Work Conflict and What to Do about It* (OUP 2000) and Grace James, *The Legal Regulation of Pregnancy and Maternity in the Labour Market* (Routledge-Cavendish 2008).
61 Michael Sandler, "The Procedural Republic and the Unencumbered Self" (1984) 12 *Political Theory* 81.
62 See also Margaret Thornton, "Work/Life or Work/Work? Corporate Legal Practice in the Twenty-first Century" (2016) 23 *Intl J Legal Profession* 13; Ruth McManus, "Work-Life Balance: A Case of Technical Disempowerment?" (2009) 16 *Social Politics: Intl Studies in Gender, State & Society* 111.

especially when they cannot rely on others to do that care.[63] A solution to this dilemma would entail a necessary increase of the share of unpaid work done by men (fathers) within the household and the use of outsourcing of some of the care through, for instance, institutional care.[64]

By contrast, supporters of the equality as difference model, or care feminists, emphasise the differences between men and women.[65] Accordingly, women's specific attributes and unique characteristics, such as care-giving, are valued and celebrated.[66] Care feminists criticise the principle of equality: as it is based on male norms, it *de facto* undermines the actual (child-bearing) or perceived/ constructed (child-rearing) unique female attributes. Based on these premises, care feminists have argued that caring work (especially for young children) is a uniquely female feature,[67] which has long been undervalued[68] and deserves compensation and (re-)evaluation. The state, in this context, would have an obligation to facilitate, remunerate and value[69] the distinctly female characteristic of care-giving.[70] Care feminism, however, goes further than simply arguing for the celebration of natural or essential differences such as women's child-bearing ability. It advocates that care is part of women's nature. The overlap of (or rather the confusion) between child-bearing, a biological issue, and child-rearing, a socially constructed reality, creates the conditions for the introduction of the gender dimension of care. Under this approach, the argument is that as women predominantly provide the unpaid care necessary for child-rearing and for other dependants, as well as the majority of unpaid domestic work, it must be part of the special female features. According to its supporters, the argument gains further weight by the fact that women are also over represented (or rather

---

63 Tamara Hervey and Jo Shaw, "Women, Work and Care: Women's Dual Role and Double Burden in EC Sex Equality Law" (1998) 8 *Journal of European Social Policy* 43. See also Janet Gornick and Marcia Meyers "Institutions that Support Gender Equality in Parenthood and Employment" in Janet Gornick and Marcia Meyers (eds), *Gender Equality, Transforming Family Divisions of Labor* (Verso 2010).
64 Sandra Fredman, "Reversing Roles: Bringing Men into the Frame" (2014) 10 *Intl J L Context* 442.
65 Julia Sohrab, "Avoiding the 'Exquisite Trap': A Critical Look at the Equal Treatment/Special Treatment Debate in Law" (1993) 1 *Feminist Legal Studies* 141; Ruth Lister, *Citizenship: Feminist Perspectives* (NYU Press 1997); Eugenia Caracciolo di Torella and Annick Masselot, "The ECJ Case Law on Issues Related to Pregnancy, Maternity and the Organisation of Family Life: An Attempt at Classification" (2001) 26 *ELR* 239.
66 Lucinda Finley, "Transcending Equality Theory: A Way Out of the Maternity and the Workplace Debate?" (1986) 86 *Colum L Rev* 1118; Robin West, "Jurisprudence and Gender" (1988) 55 *U Chi L Rev* 1.
67 Majella Kilkey and Jonathan Bradshaw, "Lone Mother, Economic Well-Being, and Policies" in Diane Sainsbury (ed), *Gender and Welfare State Regimes* (OUP 1999).
68 Julia Tolmie, Vivienne Elizabeth and Nicola Gavey, "Imposing Gender Neutral Standards in a Gendered World: Parenting Arrangements in Family Law Post Separation" (2010) 16 *Canta LR* 302; Marilyn Waring, *Counting for Nothing: What Men Value and What Women are Worth* (Allen and Unwin 1988).
69 Nancy Frazer, "After the Family Wage: Gender Equity and the Welfare State" (1994) 22 *Political Theory* 591.
70 Arnaulg Leira, *Welfare State and Working Mothers: The Scandinavian Experience* (CUP 1992).

segregated) in professions involving care. Ultimately, it is claimed that caring is in women's nature.

The question of whether men and women are equal or different in nature or whether the differences are socially constructed has always occupied thinkers in the philosophical, psychological, sociological and legal fields. Reproductive biological differences provide the perfect basis to argue for the difference between the sexes, and therefore have been used as a justification for treating women, particularly when they become mothers, differently, unfavourably. Historically, child-bearing and breast-feeding has been a source of tension between equal and differentiated treatments in the workplace. This is translated in the legal setting in the traditional pregnancy anti-discrimination provisions.[71] It has not always been the case, however. For a long time in the UK, for example, as only women could become pregnant, it was considered that there was no possible comparison with other workers and therefore no possible claim of discrimination: "when she is pregnant a woman is no longer a woman. She is a woman, as the Authorised version [of the Bible] accurately puts it, with child and there is no masculine equivalent".[72] Later, it was accepted that pregnant women could be compared to similarly situated men who are temporarily sick.[73] This conflict, although not completely resolved,[74] has been toned down by EU legislative developments, including the adoption of the Pregnant Workers Directive,[75] as well as the uncompromising case law of the CJEU.[76] This has made clear that as pregnancy is a unique feature of women, discrimination on the ground of pregnancy is prohibited direct sex discrimination.[77]

---

71 See Nicola Lacey, "Legislation against Sex Discrimination: Questions from a Feminist Perspective" (1987) 14 *J L & Society* 411 and for a US perspective on the same issue see Catherine MacKinnon, "Difference and Dominance: On Sex Discrimination" in Anne Phillips (ed), *Feminisms and Politics* (OUP 1998).
72 *Turley* v *Allders Department Stores Ltd*, [1980] IRLR 4. See Roberta Guerrina and Annick Masselot, "Walking into the Footprint of EU Law: Unpacking the Gendered Consequences of Brexit" (2018) 17 *Social Policy & Society* 319.
73 *Hayes v Malleable Working Men's Club and Institute* [1985] IRLR 367.
74 See for instance, Annick Masselot, Eugenia Caracciolo di Torella and Susanne Burri, "Thematic Report of the European Network of Legal Experts in the Field of Gender Equality: Fighting Discrimination on the Grounds of Pregnancy, Maternity and Parenthood – The application of EU and national law in practice in 33 European countries" (European Commission 2012).
75 Council Directive 92/85/EEC of 19 October 1992 on the introduction of measures to encourage improvements in the safety and health at work of pregnant workers and workers who have recently given birth or are breast-feeding (tenth individual Directive within the meaning of Article 16 (1) of Directive 89/391/EEC), O.J. [1992] L348/1.
76 See for example Case 177/88 *Elisabeth Johanna Pacifica Dekker v Stichting Vormingscentrum voor Jong Volwassenen (VJV-Centrum) Plus.* ECLI:EU:C:1990:383; Case 179/88 *Handels- og Kontorfunktionaerernes Forbund i Danmark v Dansk Arbejdsgiverforening. (Hertz)* ECLI:EU:C:1990:384 and Case C-207/98 *Silke-Karin Mahlburg v Land Mecklenburg-Vorpommern.* ECLI:EU:C:2000:64, para 29.
77 See the wealth of case law but in particular Case 177/88, *Elisabeth Johanna Pacifica Dekker v Stichting Vormingscentrum voor Jong Volwassenen (VJV-Centrum) Plus.* ECLI:EU:C:1990:383.

We argue that it might not be the best strategy for feminists to link care with an essential feminine characteristic because this proposition risks drawing serious and negative consequences for women. Indeed, as the male norm is both still prevalent and pervasive, any assertion of gender difference in a social context implies automatically the inferior status of the distinctly female.[78] It also risks presenting women as vulnerable and predisposed to domestic and care-work and this risks entrenching stereotypes about women in caring roles.[79]

Moreover, the claim that women are better at care-work because it is in their nature leads to the automatic exclusion of men from this area of life.[80] In turn, this denies men opportunities to explore their nurturing identity and limits the opportunity to think further about the organisation of family life, the relationship between work and family and the ability to break the public/private divide. In other words, linking care to women in such an essential way limits individuals' ability to change and challenge the organisation and structures of society. In turn, this is a democratic argument. The work of caring for others would be better done if it was more fairly distributed in accordance with democratic principles.[81]

Beyond the sameness/difference debate: an alternative perspective on rights

The balance between valuing women's paid employment and care is a perilous one but one that needs to be addressed.[82] For Martha Nussbaum it is a question of justice:

> [a]ny real society is a caregiving and care-receiving society, and must therefore discover ways of coping with these facts of human neediness and dependency that are compatible with the self-respect of the recipients and do not exploit the caregivers. This, as I said, is a central issue for gender justice.[83]

---

78 Joan Tronto, "Beyond Gender Difference to a Theory of Care" (1987) 12 *Signs: J Women in Culture and Society* 644.
79 Clare McGlynn, "Ideologies of Motherhood in European Community Sex Discrimination" (2000) 6 *European Law Journal* 29.
80 Eugenia Caracciolo di Torella, "Brave New Fathers for a Brave New World? Fathers as Caregivers in an Evolving European Union" (2014) 20 *European Law Journal* 88.
81 Pascale Molinier, Sandra Laugier and Patricia Paperman, "Introduction: Qu'est-ce que le Care?" in Pascale Molinier, Sandra Laugier and Patricia Paperman (eds), *Qu'est-ce que le Care? Souci des autres, sensibilité, résponsibilité* (Payot et Rivages 2009) 13; Joan Tronto, "*Care* démocratique et démocratie du *care*" in Molinier Pascale, Sandra Laugier and Patricia Paperman (eds), *Qu'est-ce que le Care? Souci des autres, sensibilié, résponsibilité* (Payot et Rivages 2009).
82 Ella Kahu and Mandy Morgan, "A Critical Discourse Analysis of New Zealand Government Policy: Women as Mothers and Workers" (2007) 30 *Women's Studies Intl Forum* 134.
83 Martha Nussbaum, "Capabilities as Fundamental Entitlements: Sen and Social Justice" (2003) 9 *Feminist Economics* 33, 41–42.

Conceptualising care 39

The sameness/difference debate surrounding equality of rights has been criticised for being counterproductive: it is divisive between feminists[84] and certainly does not represent the best way to frame care. Although the debate is in itself valuable on an intellectual level, it has not challenged the existing male norms considered as the normal work structures and with which women (most of whom are likely to be carers) continue to be confronted.[85] Equally, it has failed to address the relationship between the public and the private spheres which contributes to the invisibility of care.[86]

Legal and policy developments in the field of work-life balance[87] have provided an opportunity to disentangle the debate from between these two strands of feminist theory. The emergence of the so-called dual carer/earner model calls on the state to strengthen women's links to the labour market, while at the same time to encourage men to develop their care-giving ties.[88] It had already been theorised by Fineman, who sees the family as a bundle of caring relationships with one person assuming the "mothering" role and the other that of the "dependent child".[89] It is not crucial to this model that the mothering role is assumed by the mother as it can equally be undertaken by the father. This model is inherent in a "transformed society",[90] and has been formally endorsed by the CJEU in recent cases such as *Roca Álvarez*[91] and *Maistrellis*.[92] The EU legislator has also started to embrace it in the Work-Life Balance Directive.[93]

Although superficially attractive, this model is not above criticism. The underlying assumption of the dual carer/earner model is that all adults, whether male or

---

84 Judith Evans, *Feminist Theory Today: An Introduction to Second-Wave Feminism* (Sage 1995).
85 Vicki Schultz, "Life's Work" (2000) 100 *Colum L Rev* 1881 and more recently see Charlotte O'Brien, "Confronting the Care Penalty: The Cause for Extending Reasonable Adjustment Rights along the Disability/Care Continuum" (2012) 34 *J Social Welfare & Family L* 5.
86 Isabella Moebius and Erika Szyszczack, "Of Raising Pigs and Children" (1998) 18 *YEL* 125.
87 *Inter alia* see Rosemary Crompton, *Employment and the Family: The Reconfiguration of Work and Family Life in Contemporary Societies* (CUP 2006).
88 Birgit Pfau-Effinger, "Socio Historical Paths of The Male Breadwinner Model – An Explanation of Cross National Differences" (2004) 55 *British Journal of Sociology* 377; Rosemary Crompton, Suzan Lewis and Clare Lyonette, "Introduction: the Unravelling of the Male Breadwinner Model – And Some of Its Consequences" in Rosemary Crompton, Suzan Lewis, Clare Lyonette (eds), *Women, Men, Work and Family in Europe* (Palgrave Macmillan 2007).
89 Martha Fineman, *The Neutered Mother, the Sexual Family and Other Twentieth Century Tragedies* (Routledge 1995) 235ff.
90 Janet Gormick and Marcia Meyers, *Families that Work: Policy for Reconciling Parenthood and Employment* (Russell Sage Publication 2005).
91 Case C-104/09 *Roca Álvarez v Sesa Start España ETT SA*. ECLI:EU:C:2010:561.
92 Case C222/14 *Konstantinos Maistrellis v Ypourgos Dikaiosynis, Diafaneias kai Anthropinon Dikaiomaton*. ECLI:EU:C:2015:473.
93 Directive (EU) 2019/1158 of the European Parliament and of the Council of 20 June 2019 on work-life balance for parents and carers and repealing Council Directive 2010/18/EU, O.J. [2019] L188/79, further discussed in Chapter 4 and 5.

female, with or without children or other dependants, are potentially able to work and therefore should participate in the economy. Under this model, policy makers make the assumption that the traditional male breadwinner family model – where men would take primary responsibility for earning and women for caring – has largely disappeared from society. In reality, such assumption is simply not true: the traditional male breadwinner model has not disappeared[94] and many women remain economically dependent on their partners.[95] The other difficulty resides in the fact that this model does not take sufficiently into account contemporary societal evolutions such as the process of demographic transition, the feminisation of the workplace, the increasingly fluid model of families, or the weight of cultural traditions and economic circumstances.[96] For example, single mothers' behaviour towards paid work and care differs drastically from that of mothers with a partner.[97] The combination of encouraging female paid employment with the development of childcare services is far from suitable for all families in the EU.[98] Moreover, the dual carer/earner model does not take fully into account the reality of women's situations. Indeed, many jobs filled by women are precarious, low-quality and badly paid.[99]

In other words, while under the dual carer/earner model women are *prima facie* given more agency with regard to the organisation of care, this remains a "weighted" autonomy.[100] In reality, care-work continues to be a determinant factor in the ability of women to access paid work and the "unencumbered worker"[101] remains the norm.

---

94 Annick Masselot, Eugenia Caracciolo di Torella and Susanne Burri, "Thematic Report of the European Network of Legal Experts in the Field of Gender Equality: Fighting Discrimination on the Grounds of Pregnancy, Maternity and Parenthood – The Application of EU and National Law in Practice in 33 European Countries" (European Commission 2012).
95 Mary Daly, "What Adult Worker Model? A Critical Look at Recent Social Policy Reform in Europe from a Gender and Family Perspective" (2011) 18 *Social Politics: Intl Studies in Gender, State & Society* 1.
96 Ann Orloff, "Should Feminists Aim for Gender Symmetry? Why the Dual-earner/Dual Care Model May Not Be Every Feminist's Utopia" in Janet Gornick and Marcia Meyers (eds), *Institutions for Gender Egalitarianism: Creating the Conditions for Egalitarian Dual Earner/Dual Caregiver Families* (Verso 2009).
97 Department of Work and Pensions (DWP), "Ready for Work: Full Employment in our Generation" (2007); Simon Duncan and Rosalind Edwards, *Lone Mothers, Paid Work and Gendered Moral Rationalities* (Palgrave Macmillan 1999).
98 The Sunday Times reported in April 2016 that "a mother with two children at nursery needs to earn at least £40,000 a year to make any profit from going to work (after deducting the costs of childcare, travel and pension contributions). A salary of £60,000 would leave her with £36 a day after deductions. The average woman in a full-time job earns £24,202."
99 Catherine Hoskyns, "Mainstreaming Gender in the Macroeconomic Policies of the EU – Institutional and Conceptual Issues" (ECPR conference, Bologna, June 2004).
100 Mary Daly, "What Adult Worker Model? A Critical Look at Recent Social Policy Reform in Europe from a Gender and Family Perspective" (2011) 18 *Social Politics: Intl Studies in Gender, State & Society* 1, 17.
101 See fn 60 in this chapter.

Rights, care and capabilities

In order to move the debate forward, it is important to understand what hinders the achievement of the dual earner/carer model. We suggest that the theoretical instrument that has the potential to underpin the development of a (legal) environment where the diversity and flexibility of care relationships are valued and supported can be found in the capabilities approach. This evaluative framework was originally developed by Sen[102] as an economic theory to provide new perspectives on welfare economics. It is concerned with the evaluation of individual well-being and human development that stems from a critique of the existing philosophical and economic approaches on inequality measurement in welfare economics.[103]

It goes beyond traditional economic welfare and challenges the assumption that human well-being is based on economic success. Instead, it is centred on what people can effectively achieve because under a capabilities approach, it "is the things people are capable of doing which is the most useful indication of a successful society."[104] The core focus of the capabilities approach is on what individuals are able/capable to do and to be. The capability approach to human well-being is a "concentration on freedom to achieve in general and the capabilities to function in particular", and the central concepts of this approach are "functionings and capabilities".[105] The approach is about the empowerment of people with freedom and the development of an environment suitable for human flourishing.[106] A functioning is an achievement, whereas a capability is the ability to achieve (i.e. the freedom).[107] Sen claims that a person's well-being must be evaluated in the light of a form of assessment of the functionings achieved by that person.[108] This capability to achieve functionings reflects the person's real opportunities or freedom of choice between possible lifestyles.[109]

In other words, functionings are what people want to be capable, or should be capable, to be and/or to do. Thus, capabilities are the alternative combinations

---

102 Amartya Sen, *Commodities and Capabilities* (OUP 1987); Amartya Sen, *Development as Freedom* (Alfred Knopf 1999); Amartya Sen, "Equality of What?" in Sterling McMurrin (ed), *The Tanner Lectures on Human Values* 4 (2nd edn, CUP 2010); Amartya Sen, *Inequality Re-examined* (Harvard University Press 1992).
103 Ingrid Robeyns, "Sen's Capability Approach and Gender Inequality: Selecting Relevant Capabilities" (2003) 9 *Feminist Economics* 61.
104 Jonathan Herring, *Caring and the Law* (Hart Publishing 2013) 320.
105 Amartya Sen, "Gender Inequality and Theories of Justice" in Martha Nussbaum and Jonathan Glover (eds), *Women, Culture, and Development: A Study of Human Capabilities: A Study of Human Capabilities* (OUP 1995) 266.
106 Melanie Walker, "Amartya Sen's Capability Approach and Education" (2005) 13 *Educational Action Research* 103.
107 Amartya Sen and Geoffrey Hawthorn, *The Standard of Living* (CUP 1988) 36.
108 Amartya Sen, *Inequality Re-examined* (Harvard University Press 1992) 31.
109 Amartya Sen, "Capability and Well-being" in Martha Hausman (ed), *The Philosophy of Economics* (CUP 1993).

of functionings that are feasible for a person to achieve. Hence, the distinction between the capabilities and functionings lies in the difference between what is realised and what is effectively possible. Capabilities are considered to be our freedom, which society has an obligation to guarantee to each citizen so that they can live the life they want and be the person they want to be. There is no prescription about how life should be lived; individuals should be able to choose their path once they have the requisite capabilities.

The capability approach has further been explored by Martha Nussbaum[110] as a means to achieving effective gender equality. Indeed, it provides a suitable theoretical framework to analyse and assess social justice and care relationships. The presumption that we are (or ought to be) autonomous beings ignores the reality of the variable levels of dependency over our life cycle, as well as the risks inherent to our condition as human beings: illness, accident and old age. Care is central to human life and development. As "all societies contain people in need of care",[111] it is becoming necessary to contest the idea that "those who are dependent and 'unproductive' are not full participants."[112] Real social justice must necessarily include the need to respond to the urgency and unpredictability of care and the effects of dependency on the distribution of resources.[113] The capabilities approach goes beyond measuring well-being according to income and wealth;[114] it considers the ability of individuals to engage effectively in a wide range of human activities, of which care is an essential component.[115] Social justice cannot have any meaning without the recognition that care and dependency are significant parts of the human experience. For instance, the systematic omission of the contribution of women in their role as care-givers fails to account for social justice for all citizens. In order to frame the basic principles of capabilities as real opportunities for individuals, Nussbaum proposes a list of ten central capabilities which should enable individuals to "deal better with people's need for various types of love and

---

110 Martha Nussbaum, *Sex and Social Justice* (OUP 1999); Martha Nussbaum, "Human Capabilities, Female Human Beings" in Martha Nussbaum and Jonathan Glover (eds), *Women, Culture and Development: A Study of Human Capabilities* (OUP 1995); Martha Nussbaum, *Women and Human Development: The Capabilities Approach*, vol 3 (CUP 2001); Martha Nussbaum, "Capabilities and Social Justice" (2002) 4 *Intl Studies Rev* 123.
111 Martha Nussbaum, "Care, Dependency, and Social Justice: A Challenge to Conventional Ideas of the Social Contract" in Peter Lloyd-Sherlock (ed), *Living Longer: Ageing, Development and Social Protection* (Zed Books 2004) 275.
112 Martha Nussbaum, "Care, Dependency, and Social Justice: A Challenge to Conventional Ideas of the Social Contract" in Peter Lloyd-Sherlock (ed), *Living Longer: Ageing, Development and Social Protection* (Zed Books 2004) 293.
113 Martha Nussbaum, *Sex and Social Justice* (OUP 1999) 190.
114 Amartya Sen, "Human Rights and Capabilities" (2005) 6 *J Human Development* 151; Amartya Sen, "Equality of What?" in Sterling McMurrin (ed), *The Tanner Lectures on Human Values* 4 (2nd edn, CUP 2010); Amartya Sen, *The Idea of Justice* (Harvard University Press 2011); Martha Nussbaum, "Capabilities as Fundamental Entitlements: Sen and Social Justice" (2003) 9 *Feminist Economics* 33.
115 Martha Nussbaum, *Sex and Social Justice* (OUP 1999) 191.

care."[116] This underscores the centrality of care in the production of capabilities. People's basic needs must be met in order for them to have the capabilities to live the life they wish. Similarly, care-givers must be supported and valued to also have capabilities.

The capabilities approach goes beyond the conflict between paid work and unpaid care. It recognises that care obligations at home are not necessarily linked to income and wealth. Some people who are well-off in terms of income might at the same time experience life struggles because of their care responsibilities at home.[117] By contrast, others might only be able to secure low incomes because they cannot function well in the paid work environment due to their care obligations. Nevertheless, these individuals might at the same time be well-off because of the love they received (and give) from their valuable care contribution. Indeed, care-giving is not (and should not be construed as) a burden, but as a valuable activity which benefits society and contributes to the richness and well-being of an individual's personal life.[118] Legal rights, in particular, should exist to sustain real options for people. The law should contribute to an institutional environment in which the relevant capabilities support and enable caring relationships.[119] Such a support would sustain the dignity of human beings[120] in a caring relationship while at the same time develop the full potential of carers and those for whom they care.

Part of the solution is to challenge the perception of what constitutes *work*. Standard work is presently considered to be paid full-time work. In this context, not only unpaid work is not considered work; any form of paid work, whether made flexible or shortened, which is adopted in order to compromise for the necessity (or the choice) of unpaid care-work, is treated as atypical and carries penalties,[121] at least in terms of income. Should care-work be valued appropriately, the state would be justified in intervening in order to provide equity between the parties to a contract of employment. Essentially, this is one of the aims of the Part-Time Directive:[122] people who engage in unpaid care-work and as a result

---

116 Martha Nussbaum, *Sex and Social Justice* (OUP 1999) 192; Martha Nussbaum, *Women and Human Development: The Capabilities Approach*, vol 3 (CUP 2001) ch 7.
117 Martha Nussbaum, *Sex and Social Justice* (OUP 1999) 192.
118 Jonathan Herring, *Caring and the Law* (Hart Publishing 2013).
119 Jane Lewis and Susanna Giullari, "The Adult Worker Model Family, Gender Equality and Care: The Search for New Policy Principles and the Possibilities and Problems of a Capabilities Approach" (2005) 34 *Economy and Society* 76.
120 Gay Moon and Robin Allen, "Dignity Discourse in Discrimination Daw: A Better Route to Equality?" (2006) 6 *EHRLR* 610.
121 Charlotte O'Brien, "Confronting the Care Penalty: The Cause for Extending Reasonable Adjustment Rights along the Disability/Care Continuum" (2012) 34(1) *Journal of Social Welfare & Family Law* 5.
122 Council Directive 97/81/EC of 15 December 1997 concerning the Framework Agreement on part-time work concluded by UNICE, CEEP and the ETUC – Annex: Framework agreement on part-time work, O.J. [1998] L 14/9. Of course, the Part-Time Directive does not prohibit discrimination on the ground of caring relationship.

cannot (or choose not to) function adequately as standard workers should not be discriminated against by, for instance, being penalised on their income or on their work progression. Should the capabilities approach apply, the next step of course requires the state to intervene in order to change the perception of standard/atypical work and to integrate the requirement of unpaid care to be a part of a normal interference in paid work patterns. Such change can be done through the allocation of rights to weigh on the bargaining powers or to respond to specious prejudices and discrimination based on individual characteristics. However, as Nicole Busby cautions, such a shift in understanding labour relations is substantial because it would entail a "fundamental repositioning of the contract with greater emphasis placed on State intervention as we move from public ethic of care to the provision of a legally recognised right to care." [123] In turn, supporting caring relationships would allow for a shift in understanding of what is valued (not just income and wealth) and would support the full development of all individuals' human capabilities.[124] Thus, the capability approach is not enough by itself; it needs to be supported and complemented by an ethic of care.

The ethic of care

This section moves on to consider whether traditional rights can be interpreted through an "alternative lens" that understands, emphasises and values the responsibility and the ties that bind us to one another as a human community. Such alternative lens might come from the ethic of care[125] that focuses on attentiveness, trust, responsiveness to need, narrative nuance, and cultivating caring relations and has "at its core a central mandate to care for the relationships that sustain life".[126] Whereas an ethic of justice seeks a fair solution between competing individual interests and rights, an ethic of care sees the interests of carers and the cared for as importantly intertwined rather than as simply competing.[127]

The ethic of care is not a novel approach as its origin can be traced back to the work of Augustine[128] but its contemporary interpretation originates from developmental psychologist Carol Gilligan's seminal work in the 1980s on care

---

123 Nicole Busby, *A Right to Care?: Unpaid Care Work in European Employment Law* (OUP 2011) 36.
124 Martha Nussbaum, *Sex and Social Justice* (OUP 1999).
125 Carol Gilligan, *In a Different Voice: Psychological Theory and Women's Development* (Harvard University Press 1982). See also Selma Sevenhuijsen, *Citizenship and the Ethics of Care: Feminist Considerations on Justice, Morality, and Politics* (Psychology Press 1998); Virginia Held, *The Ethic of Care: Personal, Political, and Global* (OUP 2006); Robin West, *Caring for Justice* (NYU Press 1997).
126 Robin West, *Caring for Justice* (NYU Press 1997) 8.
127 Virginia Held, *The Ethic of Care: Personal, Political, and Global* (OUP 2006) 15.
128 Luigina Mortari, *Filosofia della Cura* (Raffaello Cortina 2015); Milton Mayeroff, *On Caring* (HarperCollins Publishers 1972). See also Jonathan Herring, *Caring and the Law* (Hart Publishing 2013) 47.

Conceptualising care 45

and morality, *In a Different Voice*.[129] This work challenged traditional gendered assumptions about moral development and reasoning in young boys and girls. Gilligan developed her moral theory in contrast to that of Lawrence Kohlberg,[130] whose model had established that boys were found to be more morally mature than girls. In particular, he argued that women became overly concerned with their conflicting responsibilities towards particular individuals, rather than viewing their position in abstract universal terms like men.[131] As a result, women were rarely able to move beyond a stage of moral development where "morality is conceived in interpersonal terms and goodness is equated with helping and pleasing others".[132]

Gilligan's theory offered an alternative perspective, namely that men and women have tendencies to view morality in different terms. She asserted that traditional moral approaches were male-biased, and that the voice of care was a legitimate alternative to the justice perspective of liberal human rights theory. Her theory claimed women tended to emphasise empathy and compassion over the notions of deontological/Kantian morality and consequentialist/utilitarian ethic privileged in Kohlberg's methodology. She argued that this did not necessarily lead to the conclusion that females were less efficient or developed than males: rather men and women are speaking with "different voices".

The ethic of care, however attractive, cannot provide a "blanket solution". To start with, the theory on the ethic of care is vast and "there is no complete agreement over what ... [it] means".[133] Furthermore, Gilligan's work has been further developed and criticised.[134] In particular, its valorisation of a female voice

---

129 Carol Gilligan, *In a Different Voice: Psychological Theory and Women's Development* (Harvard University Press 1982) 18.
130 Lawrence Kohlberg, *Essays in Moral Development Volume 1: The Philosophy of Moral Development* (Harper and Row 1981); Lawrence Kohlberg, *Essays in Moral Development Volume 2: The Psychology of Moral Development* (Harper and Row 1984).
131 Louise Campbell-Brown, "The Ethic of Care" (1997) 4 *UCL Jurisprudence Review* 272, 272.
132 Carol Gilligan, *In a Different Voice: Psychological Theory and Women's Development* (Harvard University Press 1982) 18; Fiona Kelly, "Conceptualising the Child through an 'Ethic of Care': Lessons for Family Law" (2005) 1 *Int JLC* 375, 386. For a critique of Kolberg's approach applied to the moral development the impact of concepts of moral responsibility and maturity, in relation to the development of the legal norms applied to children see Nuno Ferreira, "Putting the Age of Criminal and Tort Liability into Context: A Dialogue between Law and Psychology" (2008) 16 *Intl J Children's Rights* 29.
133 Jonathan Herring, *Caring and the Law* (Hart Publishing 2013) 49.
134 See for instance: Joan Tronto, *Moral Boundaries: A Political Argument for an Ethic of Care* (Routledge 1993); Virginia Held, *The Ethic of Care: Personal, Political, and Global* (OUP 2006); Feder Kittay, *Love's Labour Essays on Women, Equality and Dependency* (Routledge 1999); Sara Ruddick, "Maternal Thinking" (1980) 6 *Feminist Studies* 342. See Linda Kerber, "Some Cautionary Words for Historians" (1986) 11 *Signs: J Women in Culture and Society* 304, esp. 309; Catherine Greeno and Eleanor Maccoby, "How Different Is the 'Different Voice'?" (1986) 11 *Signs: J Women in Culture and Society* 310, esp. 315; Zella Luria, "A Methodological Critique" (1986) 11 *Signs: J Women in Culture and Society* 316,

has been portrayed as problematic.[135] Indeed, not all females are innately caring, self-sacrificing and nurturing, or any more capable of these traits than men.[136] Nevertheless, Gilligan's work has contributed to raising questions about the universal standards and impartiality of morality. It rests on the understanding that life is a series of mutual and interdependent relationships without which we would not exist.[137] These relationships carry responsibilities[138] and should be used as a starting point to revaluate legal norms. The ethic of care underscores the importance of a response by operating a shift in moral perspective; the question is not anymore "what is just?" or "is it my right to do X?"[139] but "how do I respond?" and "what is my proper obligation within the context of this relationship?". Thus, the ethic of care can offer an important contribution to the discourse on care and the law.[140] Placing care at the centre of the legal discourse allows us to think about the role of law and the nature of rights in different ways, and it could radically transform institutions and legal rights as well as the values that underpin them.[141] It can provide a useful means of critiquing individualistic approaches to law and policy. In practical terms, the ethic of care can support relationships by contextualising and promoting the well-being of care-givers and care-receivers in a network of social relations. In particular, it can contribute to making care visible to the policy-maker as well as accountable. Indeed, the "historical and ongoing failure to include the ethic of care when drafting social policy"[142] continues to be

---

esp. 318; Carol Stack, "The Culture of Gender: Women and Men of Color" (1986) 11 *Signs: J Women in Culture and Society* 321, 324. All of the above are cited by Joan Tronto, "Beyond Gender Difference to a Theory of Care" (1987) 12 *Signs: J Women in Culture and Society* 644. It is important, however, to clarify, as does Tronto, that Gilligan did not consider the ethic of care as a category of gender difference. While she argues that justice and care should be included in our understanding of morality, she also explains that in the context of her studies, "the focus on care ... is characteristically a female phenomenon". Carol Gilligan, "'Reply' in 'On In a Different Voice: An Interdisciplinary Forum'" (1986) 11 *Signs: J Women in Culture and Society* 324.

135 See discussion in Vanessa Munro, *Law and Politics and the Perimeter: Re-Evaluating Key Debates in Feminist Theory* (Hart Publishing 2007) 23–33.
136 Indeed, there is ample evidence that the voices of gender are far less different than Gilligan suggests – see Deborah Rhode, *Justice and Gender* (Harvard University Press 1991) 309. See also the discussion in "Setting the scene: 'Everyone cares. Everyone is cared for'".
137 Christopher Meyers, "Cruel Choices: Autonomy and Critical Care Decision-Making" (2004) 18 *Bioethics* 104.
138 Carol Gilligan, *In a Different Voice: Psychological Theory and Women's Development* (Harvard University Press 1982).
139 Virginia Held, *The Ethic of Care: Personal, Political, and Global* (OUP 2006).
140 See also Clare Ungerson, "Cash in Care" in Madonna Harrington Meyer (ed), *Care Work: Gender, Labor and the Welfare State* (Routledge 2000).
141 Selma Sevenhuijsen, "The Place of Care: the Relevance of the Feminist Ethic of Care for Social Policy" (2003) 4 *Feminist Theory* 179, 181, who argues that care is being "relocated from women to men".
142 Grace James, "Family-friendly Employment Laws (Re) assessed: The Potential of Care Ethics" (2016) 45 *Industrial Law Journal* 477.

reflected in a normative framework that promotes, prioritises and rewards autonomy, individualism and market-making above care-giving which continue to be at odds with the reality for many people.

Compassion, solidarity and dignity as an expression of the ethic of care

In practice, the ethic of care is expressed in many concepts such as compassion, dignity and solidarity. Although not strictly speaking legal, these concepts have been considered in legal contexts and we argue that taken together, they can be helpful to strengthen the legal position of carers.[143]

Compassion, from the Latin word "passio" meaning "suffer", literally means "with passion". There is a wealth of academic literature that discusses compassion. In the main, it concords that compassion is not a tangible legal concept. Rather, in the words of Nussbaum, it is "the painful *emotion* occasioned by the awareness of another person's undeserved misfortune."[144] Sir Alan Ward links compassion with the "*feeling* of concern for another who is stricken with misfortune accompanied by a strong desire to alleviate suffering."[145] There is agreement that the concept of compassion is linked to that of care. However, "care will primarily focus on activities, rather than motivations, while … compassion primarily focuses on emotions leading to care".[146] The question is whether, although not a legal concept, compassion can play a role in the legal discourse. Indeed, although occasionally it makes its way into legal judgements and legislation, compassion is not as such a legal concept.[147] We argue that it should not be used as an end in itself, but as a tool to interpret rights. Compassion does not imply that emotion triumphs over reason. It must be distinguished from concepts such as pity, sympathy or empathy. Rather, it means that a decision is reached after the concerns of all parties involved have been taken into consideration and adequately understood. In the context of care, this would mean that the interests of both care-giver and care recipient would have to be evaluated and taken into account with a view of achieving the best possible balance.

The concept of human dignity can also provide a useful lens to interpret rights when interpreting rights related to care. It broadly indicates "something that virtually all people want",[148] and many of us would feel "horror at [its]

---

143 See the discussion in Chapter 5.
144 Martha Nussbaum, *Upheavals of Thought: The Intelligence of Emotions* (CUP 2001) 301. Our emphasis.
145 Sir Alan Ward, "A Judicial perspective on the Place for Compassion in Family Law" (Institute for Advance Legal Studies Symposium, *Compassion: Child and Family Law*, 13 July 2017). Our emphasis.
146 Jonathan Herring, "Compassion, Ethic of Care and Legal Rights" (2017) 13 *Int J L Context* 158, 159.
147 The potential for incorporating compassion in the law has been explored. See Mary Schroeder, "Compassion on Appeal" (1990) 22 *Ariz St L J* 45; Claire L'Heureux-Dubè, "Making a Difference: The Pursuit of a Compassionate Justice" (1997) 31 *UBC Law Rev* 1.
148 David Mattson and Susan Clark, "Human Dignity in Concept and Practice" (2011) 44 *Policy Sciences* 303, 313.

violation",[149] yet human dignity is complex to define. The meaning of dignity has been discussed in depth by several commentators.[150] For the purpose of our argument, it denotes the intrinsic worth of human beings that applies to everybody for the simple reason of being humans, an end in themselves. It is particularly important in the context of caring relationships because, ultimately our perception of dignity is not only shaped by ourselves but also by our interactions with others. Dignity is moreover important when it comes to care because it is a valuable tool to combat stereotyping. Stereotypes are generalised views or preconceptions of attributes or characteristics possessed by, or roles that should be performed by, members of a particular group[151] and which can have a detrimental socio-economic impact on certain individuals. For example, the stereotype that "women are caring" can result in women being clustered into care related jobs.

Perhaps paradoxically, despite the complexity surrounding its interpretation, dignity has a clear legal presence. Reference to dignity appears in both international and domestic level. For example, the Preamble of the Universal Declaration on Human Rights refers to "the inherent dignity and the equal and inalienable rights of all members of the human family". The concept is further reiterated in Article 1, which states "[a]ll human beings are born free and equal in dignity and rights". Dignity has also been described as "the very essence" of the European Convention on Human Rights.[152] At the domestic level, courts have grappled with the concept of dignity in several contexts ranging from the dignity of same-sex couples,[153] patients,[154] prisoners,[155] detainees,[156] asylum seekers,[157] women seeking abortions,[158] people wishing to end their lives,[159] and, very recently, severely ill children.[160] The concept of human dignity has made its way to the EU legal system,[161] where it has become apparent that it represents a crucial principle that

---

149 David Mattson and Susan Clark, "Human Dignity in Concept and Practice" (2011) 44 *Policy Sciences* 303.
150 For an overview of the literature see David Mattson and Susan Clark, "Human Dignity in Concept and Practice" (2011) 44 *Policy Sciences* 303.
151 Rebecca Cook and Simone Cusak, *Gender Stereotyping Transnational Legal Perspectives* (University of Pennsylvania Press 2010).
152 *Pretty v United Kingdom* [2002] ECHR 427, para 65.
153 *Hall v Bull* [2012] EWCA Civ 83.
154 *R (on the application of Burke) v General Medical Council* [2005] EWCA Civ 1003.
155 *Grant v Ministry of Justice* [2011] EWHC 3379 (QB).
156 *R (on the Application of (HA) (Nigeria)) v Secretary of State for the Home Department* [2012] EWHC 979 (Admin).
157 *NS v Secretary of State for the Home Department* [2012] 2 CML Rev 9.
158 *RR v Poland* (2011) EHRR 31.
159 *Nicklinson v Ministry of Justice* [2012] EWHC 304 (QB).
160 *Alder Hey Children's NHS Foundation Trust v Evans* [2018] EWHC 308 (Fam).
161 See the discussion in Chapter 5.

can highlight and protect the needs of vulnerable individuals engaged in caring relationships, be those cared for and/or carers.[162]

Another useful concept for care is that of solidarity. It refers to the sharing of both advantages, such as prosperity, and burdens which should be distributed equally and justly among society's members. Indeed, the EU Charter of Fundamental Rights expressly places Article 33 on the Right to Reconcile Work and Family Life under the heading of "Solidarity". Solidarity is also mentioned in Article 3 TEU, which states that the Union "shall promote … solidarity between generations and protection of the rights of the child." This is an expression of the principle that "providing care for people over the life cycle is a social responsibility, an obligation that reflects our ties to one another as a human community."[163]

Ultimately, compassion, dignity and solidarity are concerned with the wellbeing of individuals. In this context, well-being is intended not merely as physical, but also as psychological and emotional.

Making care visible and accountable

> It is only with the heart that one can see rightly; what is essential is invisible to the eye.[164]

Although not above criticism, Gilligan's work and the ethic of care in general has powerfully showed the weakness of using the concept of justice and the instruments of rights as the exclusive basis for morality.[165] The public/private dichotomy that traditionally underpins legislation has placed care into the domestic sphere where it has been undervalued as a private female emotion and excluded from the more visible domain of the public sphere. Gilligan has opened the way to the reinstatement of the care perspective into the political arena. In doing so, care ethic is about making visible these invisible realities which are not being seen and which are not articulated into theory (or more exactly which have been excluded from theory). The aim of the ethic of care is almost an anthropological project designed not to discover what is invisible but rather to reveal visible realities which we do not see because they are too close and ordinary.[166] Addressing issues related to care requires looking at the ordinary life of human beings. The ethic of care forces us

---

162 Moon Gay and Robin Allen, "Dignity Discourse in Discrimination Law: A Better Route to Equality?" (2006) 6 *EHRLR* 610.
163 Johanna Brenner, "Democritizing Care" in Janet Gornick and Marcia Meyers (eds), *Gender Equality, Transforming Family Divisions of Labor* (Verso 2009) 189.
164 Antoine de Saint-Exupéry, *Le Petit Prince* (Gallimard 1946) 92.
165 Sandra Laugier, "Le sujet du *care*: vulnérabilité et expression ordinaires" in Pascale Molinier, Sandra Laugier and Patricia Paperman (eds), *Qu'est-ce que le Care? Souci des autres, sensibilité, résponsibilité* (Payot et Rivages 2009).
166 Ibid.

50 *Conceptualising care*

to pay attention to what is happening in everyday life and which we are not seeing because it is too close to our eyes.[167]

The invisibility of care-work, moreover, stems from its lack of recognition, which in turn leads to a devaluation of the work itself, a depreciation of the care provider's role and ultimately of the care recipient too.[168] Angelo Soares reminds us that the invisibility of care-work does not correspond to the non-existence of care providers in the paid employment market or in the domestic sphere, but rather to an absence of social and organisational recognition. Relying on Honneth's work, he links invisibility to a question of recognition:[169] "dominants express their social superiority by ignoring those that they dominate."[170] Recognition is linked to the acknowledgement that one's job is accomplished, useful, and of a certain standard.[171] Therefore, the non-recognition of care-work implies not only that the work done is devalued but also that the person doing the job is disregarded. This is a form of social disdain. By contrast, the ethic of care places care at the centre of the human experience. Thus, the ethic of care contributes to the social and legal visibility of care.

Care and care-work are difficult to monitor and to measure under traditional accounting methods. Accounting requires proof that the work has been done and that it has been done with high quality. However, care-work includes many dimensions that are not easily quantifiable in numbers, including love, trust and diplomacy. In addition, the requirement of cooperation between the care provider and the care recipient, the need for collaboration between the market and the unpaid care, and the personal emotional characteristics of care-work mean that in reality it is difficult to make an objective judgement with regards to the quality of care-work. It is therefore difficult to manage something that is not easily quantified. Yet quality of care is key to the adoption of legal measures.[172]

Here again, the ethic of care can help with shifting the emphasis to the value of care-work. An analysis of the ethic of care reveals that care-work goes further than simple consideration of specialisation or skills. Care-giving involves by necessity

---

167 Michel Foucault, "La philosophy analytique de la politique" (1978) in *Dits et écrits, 1976–1988* (Gallimard 2001).
168 Charlotte O'Brien, "Confronting the Care Penalty: The Cause for Extending Reasonable Adjustment Rights along the Disability/Care Continuum" (2012) 34(1) *Journal of Social Welfare & Family Law* 5.
169 Angelo Soares, *Les (in)visibles de la santé* (Université du Québec à Montréal 2010) 6.
170 Our translation from: "Les dominants expriment leur supériorité sociale en ne percevant pas ceux qu'ils dominent." Axel Honneth, *La société du mépris: vers une nouvelle théorie critique* (la Découverte 2006).
171 Angelo Soares, *Les (in)visibles de la santé* (Université du Québec à Montréal 2010); Christophe Dejours, "Intelligence ouvrière et organisation du travail (À propos du modèle japonais de production)" in Helena Sumiko Hirata (ed), *Autour du "modèle" japonais – Automatisation, nouvelles formes d'organisation et de relations de travail* (L'Harmattan 1992).
172 Council Recommendation 92/241/EEC of 31 March 1992 on child care, O.J. [1992] L123/16.

work done with the heart. Care-work includes ethics, love, common sense and attachment. The problem is that there is a semantic deficit when we try to define the caring relations that take place between human beings. Are we talking about the heart, a form of courage, a vital force? The subject of care is linked to the subconscious: care is a form of fragile sublimation. Caring for someone else is an expansion of the self, in which it is impossible not to develop attachment feelings. As such, care-work can be placed on the boundary between professional work and love. Thus, it requires perilous negotiation and management of feelings and emotions. People who care often also love the person they care for, and vice versa.

Paradoxically, experienced and/or professional care providers are not always able to articulate for themselves and for others the complexity of their activities. The kind of work done around care-giving is mostly repetitive, constant and discrete; it is only when the work is not done or not done well that it becomes visible and that everyone feels free to criticise and comment. For instance, a mother who does not love her children, a cold nurse or an unconcerned educator are shocking, whereas love, attention and availability from these same persons are considered to be normal.[173]

If the quality (and the quantity) of care is dependent on the personal and emotional relationship between the care provider and the care recipient, this emotional attachment also puts the care provider in a vulnerable position. When care-work is not just the subject of an economic exchange (which it rarely is), the emotional attachment makes it difficult, if not impossible, for the care provider to withdraw or even to threaten to withhold it. In Nancy Folbre's words, care-givers become "prisoners of love".[174] On this basis, care providers can be taken advantage of because not only are they unable to negotiate for adequate economic compensation, but also because love can be a more powerful motivator than money.[175] The historical relationship between gender and care means that these prisoners of love are disproportionately women.

The ethic of care has provided feminists with tools to unpack the elements of the caring relationship. While, traditionally, altruism and love have explained who does the care, the ethic of care itself takes into account the work done and its unequal reparation.[176] The ethic of care is linked to concrete situations, reflected by the actions of taking care of and caring for someone. It is work. The law does not acknowledge very well this work which is partly relational, partly emotional, even

---

[173] Nathalie Benelli and Marianne Modak, "Analyser un objet invisible: le travail de care" (2010) 51 *Revue française de sociologie* 39.

[174] Nancy Folbre, "Reforming Care" in Janet Gornick and Marcia Meyers (eds), *Gender Equality, Transforming Family Divisions of Labor* (Verso 2009) 114.

[175] Julie Nelson, "Of Market and Martyrs; Is It OK to Pay Well for Care?" (1999) 5 *Feminist Economics* 43; Anthony Heyes, "The Economics of Vocation or 'Why is a Badly Paid Nurse a Good Nurse?'" (2005) 24 *J Health Economics* 561; Julie Nelson and Nancy Folbre, "Why a Well-Paid Nurse is a Better Nurse!" (2006) 24 *J Nursing Economics* 127.

[176] Pascale Molinier, "Quel est le bon témoin du *care*?" in Pascale Molinier, Sandra Laugier, Patricia Paperman (eds), *Qu'est-ce que le Care? Souci des Autres, Sensibilité, Responsabilité* (Petite Bibliothèque Payot 2009).

if it is work. Adopting an ethic of care would allow for the reconciliation between emotions and rationality in policy design. It would provide a basis for enabling caring relationships by protecting care-givers and valorising their work. This can offer refreshing insights and policy recommendations.[177]

Conclusion

Despite the fact that there is widespread agreement over the role of care as a central element to the development of society, the current policy and normative framework still struggles to grapple with it. As such, it continues to fail to value care and to protect and empower carers. This is true at the domestic level and even more so at EU level. This chapter has identified several reasons for this. First, the language of rights is not suited to this discourse. Second, conceptually the current normative system remains grounded in the public/private dichotomy, where care remains relegated to the private sphere, invisible and unaccounted for. The feminist debates have been instrumental in highlighting this but have not triggered the necessary changes to valorise care and care-work within a normative framework. *Prima facie* a solution could come from a specific endorsement of the dual earner-carer model. Again, despite being celebrated this model has not succeeded, and in reality the unencumbered worker model remains dominant. A capability approach might help understanding why this is the case. However, as this approach is not a legal concept, *per se*, it remains insufficient to challenge the *status quo*.

We have suggested that the ethic of care, by having "at its core a central mandate to care for the relationships that sustain life",[178] should underpin a rights-based strategy and give "texture" to the existing rights. By valuing relationships and making care visible and accountable, the ethic of care would provide a valuable theoretical contribution to impact on the design of law making relating to care relationships.

---

[177] Nuno Ferreira, "The Human Face of the European Union. Are EU law and Policy Humane Enough? An Introduction" in Nuno Ferreira and Dora Kostakopoulou (eds), *The Human Face of the European Union: Are EU Law and Policy Humane Enough?* (CUP 2016).
[178] Robin West, *Caring for Justice* (NYU Press 1997) 8.

2 The emerging EU childcare strategy

Introduction

This chapter focuses on the European Union's (EU) engagement with childcare with a view to assess whether it has developed an efficient and coherent strategy that recognises and values the caring relationship. Although childcare is central to some of its fundamental policies, in particular gender equality and employment, the EU lacks express competencies in this area.[1] Childcare has historically been the exclusive domain of the Member States, which have traditionally been in sole charge of developing their childcare policies. The advantage is that, as Member States have a better understanding of the political, cultural and economic landscape of their own countries than the EU, they are more in tune with their needs and priorities. The drawback is that national levels of engagement vary depending on factors such as economic performance, traditions and cultural values.[2] This leads to variable results regarding the availability and the use of childcare services and, in turn, this impacts on EU policies. It is therefore unsurprising that the EU, despite its lack of competence has – timidly – intervened. Thus, over the years, a tentative EU childcare strategy has slowly emerged, and all EU institutions have played a role. As will be explored in this chapter, the Council and the European Parliament have provided crucial impetus;[3] the European Commission has put forward important initiatives[4] and the Court of Justice of the European Union

---

1 Nicole Busby, *A Right to Care? Unpaid Care Work in European Employment Law* (OUP 2011); Mark Thomson, "Social Regimes and Gender Equality: Childcare in the EU" in David Mayes and Mark Thomson (eds), *The Cost of Children* (Edward Elgar 2012).
2 European Commission Recommendation, 2013/112/EU of 20 February 2013, *Investing in children: breaking the cycle of disadvantage*, O.J. [2013] L59/5; Social Protection Committee, "Social Europe – Aiming for inclusive growth – Annual report of the Social Protection Committee on the social situation in the European Union (2014)" (European Union, 10 March 2015).
3 See for instance the European Platform for Investing in Children (EPIC), http://europa.eu/epic/studies-reports/childcare/index_en.htm. Accessed 17 December 2018.
4 Most recently see the European Commission initiative on Work-Life Balance consisting of a proposal for a Directive and a Communication (COM(2017) 252 final) to support work-life balance for working parents and carers (COM(2017) 253 final).

(CJEU or the Court), has contributed by highlighting the value of care.[5] This emerging strategy has, however, been prompted by different rationales and this has not helped coherent development. To analyse this strategy, this chapter has identified four phases, each of them triggered by a specific event that has shaped this area.

It is organised in two sections. Section one (Defining childcare) seeks to define the concept of childcare for the purpose of EU law: this is essential to discuss the development of the strategy. In this section the difficulties, different rationales and the governance of childcare are discussed. Section two (The development of the EU childcare strategy) analyses how the different rationales and forms of governance have affected the development of the childcare strategy. For this purpose, it is divided into subsections that look at the main phases of the childcare strategy. This chapter concludes that, at the time of writing, the EU childcare strategy is neither efficient nor coherent.

Defining childcare

There is no reference to childcare in the EU Treaty. Thus, to start with, we need to identify what childcare is for the purpose of EU law. It is a deceptively easy concept to define as the 'care and supervision of children',[6] yet its boundaries and meaning remain difficult to assess at EU level, for two main reasons. First, this is because of the broad diversity of the very meaning of childcare at domestic level, and second because of the different rationales underpinning the concept. As a result, different types of governance are used in this area. This section seeks to clarify the boundaries of this concept.

The diversity of childcare arrangements in the EU Member States

At the domestic level, childcare is regulated by an array of arrangements that vary considerably amongst Member States. Each country has its own unique system of provisions and structures that is influenced by a wide range of criteria including cultural aspects, social norms relating to the role of women, education and socio-economic backgrounds of the parents, as well as the age of the child.[7] Childcare can encompass elements of welfare and early education policies. Whilst some Member States draw a clear distinction between the *care* of young children and the *education* of older children, others integrate the two elements. Depending on how it is framed, childcare initiatives will receive policy support and funding accordingly. Furthermore, childcare arrangements are structured along a continuum of, often closely interconnected, formal and/or informal criteria. Formal childcare is a service provided by non-family members

---

5 See for example: Case 85/96 *María Martínez Sala v Freistaat Bayern*. ECLI:EU:C:1998:217.
6 Collins English Dictionary, *Complete and Unabridged 2012 Digital Edition*.
7 Barbara Janta, *Caring for Children in Europe* (European Union 2014).

and organised and/or controlled by public or private structures such as nurseries, preschools and registered childminders. Such services typically include elements of preschool education and sometimes are formally included in the schooling process. Formal childcare can be public or private: in some Member States, childcare is not exclusively provided by the public sector.[8] By contrast, informal childcare is provided by family, often grandparents, or friends.[9] Informal childcare is often neither paid nor subject to state control over quality, child protection and taxation.[10]

The use of formal and informal childcare varies across the Member States. In many EU countries, informal arrangements represent the main type of childcare for very young children and babies.[11] More often, the two supplement each other: informal childcare can be used to cover the care of children before and after school/nursery hours, as an emergency cover or as back-up when formal childcare arrangements break down.[12] Generally speaking, informal childcare is used on a part-time basis and therefore is unlikely to be able to support (women's) full-time employment.[13] Importantly, the two forms of childcare are intricately linked to one another: informal childcare arrangements impact on the policy development of formal childcare provisions and vice versa.

To assess the complete extent of both these types of childcare is complex, as there is no common standard for collecting data and statistics in this area. Yet there is little doubt that a childcare strategy that could deliver affordable, good quality and flexible childcare and provide parents with options can influence their choice of arrangements.

Challenges and shifting rationales

Rather than being an aim in itself, the childcare strategy at EU level has developed as a response to and is a 'by-product'[14] of a number of challenges raised in the

---

8 Ibid.
9 Karen Glaser and others, "Grandparenting in Europe: Family Policy and Grandparents' Role in Providing Childcare" (Grandparents plus 2013); Maaike Jappens and Jan Van Bavel, "Regional Family Norms and Child Care by Grandparents in Europe" (2012) 27 *Demographic Research* 85. See also Louise Spitz, "Grandparents: Their Role in the 21st Century Families" (2012) 42 *Family L* 1254.
10 Jill Rutter and Ben Evans, *Informal Childcare: Choice or Chance? A Literature Review* (Daycare Trust 2011).
11 Such as the Netherlands, Greece, Portugal, Romania and Cyprus; see Melinda Mills and others, "Use of Childcare Services in the EU Member States and Progress Towards the Barcelona Targets (Short Statistical Report 1)" (European Union 2014).
12 Ibid.
13 Ibid.
14 Eulalia Rubio, "A Policy in its Infancy: The Case for Strengthening and Rethinking EU Action on Childhood" (Notre Europe 2007).

context of broader policies.[15] Thus, its development has been reactive rather than proactive, incoherent and relatively slow. Indeed, the pace of development of the childcare strategy has coincided with the relevance and perceived importance or urgency of each of these challenges at any point in time. Furthermore, over the years, the strategy has been shaped and influenced by various overlapping and yet sometimes opposing rationales, namely: gender equality, economic imperatives and children's rights. In any event, economic considerations have constantly been prevalent in any decisions related to the advancement of the childcare strategy. These rationales will now be analysed in turn.

Gender equality and childcare

Gender equality is often seen as the natural rationale to underpin a childcare strategy: traditionally the care of young children has been – and still is – largely an activity done by women. Thus, it is women across Europe who are more likely to experience difficulties in reconciling their caring responsibilities with paid work.[16]

There is consensus that women need to be supported in performing childcare. Whilst care feminism argues that care in itself should be celebrated and valued, employment feminism has consistently argued that caring obligations have hindered women's ability to participate in the labour market, to acquire financial independence and, ultimately, to achieve gender equality.[17] In this context, a childcare strategy, in particular childcare services, can be considered an essential tool to achieve gender equality. Indeed, there is no doubt that structured, quality childcare facilities can provide women with the option and the time to participate in the employment market.[18] The creation of childcare services alone, however, is

---

15 Elissaveta Radulova, "The Construction of EU's Childcare Policy through the Open Method of Coordination" in Sandra Kröger (ed), *What We Have Learnt: Advances, Pitfalls and Remaining Questions in OMC Research*, (EIOP 2009) 13 http://eiop.or.at/eiop/texte/2009-013a.htm. Accessed 21 July 2019; Eulalia Rubio, "A Policy in Its Infancy: The Case for Strengthening and Rethinking EU Action on Childhood" (Notre Europe 2007); Carol Lee Bacchi, *Women, Policy and Politics* (SAGE 1999); Jane Lewis, "Work/Family Reconciliation, Equal Opportunities and Social Policies: The Interpretation of Policy Trajectories at the EU Level and the Meaning of Gender Equality" (2006) 13 *J Public Policy* 420; European Commission, Report of 3 October 2008, "Implementation of the Barcelona Objectives Concerning Facilities for Pre-School-Age Children", COM(2008) 638.
16 Annick Masselot, Eugenia Caracciolo di Torella and Susanne Burri, "Thematic Report of the European Network of Legal Experts in the Field of Gender Equality Fighting Discrimination on the Grounds of Pregnancy, Maternity and Parenthood – The Application of EU and National Law in Practice in 33 European Countries" (European Commission 2012); Annick Masselot, "Family Leave: enforcement of the protection against dismissal and unfavourable treatment" (European Commission 2018).
17 See the discussion in Chapter 1.
18 Mary Daly, "A Fine Balance: Women's Labour Market Participation in International Comparison" in Fritz W Scharpf and Vivien E Schmidt (eds), *Welfare and Work in the Open Economy, Vol II: Diverse Responses to Common Challenges* (OUP 2000).

not enough to achieve gender equality. Structural changes – in particular a better sharing and redistribution of domestic tasks between men and women in the private sphere – are also necessary in order to provide better opportunities for both parents.[19] If women continue to bear the vast majority of domestic unpaid care-work in the home as well as working in the labour market, regardless of the availability of childcare structures, they will simply accumulate paid and unpaid work and be liable to do the "second shift".[20] This, rather than promoting gender equality, can exacerbate inequality. To be truly underpinned by a gender equality rationale, the development of childcare structure must be complemented by measures designed to equalise the sharing and redistribute domestic tasks between partners: otherwise, any intervention will remain merely cosmetic.

The economic rationale of childcare

If gender equality might seem the obvious rationale to regulate childcare, it would be simplistic to ignore that such rationale has always had a distinctly economic flavour. This was already clear in the 1980s and has been a constant feature of any EU childcare initiatives since.

In turn, the economic rationale of childcare is instrumental in addressing three different yet interlinked issues: to encourage economic growth and raise employment rates, to reform welfare systems and reduce the culture of dependency and to address demographic concerns.

As for the first issue, the EU has historically been faced with the need to increase employment rates, especially women's. The 2000 Lisbon Council set the objective of raising female employment rates from 51% to 60% by 2010;[21] this was reiterated in the Europe 2020 Strategy.[22] The latter, although it set a gender-neutral target of 75% employment rates for the 20–64 age group, acknowledged that raising the level of women in employment was essential to achieve such a target. Simply put, if women are free from their caring responsibilities, they can take part in paid employment. For example, in 2014, across Europe, a quarter of women with

---

19 Sandra Fredman, "Reversing Roles: Bringing Men into the Frame" (2014) 10 *Intl J L Context* 442; Jane Lewis and Susanna Giullari, "The Adult Worker Model Family, Gender Equality and Care: The Search for New Policy Principles and the Possibilities and Problems of a Capabilities Approach" (2005) 34 *Economy and Society* 76.

20 For a discussion of the second shift, see also Tamara Hervey and Jo Shaw, "Women, Work and Care: Women's Dual Role and Double Burden in EC Sex Equality Law" (1998) 8 *Journal of European Social Policy* 43; Joan Williams, *Unbending Gender: Why Family and Work Conflict and What to Do About It* (OUP 2000) and Fiona Carmichael and Susan Charles, "The Opportunity Costs of Informal Care: Does Gender Matter?" (2003) 22 *J Health Economics* 781.

21 European Council, "Lisbon European Council 23 and 24 March 2000 Presidency Conclusions" (23–24 March 2000) www.europarl.europa.eu/summits/lis1_en.htm. Accessed 25 July 2019.

22 Communication from the Commission of 3 March 2010, "Europe 2020 Strategy: A Strategy for Smart, Sustainable and Inclusive Growth", COM(2010) 2020.

young children claimed that they were not in employment because of the lack of childcare services.[23]

Closely interlinked to the need to stimulate economic growth and to raise employment rates is the need to reform inefficient welfare regimes. If individuals (in reality, women) are engaged in paid employment, they will contribute to the functioning of the welfare regime as well as being less likely to claim social security benefits.[24] We have already explored how the EU aims to promote a dual earner/carer model which assumes that individuals, male or female, should be able to look after their dependents and, at the same time, take up paid work.[25] Encouraging (if not compelling) participation in paid employment is generally considered to promote financial independence, to help with the cost of care, to provide individuals with personal satisfaction and increase self-esteem. The Commission stated that "economic independence is a prerequisite for enabling both women and men to exercise control over their lives and to make genuine choices",[26] and counteracts a "culture of dependency".[27] In reality, and especially in a context where many women remain economically dependent on their partners, the assumption underpinning the dual earner/carer is simply not true.[28] The assumption is further challenged by changes in family formations such as the increase in the number of single parents, particularly single mothers. More generally, the accommodation of care-work under the dual carer/earner model remains a major concern. This can only be achieved by transferring traditional unpaid care to the formal paid sector,[29]

---

23 Melinda Mills and others, "Use of Childcare Services in the EU Member States and Progress towards the Barcelona Targets (Short Statistical Report 1)" (European Union 2014) 17.
24 Jay Wiggan, "Telling Stories of 21st Century Welfare: The UK Coalition Government and the Neo-Liberal Discourse of Worklessness and Dependency" (2012) 32 *Critical Social Policy* 383; Emmanuele Pavolini and others, "From Austerity to Permanent Strain? The EU and Welfare State Reform in Italy and Spain" (2015) 13 *Comparative European Politics* 56; Julie Windebank and Adam Whitworth, "Social Welfare and the Ethics of Austerity in Europe: Justice, Ideology and Equality" (2014) 22 *J Contemporary European Studies* 99.
25 See Jane Lewis and Susanna Giullari, "The Adult Worker Model Family, Gender Equality and Care: The Search for New Policy Principles and the Possibilities and Problems of a Capabilities Approach" (2005) 34 *Economy and Society* 76.
26 Communication from the Commission of 21 September 2010, "Strategy for Equality between Women and Men 2010–2015", COM(2010) 491 final, 5.
27 Mary Daly, "What Adult Worker Model? A Critical Look at Recent Social Policy Reform in Europe from a Gender and Family Perspective" (2011) 18 *Social Politics: Intl Studies in Gender, State & Society* 1. See also European Commission, "Increasing Labour Force Participation and Promoting Active Ageing", COM(2002) 9 (Publications Office of the European Union 2002).
28 Mary Daly, "What Adult Worker Model? A Critical Look at Recent Social Policy Reform in Europe from a Gender and Family Perspective" (2011) 18 *Social Politics: Intl Studies in Gender, State & Society* 1. See also Chapter 1.
29 Jane Lewis and Susanna Giullari, "The Adult Worker Model Family, Gender Equality and Care: The Search for New Policy Principles and the Possibilities and Problems of a Capabilities Approach" (2005) 34 *Economy and Society* 76.

which has already been identified as a potential source of new jobs.[30] In this context, childcare can play a crucial role.

Childcare has also been seen as a tool to address demographic concerns.[31] Indeed, since the 1960s fertility rates have declined steeply below the replacement level in all of the EU Member States.[32] Women in Europe now have fewer children and at a later age. These patterns – combined with an increase in life expectancy – partly explain the slowdown in the EU's population growth and the expected future decline in population size. To explain this phenomenon is rather complex. Traditional demographic theories associate economic hardship with postponement in family formation and reduced fertility rates, and economic growth with high fertility rates.[33] However, these theories have been challenged: the European demographic transition, characterised by industrialisation and economic growth, was accompanied by a rapid decline in fertility rates.[34] This has been attributed to women's emancipation and the increase in female employment rates.[35] This conclusion was based on Gary Becker's economic argument that has become a cornerstone of family economics.[36] It posits that parents not only decide the number of children (child quantity) but they also choose how much money and time they will invest in each child (child quality). As the income level rises, the demand for child quality tends to increase to a much greater extent than the demand for child quantity. It follows that income and fertility rates can have a negative relationship. Under the child quality/quantity relationship model, the economic approach to fertility assumes that women's increase in education and their involvement in the labour market amplifies the opportunity costs of childrearing and therefore this results in failing fertility rates.[37]

However, the application of this theory does not appear to have been the case in all of the EU Member States. In some countries, such as France,

---

30 Ibid, 79.
31 Janneke Plantenga and Chantal Remery, "The Provision of Childcare Services: A Comparative Review of 30 European Countries" (Office for Official Publications of the European Communities 2009).
32 Eurostat, "Fertility Statistics" (11 March 2019) https://ec.europa.eu/eurostat/statistics-explained/index.php/Fertility_statistics. Accessed 20 July 2019.
33 Tommy Bengtsson and Osamu Saito (ed), *Population and the Economy: from Hunger to Modern Economic Growth* (OUP 2000); Michaela Kreyenfeld, Gunnar Andersson and Ariane Pailhé, "Economic Uncertainty and Family Dynamics in Europe: Introduction" (2012) 27 *Demographic Research* 835.
34 Ron Lesthaeghe, "The Unfolding Story of the Second Demographic Transition" (2010) 36 *Population and Development Rev* 211.
35 Ibid.
36 Gary Becker, "An Economic Analysis of Fertility" in Gary Becker (ed), *Demographic and Economic Change in Developed Countries* (Columbia University Press 1960).
37 Gary Becker, *An Economic Analysis of Fertility: The Economic Approach to Human Behavior* (University of Chicago Press 1993) 140.

Sweden and Finland, higher female employment rates feature alongside higher fertility rates.[38]

In any case, it appears that traditional economic approaches to fertility are mitigated by work-family reconciliation law and policies.[39] As women are increasingly entering the employment market, they need law and policies that can make it possible.[40] In this context, childcare services can help women in reconciling their ambition (or need) to have paid employment while at the same time permitting them to have children.[41] Thus, a childcare strategy can be an important tool to raise fertility rates and, in turn, to address the demographic challenge.[42]

Children's rights: reducing child poverty and social exclusion

In addition to gender equality and economic imperatives, in the last decades, the reduction of child poverty has been identified as a third, and equally important, rationale for the purpose of underpinning an EU childcare strategy. Children's rights have been expressly incorporated in the Treaty on European Union (TEU) by Article 3 that states that the EU commitment to "promote the ... protection of the rights of the child". In particular, childcare has gradually been seen as a tentative solution to child poverty and social exclusion as well as a way to boost early education.

Child poverty was first addressed by the European Council in the context of the 2000 Lisbon Agenda[43] when the Open Method of Coordination (OMC) was extended to the field of social exclusion. This resulted from the acknowledgement that child poverty had increased in developed countries partly as a result of labour market transformation from industrial to more flexible service-based economies[44] and partly because of the basic withdrawal of

---

38 Janneke Plantenga and Chantal Remery, "Provision of Childcare Services: A Comparative Review of 30 European Countries" (Office for Official Publications of the European Communities 2009).
39 Ibid; Michaela Kreyenfeld, Gunnar Andersson and Ariane Pailhé, "Economic Uncertainty and Family Dynamics in Europe: Introduction" (2012) 27 *Demographic Research* 835.
40 Organisation for Economic Co-Operation and Development (OECD), "Babies and Bosses – Reconciling Work and Family Life: A Synthesis of Findings for OECD Countries" (OECD 2007) 34.
41 John Ermisch, "Purchased Child Care, Optimal Family Size and Mother's Employment Theory and Econometric Analysis" (1989) 2 *J Population Economics* 79.
42 Anna Christina D'Addio and Marco Mira d'Ercole, "Trends and Determinants of Fertility Rates in OECD Countries: The Role of Policies" (OECD Social Employment and Migration Working Paper No. 27, 2005); Ronald Rindfuss and others, "Child Care Availability and First Birth Timing in Norway" (2007) 44 *Demography* 345.
43 European Council, "Lisbon European Council 23 and 24 March 2000 Presidency Conclusions" (23–24 March 2000) www.europarl.europa.eu/summits/lis1_en.htm. Accessed 22 October 2015.

government funding from key children's services in a bid to save money. These events were coupled with the decline of the traditional family with a parent in paid employment and a parent providing full-time care. Thus, care and early education could no longer be guaranteed by an abundant reserve of full-time housewives whilst, at the same time, employment instability and family formation fluidity meant that children had become more vulnerable than ever to poverty and social exclusion. This was illustrated by figures showing that one in three lone parent families in the EU are at risk of poverty and this impacted on children.[45]

Furthermore, childcare is also considered important in boosting early education and a step towards achieving a more educated society. Whilst the EU has no express competence in matters related to education, many Member States have made links between early childcare and excellence in education. Investing in early education is generally regarded as an effective egalitarian strategy in post-industrial, knowledge-based societies. In developed countries, a relatively high level of education has become a prerequisite for participation in the labour market. Thus, guaranteeing that all children have equal access to education is essential to ensure a basic degree of equality in their adulthood. In addition, early interventions for disadvantaged children have been claimed to reduce school drop-out rates and other antisocial behaviours in teenage years.[46]

The governance of childcare

Due to the lack of specific competence, childcare at EU level has not been addressed by traditional governance involving binding measures such as regulations and directives. Instead, it has been regulated by soft law mainly with recommendations and opinions or policies such as Commission Communications and Council Resolutions.

Compared to traditional instruments, soft instruments are considered to present greater flexibility which results in a better fit with the varied national legal systems of the Member States.[47] Such instruments have also stimulated further integration by providing a useful starting point for discussion.[48] Ultimately, as the

---

44 UNICEF, "Child Poverty in Rich Countries" (Innocenti Report Card No. 6, UNICEF Innocenti Research Centre, Florence 2005).
45 Eurochild, "A Child Rights Approach to Child Poverty – Discussion Paper" (September 2007) www.eurochild.org/fileadmin/public/05_Library/Thematic_priorities/01_Childrens_Rights/ Eurochild/Eurochild_discussion_paper_child_rights__poverty.pdf. Accessed 10 December 2018.
46 Sheldon Danziger and Jane Walfogel, "Investing in Children: What Do We Know? What Should We Do?" (Centre for the Analysis of Social Exclusion, London School of Economics, Case Paper 34, 2000).
47 James Mosher and David Trubek, "Alternative Approaches to Governance in the EU: EU Social Policy and the European Employment Strategy" (2003) 41 *J Com Mar St* 63.

regulation of childcare is linked to socio-cultural characteristics of Member States, soft law is arguably a better instrument than legally binding provisions. In addition, soft law does not incorporate the inevitable compromises which can water down the substantive content of these measures.[49]

However, the benefits of soft law must be weighed against its weak legal status: by lacking binding character, soft law measures can result in a mere declaration of principles. Such measures do not create legally enforceable obligations and are therefore left to the goodwill of the Member States. Finally, soft law provisions create limited incentives for change when the national priorities do not fit with EU initiatives.[50]

In terms of historical development, in 1997 EU Member States undertook to establish a set of common objectives and targets for employment policy. The resulting European Employment Strategy (EES) aimed to create more and better jobs throughout the EU and, in doing so, it had originally placed gender equality at the centre of the emerging employment policy of the EU.[51] In the early days of the EES, women were considered key to the EU economic and demographic challenges. As such, they represented a source of labour supply, which, in turn, meant that they achieved a new legitimacy within EU employment policy.[52] The EU's commitment to gender equality was reflected in the original EES, which included gender mainstreaming as a horizontal guideline for employment policies from 1999.[53] It also established a set of specific targets for female employment rates (60%) to be reached by 2010.[54] The EU moreover

---

48 See generally the New Start Initiative: Communication from the European Commission to support work-life balance for working parents and carers, 26 April 2017, COM(2017) 252 final.
49 For example, Directive (EU) 2019/1158 of the European Parliament and of the Council of 20 June 2019 on work-life balance for parents and carers and repealing Council Directive 2010/18/EU, O.J. [2019] L188/79. See further the discussion in Chapter 5.
50 Mikkel Mailand, "The Uneven Impact of the European Employment Strategy on Member States' Employment Policies: A Comparative Analysis" (2008) 18 *Journal of European Social Policy* 353.
51 Paola Villa and Mark Smith, "Policy in the Time of Crisis: Employment Policy and Gender Equality in Europe" in Maria Karamessini and Jill Rubery (eds), *Women and Austerity: The Economic Crisis and the Future for Gender Equality* (Routledge 2014).
52 Ibid.
53 Colette Fagan and others, "Gender Mainstreaming in the Enlarged European Union: Recent Developments in the European Employment Strategy and Social Inclusion Process" (2005) 36 *Industrial Relations J* 568; Jill Rubery, "Gender Mainstreaming and Gender Equality in the EU: The Impact of the EU Employment Strategy" (2002) 33 *Industrial Relations J* 500.
54 European Council, "Council Conclusions of 17 June 2010 – A New European Strategy for Jobs and Growth" (EUCO 13/10) http://ec.europa.eu/eu2020/pdf/council_conclusion_17_june_en.pdf. Accessed 25 July 2019.

adopted quantitative targets for childcare provisions at the 2002 Barcelona Summit.[55] Although in practice it is difficult to measure the direct impact of the EES, it has been argued that it has made crucial contributions to altering national policy makers' "mental map"[56] by, in particular, raising awareness of female employment and gender equality matters.

The EES has been implemented through two new forms of governance; the OMC and, more recently, the European Semester. These have been particularly important for the development of the EU childcare strategy which now constitutes part of the Europe 2020 Growth Strategy. The OMC was first used in the context of childcare following the Lisbon (2000)[57] and Barcelona (2002)[58] Councils that extended the OMC to employment, economic reform and social exclusion. Although the OMC is considered "the chief soft law",[59] being a process, it is not strictly speaking a form of soft law. The two share some important features, however. Neither is legally binding under EU law, and there is no set mechanism to ensure enforcement. The main difference remains that, whilst the primary aim of "traditional" soft law is to emphasise general principles and declarations of intention, the OMC is a practice of cross-national policy learning where the objective is not to achieve a common policy in selected issue areas, but rather to institutionalise process for sharing policy experience and the diffusion of best practice.[60] On the one hand, the OMC was deemed the most appropriate system to overcome the asymmetry between market forces and social concerns inherent in EU law.[61] For instance, the OMC can be suitable for encouraging the development of care and childcare related issues where a strict approach will not always be successful or desirable due to wide national diversity

---

55 Communication from the Commission of 21 September 2010, Strategy for Equality between Women and Men 2010–2015, COM(2010) 491 final.
56 Jelle Visser, "Neither Convergence nor Frozen Paths: Bounded Learning, International Diffusion of Reforms, and the Open Method of Coordination" in Martin Heidenreich and Jonathan Zeitlin (eds), *Changing European Employment and Welfare Regimes: The Influence of the Open Method of Coordination on National Reforms* (Routledge 2009).
57 European Council, "Lisbon European Council 23 and 24 March 2000 Presidency Conclusions" (23–24 March 2000) www.europarl.europa.eu/summits/lis1_en.htm. Accessed 22 October 2015.
58 European Council, "Presidency Conclusions, Barcelona European Council, 15 and 16 March 2002" (SN 100/1/02 REV 1) http://ec.europa.eu/invest-in-research/pdf/download_en/barcelona_european_council.pdf. Accessed 25 July 2019.
59 Ibid.
60 Communication to the Spring European Council from President Barroso in agreement with Vice-President Verheugen, "Working Together for Growth and Jobs. A New Start for the Lisbon Strategy", COM(2005) 24.
61 Ingalill Montanari, Kenneth Nelson and Joakim Palme, "Towards a European Social Model? Trends in Social Insurance among EU Countries 1980–2000" (2008) 10 *European Societies* 787.

and variation of policies and where there is no institutional framework.[62] On the other hand, it is arguable that OMC measures lack full democratic legitimacy, as there is neither involvement of the European Parliament, the CJEU, nor the national parliaments. The absence of these institutions is regrettable as they have often supported and given a favourable input to childcare as well as promoted gender equality. The weakness of the OMC process, together with the lack of EU leadership, meant that the EU's ability to steer any development in childcare policy was severely curtailed. As a result, Member States were left to define their own objectives, often unsupported by a gender equality perspective. For example, Member States and social partners had dropped the issue of unfair distribution of care-work within the family, adopting instead a narrow vision of childcare linked to employability structures. Member States' engagement in this area fluctuated according to their economic performance and value.[63] Under the OMC, Member States can, and do, ignore EU core values such as the obligation to achieve gender equality. The Barcelona targets on childcare are a clear example of this.

The OMC has gradually been abandoned in relation to childcare and, since 2011, has been replaced by the European Semester. This was introduced in 2011 under the Europe 2020 Strategy,[64] following the 2008 financial crisis and the resulting sovereign debt crisis, *inter alia* as a mechanism to guarantee the Eurozone stability, although it applies to all the Member States.[65] It is a cycle of economic policy coordination between the EU Member States, with the aim to strengthen economic policy coordination and ex-ante assessment of structural reforms, budget plans and macroeconomic imbalances at the level of the Member States. The European Semester enables the Member States to coordinate their economic policies throughout the year and address the economic challenges facing the EU. The European Semester remains informed by the OMC, but it differs in that it does not provide a chance for feedback from the Member States themselves in the same way the OMC was meant to have these built in moments of reflexivity. Thus, the European Semester is a much more top-down process.

---

62 Paola Villa and Mark Smith, "Policy in the Time of Crisis: Employment Policy and Gender Equality in Europe" in Maria Karamessini and Jill Rubery (eds), *Women and Austerity: The Economic Crisis and the Future for Gender Equality* (Routledge 2014) 275.
63 European Commission Recommendation of 20 February 2013, "Investing in Children: Breaking the Cycle of Disadvantage", COM(2013) 778; Social Protection Committee, "Social Europe – Aiming for Inclusive Growth – Annual Report of the Social Protection Committee on the Social Situation in the European Union (2014)" (European Union 10 March 2015) http://ec.europa.eu/social/main.jsp?catId=738&langId=en&pubId=7744. Accessed 25 July 2019; Horton Rachel, "Caring for Adults in the EU: Work-Life Balance and Challenge for EU Law" (2015) 37 *Journal of Social Welfare & Family Law* 356.
64 Communication from the Commission of 3 March 2010, "Europe 2020 Strategy: A Strategy for Smart, Sustainable and Inclusive Growth", COM(2010) 2020.
65 On the European Semester, see https://ec.europa.eu/info/strategy/european-semester_en. Accessed 25 July 2019.

The EU childcare strategy is now largely embedded into the European Semester. The Commission's Communication on Work-Life Balance clearly states that the European Semester and the annual report on gender equality will monitor and provide guidance to the Member States in relation to employment friendly and accessible care services.[66] It also states that the Member States will be required to continue developing the provision of accessible, affordable and quality childcare, out-of-school and long-term care (LTC) services, including by using support from the European Social Fund and Regional Fund.[67] The Commission argues that:

> [t]he European Semester is an essential instrument for the EU to address the economic challenges Europe faces, including employment friendly and accessible care services for parents and others who need to look after dependent relatives. This policy dialogue is important in itself but it also provides the evidence basis used to guide EU funding.[68]

Although it has been argued that the European Semester has been "socialised" based on its increasing number of social policy goals,[69] this analysis has been criticised for not adequately representing the relationships between the "economic" and the "social", which feminist political economist analysis would supply.[70] As Rosalind Cavaghan explained, the European Semester is mostly concerned with "macroeconomic" goals and associated mindsets.[71] As a result, these systems of epistemology set the overall agenda, which contributes to shifting the relationship between social and economic policy.[72] In the past and under the OMC, social and

---

66 Communication from the European Commission to support work-life balance for working parents and carers, 26 April 2017, COM(2017) 252 final, 11.
67 Ibid, 14.
68 Ibid, 14.
69 Jonathan Zeitlin and Bart Vanhercke "Socializing the European Semester: EU Social and Economic Policy Co-ordination in Crisis and Beyond" (2017) 25 *J European Public Policy* 149.
70 Gary Gillespie and Uzma Khan, "Integrating Economic and Social Policy: Childcare a Transformational Policy?" in Jim Campbell and Morag Gillespie (eds), *Feminist Economics and Public Policy* (Routledge 2016); Isabella Bakker, *The Strategic Silence: Gender and Economic Policy* (Zed Books 1994); Radhika Balakrishnan, Diane Elson and Raj Patel "Rethinking Macro Economic Strategies from a Human Rights Perspective" (2010) 53 *Development* 27.
71 Rosalind Cavaghan, "The Gender Politics of EU Economic Policy: Policy Shifts and Contestations before and after the Crisis" in Johanna Kantola and Emanuela Lombardo (ed), *Gender and the Economic Crisis in Europe: Politics, Institutions and Intersectionality* (Springer 2017).
72 Ibid, 61–62.

economic policy were not well coordinated, which meant that social policy makers were able to "get away" with interesting, and at time unexpected, policy development whilst macroeconomic policy might have pulled in a different direction. Cavaghan argues that since the introduction of the integrated guidelines in 2005 and the European Semester, social policy has been increasingly subordinated to macroeconomic goals and assumptions.[73]

Over the years, and particularly since being embedded in the European Semester, the EES has gradually abandoned the gender equality goals, which have been reflected by a parallel decline in gender priorities at national level.[74] The Europe 2020 Growth Strategy, which talks about a "changing world", in reality entrenches the traditional gendered vision of production and reproduction where the former is valued and the latter is not. The European Semester represents a strong instrument of economic governance focused on competitivity and productivity. It has been criticised for pursuing "gender-blind and gender-biased economic goals".[75] It is submitted that the new model of governances has contributed to shifting the focus of childcare away from gender equality,[76] representing a real setback from the feminist perspective. Arguably, the method of governance adopted to manage the development of the EU childcare strategy goes a long way to explain the mediocre results in the area. However, in the most recent employment guidelines (2018), the European Semester has been aligned to the principles of the European Pillar of Social Rights (EPSR)[77] to target *inter alia* fairness, the combat against poverty and the promotion of equal opportunities for all. It remains to be seen whether this will contribute to bring gender equality goals back.

Finally, it is important to mention that to overcome its lack of competencies in the area of care, the EU has also supplemented its governance with a number of financial mechanisms. The Structural Funds, for example, have been

---

73 Ibid, 61–62.
74 Paola Villa and Mark Smith, "Policy in the Time of Crisis: Employment Policy and Gender Equality in Europe" in Maria Karamessini and Jill Rubery (eds), *Women and Austerity: The Economic Crisis and the Future for Gender Equality* (Routledge 2014); Mark Smith and Paola Villa, "The Ever-Declining Role of Gender Equality in the European Employment Strategy" (2010) 41 *Industrial Relations J* 526.
75 Rosalind Cavaghan and Muireann O'Dwyer, "European Economic Governance in 2017: A Recovery for Whom?" 56 (2018) *JCMS* 96.
76 Elissaveta Radulova, "The Construction of EU's Childcare Policy through the Open Method of Coordination" in Kröger S (ed), *What We Have Learnt: Advances, Pitfalls and Remaining Questions in OMC Research*, (EIOP 2009) 13 http://eiop.or.at/eiop/texte/2009-013a.htm. Accessed 25 July 2019.
77 Interinstitutional Proclamation on the European Pillar of Social Rights, O.J. [2017] C428/15.

utilised to provide resources to co-finance the construction of childcare facilities, training of personnel and the provision of childcare services for parents seeking employment.[78]

The development of the EU childcare strategy

Based on shifting rationales and using the types of governance discussed above, an EU childcare strategy has, slowly but steadily, emerged. This section identifies four phases, each of which has been triggered by a specific event. It examines how at any given time different rationales have been put forward to justify specific EU intervention and analyses how these rationales, using different governance, have contributed to shape the EU position in this area.

The first phase: early developments

During the first phase childcare was expressly included in the EU agenda. A childcare strategy was first discussed in the 1980s. It was promoted by the European Commission within the context of the Second Action Program (1986–1989)[79] and the creation of the European Childcare Network that ran between 1986 and 1996. These marked the formal beginning of the EU discourse on childcare.[80] The Network focused mainly on three areas: services for children; leave for parents; and men as carers. It argued in favour of a Directive on childcare, which should have emphasised the need for public support, the better sharing of care-work within

---

78 The Structural Funds Regulations (Regulation (EU) No 1303/2013 of the European Parliament and of the Council of 17 December 2013 laying down common provisions on the European Regional Development Fund, the European Social Fund, the Cohesion Fund, the European Agricultural Fund for Rural Development and the European Maritime and Fisheries Fund and laying down general provisions on the European Regional Development Fund, the European Social Fund, the Cohesion Fund and the European Maritime and Fisheries Fund and repealing Council Regulation (EC), O.J. [2013] L347/320) provides that childcare is an investment priority. The European Social Fund (ESF) Regulation, moreover, provides for financial assistance for measures to reconcile work and private life, notably by supporting childcare facilities. Regulation (EU) No 1300/2013, Preamble 6 states: "The ESF may be used to enhance access to affordable, sustainable and high quality services of general interest, in particular in the fields of health care, employment and training services, services for the homeless, out of school care, childcare and long-term care service."
79 Communication from the Commission of 19 December 1985, "Equal opportunities for women. Medium-term Community Programme (1986–1990)", COM(1985) 801 final and final/2. By contrast, the Community First Action Programme (1982–1985) focussed on the sharing domestic tasks but did not include measures on childcare. See: Communication from the Commission of 9 December 1981, "A New Community Action Programme on the Promotion of Equal Opportunity for Women", COM(1981) 758.
80 Maria Stratigaki, "The European Union and the Equal Opportunities Process" in Linda Hantrais (ed), *Gendered Policies in Europe: Reconciling Employment and Family Life* (Macmillan and St. Martin's Press 2000).

the family and an improvement of work-family reconciliation through structural changes in workplace and access to leave.[81] Unsurprisingly, however, the necessary majority could never be reached and the 1992 Childcare Recommendation[82] was adopted instead. Although the gender equality rationale is clear, economic concerns also played a role: the main aim of the Recommendation remains to guarantee women's access to the market rather than raising men's opportunities to care. As the first initiative in this area, it was, perhaps an important symbolic achievement,[83] yet it was a weak instrument on two grounds. First, it was not legally binding and thus merely *advised* and *recommended* Member States to *encourage* initiatives such as childcare services. Second, it was not part of broader policymaking and *de facto* had the flavour of a one-off action. It therefore yielded very little traction and failed to generate substantial change in domestic policies. The fact that the Childcare Recommendation was a weak instrument was confirmed by the inactivity in this area in the decade following its adoption: childcare was simply not seen as a priority.

The second phase: the Treaty of Amsterdam

The second phase was triggered by the 1999 Treaty of Amsterdam. With its renewed commitment to gender equality and full employment, it brought new impetus to the issue of reconciliation between work and family life, and with it, to childcare. The introduction of a new Employment Title in the Treaty[84] gave the EU responsibility to coordinate employment policies with specific emphasis on the employability of men and women. There was awareness that, because of structural constraints, in particular caring responsibilities, *de facto* women had limited access to the labour market.[85] Therefore, a successful employment policy was to reflect the reality of gender relations both inside and outside work. In the Treaty of Amsterdam, the social partners (representatives of management and labour) were provided with full recognition in order to contribute to social dialogue as well as to actively design European social policy.[86]

Effectively, the new Employment Title merged the equal opportunity and employment agendas. In essence, this meant that, for the first time, the EU was able to

---

81 Bronwen Cohen and Neil Frazer, *Childcare in a Modern Welfare System* (Institute of Public Policy Research 1991).
82 Council Recommendation 92/241/EEC of 31 March 1992 on childcare, O.J. [1992] L123/16.
83 Clare McGlynn, "Ideologies of Motherhood in European Community Sex Discrimination" (2000) 6 *European Law Journal* 29.
84 Title IX of the TFEU includes Articles 145–150 TFEU (formerly Articles 125–130 of the EC Treaty).
85 Jill Rubery and Colette Fagan, "Equal Opportunities and Employment in the European Union" (Federal Ministry of Labour, Health and Social Affairs 1998) 99.
86 Article 151–156 TFEU.

support the development of a childcare strategy with an implementation system under the Council Employment Guidelines[87] and their application through the EES.[88]

At the same time, the focus of the EU employment policy shifted from fighting unemployment to raising employment levels through growth and opportunities for skilled workers.[89] The 1998 Employment Guidelines, adopted at the Luxembourg European Council, asked Member States "to strive to raise levels of access to care services where some needs are not met".[90] The 1999 European Council provided further guidelines on childcare, including the active involvement of both Member States social partners who were encouraged to:

> design, implement and promote family friendly policies, including affordable, accessible and high-quality care services for children and other dependants, as well as other leave schemes.[91]

The following year, the Lisbon European Council agreed on a new agenda to achieve "the most competitive and dynamic knowledge economy in the world, capable of durable economic growth, of high employment levels and jobs of a better quality and of improved social cohesion".[92] This agenda included various targets to be achieved by 2010 and, in particular, it demanded an increase in female employment rates to 60% (70% for men). To achieve this, the European Council adopted a series of objectives aimed at removing the obstacles to women participating in the labour market. Member States were, again, encouraged to work with their competent authorities at national, regional and local levels and their social partners to ensure access to quality and affordable childcare facilities. In 2002,

---

87 Employment guidelines are common priorities and targets for employment policies proposed by the Commission, agreed by national governments and adopted by the EU Council. On 22 November 2017, The Commission has adopted a proposal to amend the guidelines on 22 November 2017 to align the text with the principles of the European Pillar of Social Rights. See: Proposal for a Council Decision on guidelines for the employment policies of the Member States, COM(2017) 677 final.
88 After inclusion of the new title "Employment" in the Treaty on European Union, the Heads of State and Government launched a European Employment Strategy (EES) at the Luxembourg Jobs Summit with a view to coordinating national employment policies. The EES aims to improve employability, entrepreneurship, adaptability and equal opportunities at the level of the European labour market. See James Mosher and David Trubek, "Alternative Approaches to Governance in the EU: EU Social Policy and the European Employment Strategy" (2003) 41 *J Common Market Studies* 63.
89 Maurizio Ferrera, Anton Hemerijck and Martin Rhodes, *The Future of Social Europe: Recasting Work and Welfare in the New Economy* (Celta Editora 2000) 77–78.
90 Council Resolution of 15 December 1997 on the 1998 Employment Guidelines, O.J [1998] C30/1.
91 Council Resolution of 22 February 1999 on the 1999 Employment Guidelines, O.J. [1999] C69/2.
92 European Council, "Lisbon European Council 23 and 24 March 2000 Presidency Conclusions" (23–24 March 2000) www.europarl.europa.eu/summits/lis1_en.htm. Accessed 22 October 2015.

70 *The emerging EU childcare strategy*

the Barcelona European Council set specific targets requiring Member States "to provide childcare by 2010 to at least 90% of children between 3 years old and the mandatory school age and at least 33% of children under 3 years of age".[93] The Commission was quick to express concerns:

> [e]ven though a growing number of Member States have introduced new measures, quantitative targets and deadlines to improve childcare facilities, good and affordable services are still not sufficient to meet the demand or to reach the new Barcelona targets ... [Furthermore] the issue of improving care for other dependents has, as last year, received very little attention.[94]

Unsurprisingly, these predictions were confirmed. In 2010, only ten Member States[95] had achieved the Barcelona targets for children under three and only 11 had achieved the objectives for children between three years and school age. In 2013, targets were still far from being achieved – in particular for children under the age of three – and in some countries "the situation appears to deteriorate".[96] In 2016, six years after the deadline, the overall rate of children under three years of age in childcare was 32.9%, although there were vast disparities amongst the Member States: only 12 Member States had reached the 33% target in 2016,[97] whilst in the remaining countries, only in six access to childcare for children aged zero to three had reached 25%.[98] For children aged three to mandatory school age, the Barcelona targets have also not quite been reached and only 86.3% had access to formal childcare or attended preschool. It was only in 2018 that the Barcelona targets for children aged between zero and three have finally been reached, although only on average in the EU-28.[99] This failure prompted the Commission

---

93 European Council, 'Presidency Conclusions, Barcelona European Council, 15 and 16 March 2002' (SN 100/1/02 REV 1) http://ec.europa.eu/invest-in-research/pdf/download_en/barcelona_european_council.pdf. Accessed 25 July 2019.
94 Communication from the Commission of 13 November 2002, "Draft Joint Employment Report 2002", COM(2002) 621 final 54.
95 Denmark, Sweden, The Netherlands, France, Spain, Portugal, Slovenia, Belgium, Luxembourg and the UK.
96 European Commission, "Barcelona objectives: The development of childcare facilities for young children in Europe with a view to sustainable and inclusive growth. Report from the Commission to the European Parliament, the Council, the European Economic and Social Committee and the Committee of the Regions" (Publications Office of the European Union 2013). See also, Council of the European Union, Council conclusions of 7 March 2011 on European Pact for Gender Equality (2011–2020), (2011/C 155/02), O.J. [2011] C155/10;
97 Belgium, Denmark, Finland, France, Germany, Italy, Luxembourg, the Netherlands, Portugal, Slovenia, Spain and Sweden.
98 Cyprus, Estonia, Ireland, Latvia, Malta and the United Kingdom.
99 European Commission Report, "The development of childcare facilities for young children with a view to increase female labour participation, strike a work-life balance for working parents and bring about sustainable and inclusive growth in Europe (the 'Barcelona objectives')", COM(2018) 273 final.

to emphasise the need for the EU to take stronger leadership in this area since childcare directly contributes to the (economic) objectives of the EU.

Furthermore, the assessment of the targets at national level remains particularly challenging "because of the lack of appropriate and/or comparable data".[100] As Member States were originally not obliged to disclose their national childcare targets in terms of the percentage of children covered in each age group as defined by the EES, some states limited the information provided to the Commission to their spending and the creation of childcare facilities. Although the information gathered has improved over the years, it remains incomplete and does not provide adequate comparative data on childcare.[101] Moreover, the link between formal childcare usage and employment rates is problematic, particularly when reference is made to the concept of "full-time". In the context of formal childcare, "full-time" is defined by the usage of 30 hours or more per week. However, "full-time" employment generally refers to 40 hours per week (plus commuting time). As the two definitions of "full-time" are not compatible, it means that the link between employment (or full-time employment) and childcare usage is problematic to establish.[102] As a result, it might not be enough that a child attends full-time childcare for the mother to be able to be employed full-time. Complementary informal childcare might also be needed. Alternatively, the mother might remain in part-time employment. This is extremely problematic because the Barcelona targets were set with the clear understanding that parenthood strongly influences female employment rates.[103]

Regardless of their success levels, it is important to emphasise that the Barcelona targets were firmly underpinned by an economic-oriented rationale rather than a gender equality one.[104] This is also evident by the lack of reference to other forms of care for school age children, or to the role of men as carers. In other words, the concept of gender equality was fast fading and the equal opportunity debate was reframed to fit the necessity of the labour market, the economic growth narrative and in particular, parents' employability. In the case of *Lommers*,[105] which to date

---

100 Communication from the Commission of 13 November 2002, "Draft Joint Employment Report 2002", COM(2002)621 final, 54.
101 Nicole Richardt, "European Employment Strategy, Childcare, Welfare State Redesign: Germany and the United Kingdom Compared" (Conference of Europeanists, Chicago, March 2004) http://citeseerx.ist.psu.edu/viewdoc/download;jsessionid=5557F13384911 34E9272F3C8FEEAD63A?doi=10.1.1.497.9971&rep=rep1&type=pdf. Accessed 25 July 2019.
102 Melinda Mills and others, "Use of Childcare Services in the EU Member States and Progress Towards the Barcelona Targets (Short Statistical Report 1)" (European Union 2014) 12–13.
103 Ibid, 11.
104 Elissaveta Radulova, "The Construction of EU's Childcare Policy through the Open Method of Coordination" in Kröger S (ed), *What We Have Learnt: Advances, Pitfalls and Remaining Questions in OMC Research*, (EIOP 2009) 13 http://eiop.or.at/eiop/texte/2009-013a.htm. Accessed 25 July 2019.
105 Case C-476/99 *Lommers v Minister van Landbouw, Natuurbeheer en Visserij*. ECLI: EU:C:2002:183.

remains the only case that directly addresses childcare, the CJEU confirmed this stance. The case involved the Dutch Ministry of Agriculture's childcare policy, which provided access to childcare facilities primarily to its female employees whilst granting male employees access only in emergencies such as in the case of a single father who was the sole care-giver. The Ministry had justified its position as the only way:

> to tackle inequalities existing between male and female officials, as regard both the number of women working at the Ministry and their representation across the grades. The creation of subsidised nursery places *is precisely the kind of measure needed to help to eliminate this de facto inequality.*[106]

The emphasis on parental employability and the lack of a gender equality rationale are clear. The Court was satisfied that there was no breach of the Equal Treatment Directive because when men were fulfilling a primary caring role, they were not excluded from the policy. In doing so, however, it omitted to consider that this policy could have created difficulties for Mrs Lommers. Ultimately, it sent the message that *normally* "care-work is for women" and men enter the picture only in *exceptional* circumstances.

On the one hand, there is little doubt that in this second phase there is clear momentum for the creation of an EU childcare strategy. On the other hand, there are two main drawbacks. First, the conceptual underpinning of gender equality gradually disappeared to be replaced by the systematic incorporation of childcare into the broader policy framework of employment and economic competitiveness. Equal opportunities as a feminist vision (including the equal sharing of care-work) has progressively been replaced by equal opportunities as part of economic and strategic concerns.[107] Second, there was a strong emphasis on the supply side of childcare: the emphasis was on the quantity of childcare services rather than the quality.[108] Under this phase, and in particular under the Barcelona objectives, childcare was conceptualised as a service for adult workers: it was blind to the needs of children *and* parents. It did not include any information about the quality of the childcare services and whether those services should serve the educational needs of children and the care relationship between parents (carers) and children.

---

106 Ibid, para 21, emphasis added.
107 Elissaveta Radulova, "The Construction of EU's Childcare Policy through the Open Method of Coordination" in S. Kröger (ed), *What We Have Learnt: Advances, Pitfalls and Remaining Questions in OMC Research*, (EIOP 2009) 13 http://eiop.or.at/eiop/texte/2009-013a.htm. Accessed 25 July 2019.
108 Council of the European Union, "Joint Employment Report 2003/2004" 5 March 2004 (7069/04).

Although the EU strategy provided broad principles such as quality and affordability, it left the Member States to design their practical operation, including the payment and training of care workers. In other words, the demand side of childcare was a matter for national law.[109]

The third phase: the Work-Life Balance Package and the 2008 financial crisis

The third phase saw a quick turn of events. Until now, even if the gender equality rationale was fast fading, a number of legal provisions had been adopted in relevant areas such as in the area of working time[110] and leave from work.[111] These provisions had created the right environment to build a strong legal strategy designed to facilitate work-family reconciliation[112] and culminated with the adoption of the Work-Life Balance Package in 2008.[113] The Work-Life Balance Package contributed actively to EU childcare strategy: it included a report monitoring the national progress towards the childcare targets set by the 2002 Barcelona Council[114] and, more generally, indicated that childcare was one aspect of the work-life reconciliation discourse.

---

109 Marcia Meyers, Janet Gornick and Katherin Ross, "Public Childcare, Parental Leave and Employment" in Diane Sainsbury (ed), *Gender and Welfare State Regimes* (OUP 1999).
110 Council Directive 97/81/EC of 15 December 1997 concerning the Framework Agreement on part-time work concluded by UNICE, CEEP and the ETUC – Annex: Framework agreement on part-time work, O.J. [1998] L14/9; Council Directive 99/70/EC of 28 June 1999 concerning the framework agreement on fixed-term work concluded by ETUC, UNICE and CEEP, O.J. [1999] L175/43, corrigendum at O.J. [1999] L244/64; Directive 2003/88/EC of the European Parliament and of the Council of 4 November 2003 concerning certain aspects of the organisation of working time, O.J. [2003] L 299/9.
111 Council Directive 92/85/EEC, O.J. [1992] L348/1; Council Directive 2010/18/EU, O.J. [2010] L68/13.
112 Eugenia Caracciolo di Torella and Annick Masselot, *Reconciling Work and Family Life in EU Law and Policy* (Palgrave Macmillan 2010).
113 The European Commission proposed Work-Life Package (MEMO/08/603 of 03 October 2008). The Work-Life Package included four documents: a Communication from the European Commission setting the context (Communication from the Commission of 3 October 2008, "A Better Work-Life Balance: Stronger Support for Reconciling Professional, Private and Family Life", COM(2008) 635 final); two legislative proposals to revise existing directives, the Pregnant Workers Directive (Proposal for a Directive amending Council Directive 92/85/EEC on the introduction of measures to encourage improvements in the safety and health at work of pregnant workers and workers who have recently given birth or are breastfeeding, COM(2008) 637) and the Self-Employed Directive (Proposal for a Directive on the application of the principle of equal treatment between men and women engaged in an activity in a self-employed capacity and repealing Directive 86/613/EEC, COM(2008) 636); finally a report monitoring the national progress towards the childcare targets set by the 2002 Barcelona Council (European Commission Report, "Implementation of the Barcelona Objectives Concerning Facilities for Pre-School-Age Children" 03/10/2008, COM(2008) 638).
114 European Commission Report, "Implementation of the Barcelona Objectives Concerning Facilities for Pre-School-Age Children" 03/10/2008, COM(2008) 638.

The success was short-lived, however. A few weeks later, the 2008 financial crisis[115] engulfed the EU. The recession that followed did not provide the optimal political and economic context from which to build and develop the nascent childcare strategy into a fully-fledged policy. Unsurprisingly, in the immediate aftermath of the crisis, the EU, occupied with reforming banking and financial markets, was not concerned with childcare. By then, gender equality was clearly no longer at the heart of policy development on work-family reconciliation[116] and any EU activity was strongly tainted by economic motives. In many Member States, the crisis deeply affected national welfare policies in general[117] and specifically, those aimed at supporting working parents which have been cut back, postponed or abandoned in many countries.[118] In this new economic context, austerity measures sprouted and fundamental rights, such as gender equality, have either been considered too costly or subordinated to the demand of market necessity. Not surprisingly, the tendency, which began with the Lisbon Agenda, to use childcare as a tool to support economic competitiveness and employment strategy goals, was staunchly entrenched post-crisis.

Although the consequences of the recession were felt by both men and women (but negative overall), in the sense that unemployment levels for both men and women were equalised,[119] women generally remained in segregated, underpaid and precarious jobs. In some countries, unemployment levels accelerated, especially for women as the public sector was shrinking. Public sector cuts disproportionately affect women both as employees and as service users. Indeed, in this

---

115 The chapter does not aim to define the crisis or its transformations. See Sylvia Walby, *Crisis* (Polity 2015).
116 Abigail Gregory, Sue Milner and Jan Windebank, "Work-Life Balance in Times of Economic Crisis and Austerity" (2013) 33 *Intl Journal of Sociology and Social Policy* 528.
117 Ibid.
118 Roberta Guerrina, "Socio-Economic Challenges to Work-Life Balance at Times of Crisis" (2015) 37 *Journal of Social Welfare & Family Law* 368. See also Jude Towers and Sylvia Walby, "Measuring the Impact of Cuts in Public Expenditure on the Provision of Services to Prevent Violence against Women" (Report for Northern Rock Foundation and Trust for London, 30 January 2012) http://eprints.lancs.ac.uk/55165/1/Measuring_the_impact_of_cuts_in_public_expenditure_on_the_provision_of_services_to_prevent_violence_against_women_and_girls_Full_report_3.pdf. Accessed 25 July 2019; Sylvia Walby, "Enquête on the Current Financial Crisis: the UK" (2012) 14 *European Societies* 151.
119 Women are not significantly more likely to face unemployment (9.8% compared to 9.7% for men) but they face a higher risk of poverty and exclusion (25.2%) than men (23%) as stated by European Commission, "Barcelona Objectives: The Development of Childcare Facilities for Young Children in Europe with a View to Sustainable and Inclusive Growth" (Publications Office of the European Union 2013) 5. See also Cristina Solera and Francesca Bettio, "Women's Continuous Careers in Italy: The Education and Public Sector Divide" (2013) 52 *Population Review* 129; Maria Karamessini and Jill Rubery, "The Challenge of Austerity for Equality. A Consideration of Eight European Countries in the Crisis" (2014) 2 *Revue de l'OFCE* 15; Jill Rubery and Anthony Rafferty, "Women and Recession Revisited" (2013) 27 *Work, Employment & Society* 414.

context, funding for childcare provision was seen more as a luxury for women rather than a necessity in a time of crisis. In other words, the recession "appears to have exacerbated the earlier gendered and sectoral pattern of work-life conflict".[120] Furthermore, the crisis also highlighted the deeply ingrained gender stereotypes in Europe.[121] Women are still perceived as the main caregivers, and thus childcare is conceived as a service for them. The persisting gender pay gap of 16% (in the average hourly gross wage)[122] due in part to women earning lower pay for work of equal value, and in part to job segregation, continues to shape the perception of entitlement and preference in the workplace.

Nevertheless, despite claims to the contrary,[123] women's labour market participation appears to have become a lasting feature of contemporary capitalism.[124] Despite the difficulties, the crisis has revealed some durable transformed structures: the majority of women are in paid employment and the crisis has not led to them returning (voluntarily) to traditional unpaid roles.[125]

The fourth phase: childcare post-2010 – an emerging children's rights framework?

The final phase spans from 2010 to the present day. If the initial reaction to the financial crisis was to introduce a raft of austerity measures that exacerbated the soaring levels of poverty, after 2010 the EU devised a plan to counteract the Member States' cycle of austerity measures which had increasingly involved cutting welfare state and social protection. *Prima facie*, this phase shows an increase of EU activities in relation to childcare and culminates with Principle 11 of the EPSR[126] that specifically states that "[c]hildren have the right to affordable early childhood

---

120 Abigail Gregory, Sue Milner and Jan Windebank, "Work-Life Balance in Times of Economic Crisis and Austerity" (2013) 33 *Intl Journal of Sociology and Social Policy* 528. See also European Commission, 'Report on Equality between Women and Men 2014' (Publications Office of the European Union 2015).
121 Annick Masselot, Eugenia Caracciolo di Torella and Susan Burri, "Thematic Report of the European Network of Legal Experts in the Field of Gender Equality "Fighting Discrimination on the Grounds of Pregnancy, Maternity and Parenthood – The Application of EU and National law in Practice in 33 European Countries" (European Commission, 2012). See also European Commission, "Report on Equality between Women and Men 2014" (Publications Office of the European Union 2015).
122 Eurostat, "Gender Pay Gap Statistics" (2017) http://ec.europa.eu/eurostat/statistics-explained/index.php/Gender_pay_gap_statistics#cite_note-1. Accessed 24 July 2019.
123 Neil Gilbert, *A Mother's Work: How Feminism, the Market and Policy Shape Family Life* (Yale University Press 2008) 10.
124 Maria Karamessini and Jill Rubery, "The Challenge of Austerity for Equality. A Consideration of Eight European Countries in the Crisis" (2014) 2 *Revue de l'OFCE* 15.
125 See generally: Maria Karamessini and Jill Rubery, *Women and Austerity – The Economic Crisis and the Future for Gender Equality* (Routledge 2014).
126 Interinstitutional Proclamation on the European Pillar of Social Rights, O.J. [2017] C428/10.

education and care of good quality" and that they "have the right to protection from poverty". Indeed, in this phase, the number of EU measures relating to childcare dramatically increased and have now surpassed any such activities prior to 2008. All of the EU political institutions have been involved. The Council issued the European Pact for Gender Equality (2011–2020)[127] where it reiterated its commitment to the Barcelona childcare targets and the European Commission adopted at least four communications.[128] The European Parliament created the European Platform for Investing in Children (EPIC)[129] to inform Member States on evidence-based practices that have been found to have a positive impact on children and families.

Yet the childcare strategy is now clearly constructed to support economic competitiveness and employment strategy goals as well to complement and support the policy response to the recession,[130] in the form of measures designed to limit or avoid job losses and to support companies in retaining their workforce. Indeed, childcare measures have been identified by the EU as contributing to the creation of new jobs. However, most of these care-related jobs are undervalued, heavily gender-segregated, underpaid and often precarious.[131] A closer look at the 2020 Strategy shows that it does not appear to be primarily concerned with social issues: indeed, it clearly outlines a business framework. Employment rates are to be raised, with special emphasis on the participation of women, the young and the old in the workforce. The increase of women's work rate was judged to not have progressed fast enough by comparison to the rest of the world (especially when compared with the USA and Japan): "only 63% of women are in work compared to 76% of men."[132] Thus, the 2020 Strategy requires greater effort to involve women in paid employment, which will be achieved by providing "access and opportunities for all

---

127 Council of the European Union, "Council Conclusions of 7 March 2011 on European Pact for Gender Equality (2011–2020)" (2011/C 155/02), O.J. [2011] C155/10.
128 Communication from the Commission of 21 September 2010, "Strategy for Equality between Women and Men 2010–2015", COM(2010) 491 final; Communication from the Commission of 3 March 2010, "Europe 2020 Strategy, A Strategy for Smart, Sustainable and Inclusive Growth", COM(2010) 2020; Communication from the Commission of 17 February 2011, "Early Childhood Education and Care: Providing all Our Children with the Best Start for the World of Tomorrow", COM(2011) 66; Communication from the European Commission of 26 April 2017 to support work-life balance for working parents and carers, COM(2017) 252 final.
129 European Platform for Investing in Children (EPIC), https://ec.europa.eu/social/main.jsp?catId=1246&langId=en. Accessed 25 July 2019.
130 Andreas Crimman, Frank Wiener and Lutz Bellman, "The German Work-sharing Scheme: An Instrument for the Crisis" (International Labour Organization, Conditions of Work and Employment Series No. 25, 2010).
131 It must be noted, however, that these care-related jobs are typically filled by women, are undervalued, heavily segregated, under paid and often precarious. See further Jill Rubery and Anthony Rafferty, "Women and Recession Revisited" (2013) 27 *Work, Employment & Society* 414.
132 Communication from the Commission of 3 March 2010, "Europe 2020 Strategy, A Strategy for Smart, Sustainable and Inclusive Growth", COM(2010) 2020, 5.

throughout the lifecycle"[133] and by using "[p]olicies to promote gender equality ... to increase labour force participation thus adding to growth and social cohesion."[134] The 2020 Strategy mentions the importance of childcare facilities and of the care for other dependants but the Member States remain in charge of the care strategy which continues to be a national competence. Member States would be required under the new strategy to facilitate "the reconciliation of work and family life" as well as to "promote new forms of work-life balance ... and to increase gender equality."[135]

Thus, following the global economic crisis, the problems which existed with regards to raising women's employment rate prior to 2010 remain the same, if not more acute. Despite the existence of EU gender equality legislation, women continue to provide most of the care-work in Europe. Policy to encourage the increase of women's employment rate cannot be successful without policies aimed at a more equitable division of the care and, more generally, family responsibilities[136].

Against this background, in an attempt to counteract the influx of national austerity measures arising from combating the crisis, the Commission adopted the 2013 Social Investment Package (SIP), which places childcare at the heart of the economic recovery. In particular, it makes the achievement of the Barcelona objectives central to European Union priorities in line with both the Lisbon Strategy and in the Europe 2020 Strategy.[137] The SIP is made up of a Commission *Communication on Growth and Cohesion*[138] together with a Commission Recommendation on *Investing in Children: Breaking the Cycle of Disadvantage*[139] and a series of staff working documents.[140] In addition, to help Member States

---

133 Ibid, 16
134 Ibid, 16
135 Ibid, 17
136 Veerle Miranda, "Cooking, Caring and Volunteering: Unpaid Work around the World" (OECD Social, Employment and Migration Working Papers No. 116, OECD Publishing, 2011); Colette Fagan and Helen Norman, "Men and gender equality: Tackling gender segregation in family roles and in social care jobs" in F Bettio, J Plantenga and M Smith (eds), *Gender and the European Labour Market* (Routledge 2013); Equality and Human Right Commission (EHRC), "Working Better: Fathers, Family and Work – Contemporary Perspectives" (2009).
137 European Commission, "Social Investment Package: Key Facts and Figures" (Publications Office of the European Union 2013) 4.
138 Communication from the Commission to the European Parliament, the Council, the European Economic and Social Committee and the Committee of the Regions, "Towards Social Investment for Growth and Cohesion – including implementing the European Social Fund 2014–2020", COM(2013) 83.
139 European Commission Recommendation, 2013/112/EU of 20 February 2013, "Investing in Children: Breaking the Cycle of Disadvantage", O.J. [2013] L59/5.
140 For an overview of the various documents adopted by the EU on the SIP, see: http://ec.europa.eu/social/main.jsp?catId=1044&langId=en&newsId=1807&moreDocuments=yes&tableName=news. Accessed 25 July 2019.

implement the SIP in 2013, the European Parliament has also been supporting of the creation of the EPIC,[141] which serves to feed into the European Semesters as a platform for sharing the best of policymaking for children and families and to foster cooperation and mutual learning in the field.

By providing guidance for Member States on how to tackle child poverty and social exclusion through measures such as family support and benefits, quality childcare and early childhood education, the Recommendation on *Investing in Children* puts forward a long-term social strategy to support children and to help mitigate the effects of the economic crisis. Specifically, it emphasises the importance of improving *access* to quality and affordable early childhood education and care services as well as encouraging Member States to support children's participation in extracurricular activities.

Without doubt, the SIP is inextricably linked to the achievement of economic growth and underlines the importance of an economic perspective. The aim of the policy is to entice and support Member States into investing in people's social capital in order to prevent social risks. The SIP aims to reconcile social investment with adequate social protections. In particular, the 2013 Recommendation aims to support parents' access to the labour market and to make sure that work "pays" for them. It also recommends the provision of adequate income support in the form of measures such as child and family benefits, which should be redistributive across income groups. It urges the need to avoid inactivity traps and stigmatisation. Under the Recommendation, childcare becomes an investment in individual capacities during the early years. This economic perspective is important because it provides momentum for policy development around childcare.

The introduction of the perspective of the child in the SIP is *prima facie* a new and welcome development. The Recommendation states that it aims to improve the well-being and the protection of the rights of children.[142] Arguably, the SIP mitigates its economic competitiveness objectives by including more human concerns in the form of children's interests. This perspective has been called for by scholars[143] who have persuasively argued that the reconciliation discourse has too often neglected addressing children's needs. The SIP introduces for the first time the notion that childcare is important not just for the economy, rising employment rates or the concept of reconciliation between work and family life, but it

---

141 European Platform for Investing in Children (EPIC) http://europa.eu/epic/studies-reports/childcare/index_en.htm. Accessed 25 July 2019.
142 European Commission Recommendation, 2013/112/EU of 20 February 2013, "Investing in Children: Breaking the Cycle of Disadvantage", O.J. [2013] L59/5, preamble s1.
143 Eulalia Rubio, "A Policy in its Infancy: The Case for Strengthening and Rethinking EU Action on Childhood" (Notre Europe 2007); Louise Ackers and Helen Stalford, *A Community for Children? Children, Citizenship and Internal Migration in the EU* (Ashgate 2004); Helen Stalford and Eleanor Drywood, "Coming of Age? Children's Rights in the European Union" (2009) 46 *CML Rev* 143; Grace James, "Forgotten Children: Work-Family Reconciliation in the EU" (2012) 34 *Journal of Social Welfare & Family Law* 363.

is relevant also to children. Giving children rights in the building of a childcare strategy makes sense as they are directly impacted. In addition, a child perspective is long overdue in EU law as "children are coming to be recognised as political citizens".[144] However, as Daly argues, the tendency to grant children some individual rights can also contribute to increasing the individualisation of family members and creates a distance between the child and the family.[145] In addition, social reforms which promote the individualisation of family members have gender implications but often are blind to them.[146] The SIP valorises out-of-home childcare facilities as a social investment designed to build children's social capital, but in doing so, it also risks distancing itself from feminist concerns and the principle of gender equality. Additionally, the tendency to individualise rights blanks out the ethic of care insight to focus on relationships rather than on individuals.[147]

The 2017 European Commission New Start Initiative[148] appears to have counterbalanced some of these criticisms. It adopted a proposal for a Directive[149] and a Communication[150] to support work-life balance for working parents and carers. The latter, in particular, aims to support the economic aim of raising female employment rate together with encouraging a better sharing of caring responsibilities between women and men, hereby reintroducing gender equality concerns into the EU childcare strategy. Moreover, the Communication addresses the need to improve childcare services, which it frames, in line with the 2013 SIP, explicitly

---

144 Mary Daly, "What Adult Worker Model? A Critical Look at Recent Social Policy Reform in Europe from a Gender and Family Perspective" (2011) 18(1) *Social Politics: Intl Studies in Gender, State & Society* 1, 10.
145 Ibid, 10; Ruth Lister, "Children (But Not Women) First: New Labour, Child Welfare and Gender" (2006) 26 *Critical Social Policy* 315.
146 Mary Daly, "What Adult Worker Model? A Critical Look at Recent Social Policy Reform in Europe from a Gender and Family Perspective" (2011) 18 *Social Politics: Intl Studies in Gender, State & Society* 1, 10; Barbara Hobson, "The Individualised Worker, the Gender Participatory and the Gender Equity Models in Sweden"(2004) 3 *Social Policy & Society* 75; Rebecca Ray, Janet Gornick and John Schmitt, "Who Cares? Assessing Generosity and Gender Equality in parental Leave Policy Designs in 21 Countries" (2010) 20 *Journal of European Social Policy* 196.
147 Mary Daly and Kirsten Scheiwe, "Individualisation and Personal Obligations: Social Policy, Family Policy and Law Reform in Germany and the UK" (2010) 24 *Intl J L, Policy and the Family* 177; Göran Therborn, *Between Sex and Power: Family in the World 1900–2000* (Routledge 2004); Fiona Williams, "A Good-Enough Life: Developing the Grounds for a Political Ethic of Care" (2005) 30 *Soundings* 17.
148 "A New Start Initiative to Support Work-Life Balance for Parents and Carers" https://ec.europa.eu/info/law/better-regulation/initiatives/com-2017-253_en. Accessed on 25 July 2019. See also Chapter 5.
149 Proposal for a Directive of the European Parliament and of the Council on work-life balance for parents and carers and repealing Council Directive 2010/18/EU, 26 April 2017, COM(2017) 253 final.
150 Communication from the European Commission to support work-life balance for working parents and carers, 26 April 2017, COM(2017) 252 final.

as social investment.[151] Specifically, it states that "[i]nvesting in early childhood education and good-quality care is also recognised as an effective social investment to address inequality and the challenges faced by disadvantaged children."[152] It finally highlights the positive impact of childcare on children's development and the contribution it makes to reduce the risk of poverty and social exclusion for children.[153]

While the SIP did not address the gender imbalance which underlines childcare, the New Start Initiative reintroduced gender equality as one of the aims of the childcare strategy. There is a risk, nevertheless, that the various rationales will compete against each other to the detriment of the achievement of gender equality. While it is noticeable that the EU does restate its commitment to the promotion of gender equality in the labour market and in family responsibilities,[154] gender equality principles have mainly become instrumental to the realisation of both economic perspectives and children's rights. The new child perspective represents an interesting development. However, if the individual rights of the child take precedence over gender equality, it risks confirming the so-called dominant ideology of motherhood[155] where childcare remains gendered, under- or unvalued, unaccounted for and largely unpaid. The danger is that this is likely to entrench women in traditional domestic roles, or worse, to legitimise the "second shift".[156] Consequently, one might question whether the childcare strategy is contributing to the retrenchment of the core EU values. It should be noted, however, that the EU appears to have strengthened the core values in its childcare strategy though the proclamation in 2016 of the European Pillar of Social Rights[157] and the 2019 Work-life Balance Directive,[158] which both show a renewed commitment toward EU core values.

---

151 Ibid.
152 Ibid.
153 Ibid.
154 Article 2.1, European Commission Recommendation, 2013/112/EU of 20 February 2013, "Investing in Children: Breaking the Cycle of Disadvantage", O.J. [2013] L59/5.
155 Clare McGlynn, "Ideologies of Motherhood in European Community Sex Discrimination" (2000) 6 *European Law Journal* 29.
156 Arlie Hochschild and Anne Machung, *The Second Shift: Working Parents and the Revolution at Home* (Viking Penguin 1989); Tamara Hervey and Jo Shaw, "Women, Work and Care: Women's Dual Role and Double Burden in EC Sex Equality Law" (1998) 8 *Journal of European Social Policy* 43.
157 Communication from the Commission to the European Parliament, the Council, the European Economic and Social Committee and the Committee of the Regions Launching a consultation on a European Pillar of Social Rights, COM(2016) 127 final.
158 Directive (EU) 2019/1158 of the European Parliament and of the Council of 20 June 2019 on work-life balance for parents and carers and repealing Council Directive 2010/18/EU, O.J. [2019] L188/79.

Moreover, although gender equality appears to be fading from the picture, the SIP highlights the EU's commitments in combating social exclusion and discrimination.[159] The SIP also identifies social exclusion (but not inequality) as a cost to the economy and as a threat to achieving the economic targets set by the Europe 2020 Strategy.[160] The introduction of core values such as social exclusion and social justice are to be welcomed and it is possible that the economic crisis has served to highlight existing structural inequalities.

Conclusion

This chapter has mapped the development of the EU "childcare strategy". It has emphasised that this strategy, rather than being constructed as an aim in itself, has responded to different goals, unrelated to childcare and/or in reaction to external events, perceived as important at any given time. As such, it has been underpinned and shaped by different rationales, namely gender equality, economic imperatives and children's rights. Amongst these rationales, economic imperatives have clearly remained the constant thread that has shaped the other two. As for gender equality, despite the EU commitment to promote it and despite being a core element of the caring relationship,[161] it has taken a back seat. The fading emphasis on gender equality has further entrenched the traditional gendered vision of production and reproduction where only the former is valued. Accordingly, childcare remains gendered, undervalued, unaccounted for and largely unpaid or poorly paid, and women pay the brunt of this. The children's rights rationale, although *prima facie* might be seen as a tool to empower children, has also shown a clear market connotation. Not only does it consider children only in so far as they are an "investment for the future",[162] but it obscures the fact that the need for care is broader than just "child"-care.[163]

---

159 Communication from the Commission to the European Parliament, the Council, the European Economic and Social Committee and the Committee of the Regions, "Towards Social Investment for Growth and Cohesion – including implementing the European Social Fund 2014–2020", COM(2013) 83, 1.
160 Communication from the Commission of 3 March 2010, "Europe 2020 Strategy: A Strategy for Smart, Sustainable and Inclusive Growth", COM(2010) 2020; Council of the European Union, "Council Conclusions of 17 June 2010 – A New European Strategy for Jobs and Growth" EUCO 13/10 http://ec.europa.eu/eu2020/pdf/council_conclusion_17_june_en.pdf. Accessed 24 October 2015.
161 European Commission Recommendation, 2013/112/EU of 20 February 2013, "Investing in Children: Breaking the Cycle of Disadvantage", O.J. [2013] L59/5.
162 Annick Masselot, "Reformulating Gender Equality in the EU: Social Investment and Childcare as a Central Element of the Economic Recovery" in Paolo Canelas de Castro (ed), *60 Years after the Treaties of Rome: What is the Future for the European Union?*, (University of Macau Publication 2020). See also Jane Jenson, "Social Investment for New Social Risks: Consequences of the LEGO Paradigm for Children" in Jane Lewis (ed), *Children in Context: Changing Families and Welfare States* (Edward Elgar Publishing 2006); Ruth Lister, "Children (But Not Women) First: New Labour, Child Welfare and Gender" (2006) 26 *Critical Social Policy* 315.
163 See the discussion in Chapter 3.

A further issue with the childcare strategy is that, because the EU lacks express competences, it has developed through alternative forms of governance. These are either measures that are soft in nature and merely aim to encourage Member States to develop accessible, affordable and quality childcare facilities, or measures adopted under the umbrella of the OMC and the European Semester in the context of the EES. Thus, *de facto*, Member States set their own objectives, whilst the EU's role is largely, although not exclusively, limited to that of facilitator.[164] It is hardly surprising, therefore, that so far, the childcare strategy is neither coherent nor comprehensive.

By contrast, we argue that the EU should be more proactive, although it is unlikely and perhaps even undesirable for the EU to be in the position to legislate at this stage. The EU should strengthen its current childcare strategy to acknowledge and "facilitate the recognition and intrinsic value of child care" not so much as a means to a specific end or as an investment for the future but as "part of the achievement of human well-being".[165] Thus, it should take the lead in this area and develop a strategy where all the existing rationales are equally important. Using its fundamental values, such as gender equality, human dignity and solidarity, the EU should also develop clear guiding principles that enable childcare to flourish and the caring relationship to be valued. The European Pillar of Social Rights and the Commission's Communication on Work-Life Balance represent steps in the right direction. Finally, such a cohesive childcare strategy has the potential to serve as a blue print for developing strategies for other forms of care.

---

164 In 2010, the EU set in certain policy areas targets that EU should meet by 2020. These were translated into national targets so that each Member State can check its own progress towards each goal. The Commission monitors the progress towards these targets, both at EU and national level.
165 Sandra Fredman, *Women and the Law* (Clarendon Press 1997) 24.

3 The EU and long-term care

Introduction

In the previous chapter, we discussed how the European Union (EU) has addressed the challenges of childcare and has accordingly developed a policy and legislative strategy. Caring needs, however, are not limited to young and healthy children and in the cases of *Ibrahim* and *Teixeira*, the Court of Justice of the European Union (CJEU or the Court) confirmed that such needs cannot be subject to age.[1] Apart from young age, instances where care is needed include, *inter alia*, the case of disabled children, chronically ill partners or elderly and frail relatives or dependants. Although there are marked differences between these situations, this chapter groups them under the term of long-term care (LTC) that broadly indicates the support that certain individuals need over an extended period of time to enable them to perform basic tasks necessary for their daily living.[2]

Some individuals (be they children or adults) have long-term needs because of disability and, increasingly, because of old age. The latter in particular is the focus of this chapter.

The rise of life expectancy means that old age is "a stage that each of us will reach if we live out our normal span".[3] It is a well-established fact that the population is ageing in post-industrial countries,[4] and the EU is no exception. The European Commission, on several occasions, has highlighted that the ageing of the European population has accelerated: "the number of people aged over 60 is now increasing twice as fast as it did before 2007 – by about two million every year

---

1 Case C-310/08 *London Borough of Harrow v Nimco Hassan Ibrahim.* ECLI:EU:C:2010:80 and Case C-480/08, *Maria Teixeira v London Borough of Lambeth and Secretary of State for the Home Department.* EU:C:2010:83, in particular para 28.
2 European Commission, Commission Staff Working Document of 20 February 2013, "Long-Term Care in an Ageing Society – Challenges and Policy Options" SWD(2013) 41 final.
3 *Massachusetts Board of Retirement v Murgia* (1976) 438 US 285.
4 See e.g. Jonathan Herring *Older People in Law and Society* (OUP 2009); Jonathan Herring, *Caring and the Law* (Hart Publishing 2013) 1.

compared to one million previously."[5] Although ageing is experienced in different ways,[6] it affects all of the Member States. A greater life expectancy, combined with declining birth rates, has meant that the number of older (55–64), elderly (65–79) and very elderly (80+) people has grown to an unprecedented level and this trend is steadily increasing.[7] It is estimated that those over the age of 79 are expected to triple across the EU by 2060.[8] Specifically, by then, the age band 80+ is expected to increase from 5% to 28% of the population, whilst those aged 55+ are expected to rise from 18% to 28%.[9] It will therefore not be unusual to see four surviving generations of the same family. Whilst this "longevity revolution"[10] may be "wonderful news",[11] and a "very positive trend",[12] it also creates multiple and complex challenges that cannot be ignored.[13] These include, *inter alia*, the sustainability of the pension system, the inclusion into the labour market of both individuals who need care and those who care for, and the establishment of adequate health and social care services and provisions. Indeed, rising life expectancy does not necessarily mean that healthy life expectancy is rising accordingly: it is not old age in itself that triggers the need for care but the frailty and impairment that old age almost inevitably brings.[14] Today, more people than ever reach an age where declining physical and mental health make them dependent on others.

---

5 See *inter alia* the Communication from the Commission, "Europe 2020: A Strategy for Smart, Sustainable and Inclusive Growth", COM(2010) 2020 final, 7.
6 Ann Numhauser-Henning (ed), *Elder Law: Evolving European Perspectives* (Edward Elgar 2017).
7 See also European Commission, "Demography Report 2010 – Older, More Numerous and Diverse Europeans" (2011) http://senas.lnb.lt/stotisFiles/uploadedAttachments/es320111028114623.pdf. Accessed 25 July 2019.
8 European Commission, "The 2015 Ageing Report" (European Union 2015). See also earlier reports such as Communication from the Commission, Green Paper, "Confronting Demographic Change: A New Solidarity between Generations", COM(2005) 94.
9 European Commission, "The 2015 Ageing Report" (European Union 2015).
10 Robert Butler, *The Longevity Revolution: The Benefits and the Challenges of Living a Long Life* (Public Affairs 2008).
11 Jonathan Herring, *Older People in Law and Society* (OUP 2009).
12 Social Protection Committee and European commission Services, "Adequate Social Protection for Long-Term Care Needs in an Ageing Society" 2014 SOC 403 ECOFIN 525.
13 See Louise Ackers and Peter Dwyer, *Senior Citizenship? Retirement, Migration and Welfare in the European Union* (Policy Press 2002); Naoki Ikegami, John Hirdes and Ian Carpenter, "Long-Term Care: A Complex Challenge" (2001) 229 *OECD Observer* 27.
14 Gaetan Lafortune and Gaëlle Balestrat, "Trends in Severe Disability among Elderly People: Assessing the Evidence in 12 OECD Countries and the Future Implications" (OECD Health Working Papers, No. 26, OECD Publishing, 2007), https://doi.org/10.1787/217072070078. Accessed 25 July 2019. Indeed, UK research has challenged the link between age and health related issues, see Office for National Statistics, "Sustainable Development Indicators" (July 2015) www.ons.gov.uk/peoplepopulationandcommunity/wellbeing/datasets/sustainabledevelopmentindicators. Accessed 25 July 2019. Furthermore it has been argued that "longevity achieved by the

These challenges have been exacerbated by the increasing lack of available and adequate care due to circumstances such as migration, transformation of the social welfare and changes in family structure.

Therefore, a society with a rising number of individuals[15] who need care represents a key challenge for domestic governments and the EU respectively:

> the previously held assumption that that EU law has little relevance for … the long-term care of older people is increasingly under question … EU law is [now] an important element of the policy context within which changes to the long-term of care for older people … are taking place.[16]

It is against this background that this chapter explores the extent to which the law and policy of the European Union have engaged with the multiple and complex challenges inherent in LTC related issues.[17] Although there is agreement on the need for high quality, financially sustainable and accessible LTC care services,[18] progress in this area remains limited and very slow.

For this purpose, this chapter is organised in two main sections. The first section (Long-term care: the main features) starts by exploring the meaning of LTC, its specific challenges and opportunities before turning to the EU rationale for engaging with it. for. The second section (LTC policy developments in the Member States) reviews the EU involvement in this area. It will consider the European

---

right mechanisms is likely to reduce the costs of care in later life", John Grimley Evans, "Age Discrimination: Implications of the Ageing Process" in Sandra Fredman and Sarah Spencer (eds), *Age as an Equality Issue* (Hart Publishing 2003). For a comprehensive discussion, see Rachel Horton, "Dignity and the legal justification of age discrimination in health care" (PhD thesis, Middlesex University 2016).

15 In Italy, for example, it is estimated that three quarters of all carers are (often undeclared) migrants, see Mirko Di Rosa and others, "The Impact of Migrant Work in the Elder Care Sector: Recent Trends and Empirical Evidence in Italy" (2012) 15 *European J Social Care* 9. More generally see also Organisation for Economic Co-operation and Development, "Health at a Glance 2013: OECD Indicators" (2013).

16 Tamara Hervey and others, "Long-Term Care for Older People and EU Law: The Position in England and Scotland" (2012) 34 *Journal of Social Welfare & Family Law* 105.

17 Although the two terms are sometimes used interchangeably, they indicate two different situations: eldercare is a form of long-term care. They can both be particularly challenging older people. In fact, both might require care and at the same time often, they might themselves be (informal) carers to others.

18 See e.g. Communication from the Commission, "The Future of Health Care and Care for the Elderly: Guaranteeing Accessibility, Quality and Financial Viability", COM(2001) 723; Communication from the Commission "Health Care and Care for the Elderly: Supporting National Strategies for Ensuring a High Level of Social Protection", COM(2002) 774; Communication from the Commission "Promoting Solidarity between the Generations", COM(2007) 244 final and Communication from the Commission "A Better Work-life Balance: Stronger Support for Reconciling Professional, Private and Family Life", COM(2008) 635.

Pillar of Social Rights (EPSR)[19] and the Commission's Communication on the New Start Initiative[20] In light of this discussion, this chapter maintains that the regulation of LTC at EU level remains limited and has had even less traction than the regulation of childcare. Although this is understandable, the EU should ensure that Member States, when approaching LTC issues, do so within the framework of EU general principles as well as the Charter of Fundamental Rights (CFR) and the EPSR.

Long-term care: the main features

The need to provide for LTC is relatively recent in social protection systems. As LTC is neither a legal nor a traditional concept of EU law, there is not a set definition for the purpose of developing an EU framework. Indeed, as the EU legal institutions have not addressed this issue before, we will need to identify a working definition and, for this purpose, we have explored definitions available elsewhere. The definition provided by the Organisation for Economic Cooperation and Development (OECD) sees LTC as a variety of health and social services provided for an *on-going* or extended period to individuals *who need assistance* on a continuing basis due to physical or mental disability.[21] In the same vein, a report of the Social Protection Committee defines it as:

> a range of services and assistance for people who, as a result of mental and/or physical disability over an *extended* period of time, depend on help with daily living activities and/or are in need of some permanent nursing care.[22]

Both definitions emphasise the need for on-going assistance for an extended period of time. However, no explanation is provided with regard to what the required assistance might be and how it could be structured. Broadly, we can say that it involves both the organisation and delivery of a range of services to assist people who have limited ability to function independently because of a mental and/or physical disability. Within this context, care means different things to different people. For some, care might mean medical support; for others it might represent

---

19 Interinstitutional Proclamation on the European Pillar of Social Rights, O.J. [2017] C428/10. See also the Communication from the Commission, Launching a consultation on a European Pillar of Social Rights, COM(2016) 127 final, for information on the European Pillar of Social Rights see: https://ec.europa.eu/commission/priorities/deeper-and-fairer-economic-and-monetary-union/european-pillar-social-rights_en. Accessed 25 July 2019.
20 Communication from the European Commission, An Initiative to Support Work-life Balance for Working Parents and Carers, COM(2017) 252 final.
21 Naoki Ikegami, John Hirdes and Ian Carpenter, "Long-Term Care: A Complex Challenge" (2001) 229 *OECD Observer* 27.
22 Joint Report by the Social Protection Committee and the European Commission Services, "Adequate Social Protection for Long-Term Care Needs in an Ageing Society" (European Union 2014) 12.

help with daily living activities, such as getting out of bed and getting dressed; to others it might mean help with housework (cooking and shopping); to others it could be synonymous to company and emotional support;[23] and to yet others, it might be about help with caring for somebody else.

As a result of these multiple quests, LTC has been organised – and financed – in different ways across Europe: as part of healthcare or welfare/social care.[24] The latter is the focus of this chapter. Similarly to the organisation of childcare, LTC consists of a combination of formal and informal measures.[25]

Formal care involves a specific range of services, from home help to community-based services to providing care in an institutional setting. Its importance has recently been emphasised by Principle 18 EPSR that highlights "[t]he right to affordable long-term care services of good quality". People whose professional qualification is to provide these services are "formal" carers: they are typically (poorly) paid and work under a contract that entitles them to holidays and determines how many hours they can work.

By contrast, informal care is often provided by family or friends, often women. Although informal carers play a key role in delivering high levels of care,[26] they are untrained and, in the main, unpaid.[27] In other words, informal care is not a service that can be purchased. Informal care is the most common approach, perhaps because in many instances it is perceived as being the only available option, or possibly because the parties concerned prefer it.[28] It is estimated that today

---

23 See for example, Case C-77/95 *Bruna-Alessandra Züchner v Handelskrankenkasse (Ersatzkasse) Bremen*. ECLI:EU:C:1996:425, para 14 where the Court acknowledged that "a person may be obliged to have recourse to the services of another when he is unable, or no longer able, to perform a particular activity himself, whether it be the education of children, housework, management of private property or *mere incidents of daily life*. In the main, such activities call for a degree of competence, are of a certain scope and must be provided by an outsider in return for remuneration if there is no-one else, whether or not a member of the family, who will do so without payment" (emphasis added).
24 See Annick Masselot, "Family Leave: Enforcement of the Protection against Dismissal and Unfavourable Treatment" (European Union 2018).
25 Communication from the Commission, Green Paper, "Confronting Demographic Change: A New Solidarity between Generations", COM(2005) 94; European Commission, "The 2015 Ageing Report" (European Union 2015), http://ec.europa.eu/economy_finance/publications/european_economy/2015/pdf/ee3_en.pdf. Accessed 20 July 2019.
26 European Parliament Report of 4 July 2013, "Impact of the Crisis on Access to care for Vulnerable Groups" (2013/2044(INI)), www.europarl.europa.eu/sides/getDoc.do?pubRef=-//EP//NONSGML+REPORT+A7-2013-0221+0+DOC+PDF+V0//EN. Accessed 25 July 2019.
27 However, some countries provide some basic financial support, such as carers allowance in the UK. See further European Commission, Commission Staff Working Document of 20 February 2013, "Long-Term Care in an Ageing Society – Challenges and Policy Options" SWD(2013) 41 final.
28 Home care is what most elderly people want. The Special Eurobarometer survey of 2007 asked how they would prefer to be assisted with long-term care if the need arose, 45% of respondents said "in my own home by a relative", 24% said "in my own home by a professional

20 million people across Europe care for older members of their family and they provide for around 80% of the care needs.[29] Even in Scandinavia, where relatively generous care provisions are in place, the vast majority of eldercare is performed informally by family and friends.[30] Under traditional accounting systems, this work is unaccounted,[31] but it comes at a cost for women as they represent the majority of carers, both formal and informal.

It is not the aim of this chapter to argue that one form of care should be preferable or better than the other. Equally, it is neither possible nor, arguably, desirable to commodify all the care needed in the family. Formal and informal care might substitute or complement each other, depending on individual circumstances. Therefore, each case should be determined according to the preference, needs and interests of the parties of the caring relationship in each individual case.[32] Too often, however, it is not a question of individual choice: for example, the austerity measures introduced by national governments to address the 2008 financial crisis and its aftermath, have resulted in a lack of eligibility for free or affordable care and lack of support for informal carers in the workplace, thus arguably dictating the "appropriate" type of care available.[33]

Yet the fact that informal care is a common occurrence does not exempt Member States from responsibility to provide care structures. The lack of care structure has a profound impact on those who are cared for, as well as on their carers. This,

---

care service", 12% said "in my own home by a hired carer" and 5% said "in the home of a close family member"; in total, 86% chose some form of home care and only 8% said "in a nursing home". See European Commission, "Health and Long-Term Care in the European Union" (Special Eurobarometer 283, European Union 2007) http://ec.europa.eu/public_opinion/archives/ebs/ebs_283_en.pdf. Accessed 25 July 2019.

29 European Parliament, "European Parliament Resolution of 13 September 2016 on Creating Labour Market Conditions Favourable for Work-life Balance (2016/2017(INI))" (13 September 2016) www.europarl.europa.eu/sides/getDoc.do?type=TA&reference=P8-TA-2016-0338&language=EN. Accessed 25 July 2019. The position of informal carers is further discussed in Chapter 4.
30 Eva Ryrstedt, "Dementia and Autonomy" in Ann Numhauser-Henning (ed), *Elder Law: Evolving European Perspectives* (Edward Elgar 2017).
31 Marilyn Waring, *Counting for Nothing: What Men Value and What Women are Worth* (Allen and Unwin 1988).
32 Not surprisingly an EU survey reports that a high number of elderly people indicated that they prefer home care to be done by a relative; see European Commission, "Health and Long-Term Care in the European Union" (Special Eurobarometer 283, European Union 2007) http://ec.europa.eu/public_opinion/archives/ebs/ebs_283_en.pdf. Accessed 25 July 2019.
33 See also, European Parliament Report of 4 July 2013, "Impact of the Crisis on Access to care for Vulnerable Groups" (2013/2044(INI)) www.europarl.europa.eu/sides/getDoc.do?pubRef=-//EP//NONSGML+REPORT+A7-2013-0221+0+DOC+PDF+V0//EN. Accessed 25 July 2019. The Report expresses concerns about the percentage of those giving up work altogether in order to care and expects that this number will rise over the coming years as a result of the increased demand for care and the reductions in state support for care due to austerity measures.

in particular, affects the ability of individuals to take up jobs in the labour market, a concern for the EU in the context of its Growth Strategy.[34] The European Parliament has suggested that about 3.3 million Europeans aged between 15 and 34 have had to give up full-time work because of the lack of care facilities for dependent children or older relatives.[35]

LTC challenges...

Historically, the EU has rarely engaged with the issue of LTC, whether formal or informal. When it has, the EU has done so indirectly and in a reactive rather than a proactive fashion. In other words, this type of care has been addressed only when it has become a challenge for other EU related policies. For example, it has been discussed in the context of third country migrants. The questions raised in this context covered the circumstances and the extent under which third country nationals can be allowed to come to the EU to be cared for by a relative already living in one of the EU Member States or when a non-EU national can be entitled to remain in order to care for an EU citizen.[36] Although we must remain aware of the impact that LTC can have on a diverse range of EU policies, this chapter focuses on the type of support the EU should offer to allow its citizens to care and to be cared for. Some very specific challenges need to be considered.[37] The first challenge is linked to the sheer numbers of individuals in need of care. The rapidly raising age of the population means that those in need of LTC are expected to triple by 2060.[38] In turn, the age-related expenditure will increase correspondingly. Indeed, the 2012 Ageing report highlighted that the health care expenditure in the EU27 is expected to increase from 7.1% of GDP in 2010 to 8.3% in 2060, and the public spending on long-term care is projected to double from 1.8% in 2010

---

34 Communication from the Commission to the European Parliament, the Council, the European Economic and Social Committee and the Committee of the Regions, "Towards Social Investment for Growth and Cohesion – including implementing the European Social Fund 2014–2020", COM(2013) 83.
35 European Parliament, "European Parliament Resolution of 13 September 2016 on Creating Labour Market Conditions Favourable for Work-life Balance (2016/2017(INI))" (13 September 2016) www.europarl.europa.eu/sides/getDoc.do?type=TA&reference=P8-TA-2016-0338&language=EN. Accessed 20 December 2018. The position of informal carers is further discussed in Chapter 4.
36 *Inter alia*, Case C-34/09 *Gerardo Ruiz Zambrano v Office national de l'emploi (ONEm)*. ECLI:EU:C:2011:124; Case C-413/99 *Baumbast and R. v Secretary of State for the Home Department*. ECLI:EU:C:2002:493 and Case C-60/00 *Mary Carpenter* v *Secretary of State for the Home Department*. ECLI:EU:C:2002:434.
37 See, *inter alia*, Social Protection Committee and the European Commission, "Adequate Social Protection for Long-Term Care Needs in an Aging Society" 18 June 2014, 10,406/14 ADD 1; SOC 403 ECOFIN 525.
38 See Francesca Bettio and Alina Verashchagina, "Long-Term Care for the Elderly: Provisions and Providers in 33 Countries" (Publication Office of the European Union 2013).

to 3.4% of GDP in 2060 in the EU as a whole.[39] In this context, the sustainability of the existing framework to cater for LTC will be seriously challenged. In other words, an ageing population implies careful management of LTC policies to avoid prohibitive costs for both individuals and society. Related to this, is a second challenge namely that, whilst the number of people in need of care will increase, the availability of carers is expected to decline. Stagnation and/or falling birth rates contribute to an expected 14.2% (2010–2060) decrease in the EU27's working age population. Therefore, fewer people will be able to provide formal care. By 2020, a shortage of up to 2 million health carers is predicted.[40] Equally, the capacity of family and friends (mainly spouses, daughters and daughters-in-law),[41] who are currently estimated to provide around 80% of care,[42] is projected to decline as a result of changes to society, and family structures. As to the former, higher pensionable ages require people to work longer, therefore affecting their availability to provide care.[43] As to the latter, increasing numbers of fluid relationships reduce the possibility of partner's support in old age as well as, in particular, in the case of men, children's support.[44] Moreover, people are having fewer children; children tend to live further away from their elderly parents and as a result are unable to provide the required care.[45] Should no action be taken, it is estimated that at least 15% of necessary care will not be covered by 2020.[46] The increase in the number

---

39 European Commission and Economic Policy Committee, "The 2012 Ageing Report Economic and budgetary projections for the 27 EU Member States (2010–2060)" (European Economy 2/2012, European Union 2012) http://ec.europa.eu/economy_finance/publications/european_economy/2012/pdf/ee-2012-2_en.pdf. Accessed 25 July 2019.

40 European Commission, "Growing the European Silver Economy" (Background Paper, 23 February 2015) http://ec.europa.eu/research/innovation-union/pdf/active-healthy-ageing/silvereco.pdf. Accessed 25 July 2019.

41 Ricardo Rodrigues, Manfred Huber, and Giovanni Lamura (eds), *Facts and Figures on Healthy Ageing and Long-term Care: Europe and North America* (European Centre for Social Welfare Policy and Research 2012) www.euro.centre.org/publications/detail/403. Accessed 25 July 2019.

42 Francesca Bettio and Alina Verashchagina, "Long-Term Care for the Elderly: Provisions and Providers in 33 Countries" (Publication Office of the European Union 2013).

43 Denis Bouget, Chiara Saraceno and Slavina Spasova, "Towards New Work-Life Balance Policies for those caring for Dependent Relatives?" in Bart Vanhercke, Sebastiano Sabato, Denis Bouget (eds), *Social Policy in the European Union: State of Play 2017* (ETUI 2017).

44 Marco Albertini and Chiara Saraceno, "Intergenerational Contact and Support: The Long-Term Effects of Marital Instability in Italy" in Chiara Saraceno (ed), *Families Ageing and Social Policy, Intergeneration Solidarity in European Welfare States* (Edward Elgar 2008).

45 Joëlle Gaymu and others, "Who Will be Caring for Europe's Dependent Elders in 2030?" (2007) 62 *Population* 675; Linda Pickard, "A Growing Care Gap? The Supply of Unpaid Care for Older People by their Adult Children in England to 2032" (2015) 35 *Ageing and Society* 96 and European Commission, "Proposal for Multi-annual Programme of Action for Health (2014–2020)", COM(2011) 709 final.

46 Ibid.

of people needing care and the decrease in the number of people who can offer care creates a "care-gap" which, in turn, is predicted to make it difficult to ensure the availability, affordability and quality of the care offered.

This brings us to a third challenge which will be discussed in detail in the next chapter, namely, the acknowledgement of the vital connection between care-givers and care recipients.[47] The role of carers is crucial to secure the well-being of those in receipt of care. The development of an EU LTC strategy should therefore prioritise carers.[48] Yet, although the needs of carers and cared for are interconnected, it is important to acknowledge that both groups deserve independent recognition. Accordingly, carers should not be protected exclusively because of their association with people in need of care[49] but also, because they themselves represent a vulnerable group.[50] For example, it is not unusual for care-givers to be simultaneously care recipients themselves.

... and opportunities

LTC does not necessarily only pose threats and challenges. It is becoming increasingly clear that, especially when addressing the ageing population, LTC has the potential to open up opportunities for new jobs and to contribute to economic growth. There is a compelling argument to support public investment in both physical and social infrastructures for LTC. Physical infrastructures cover a traditional terrain, namely the constructions of buildings and facilities to cater for LTC, which can result in an indirect boosting economic effect. Social infrastructures, namely those related to health services as well as social care activities for the elderly and disabled, are perhaps even more important. The EU will need to provide appropriate care goods and services to target active and healthy ageing; these will be structured taking into account the age and the level of dependency of the potential users. In turn, a strong market in this area is likely to contribute to the significant improvement of the efficiency and sustainability of health and social care systems.

In 2007, the EU Council started to define a policy position in this respect and called upon the Commission to seize the opportunity and develop a Silver

---

47 Rachel Horton, "Caring for Adults in the EU: Work-Life Balance and Challenge for EU Law" (2015) 37 *Journal of Social Welfare & Family Law* 356. See also Chapter 4.
48 E.g. Ikegami Naoki, John Hirdes and Ian Carpenter, "Long-Term Care: A Complex Challenge" (2001) 229 *OECD Observer* 27. See also Herring who argues that it is a recognition of the caring relationship and mutual vulnerability of the parties, rather than the separate rights and interests of each, that should underpin legal and policy approaches to care, Jonathan Herring, *Caring and the Law* (Hart Publishing 2013).
49 See Case C-303/06 *Coleman* v *Attridge Law and Steve Law*. ECLI:EU:C:2008:415 and *Kulikauskas v Macduff Shellfish* UKEATS/62/09 [2011] ICT 48 and *Hainsworth v Ministry of Defence* UKEATPA/0227/13/GE [2013].
50 See the discussion in Chapter 1.

Economy.[51] There is no set definition of the Silver Economy, but it is accepted that it indicates the creation of a framework to facilitate the development of a specific section of the economy concerned with Europe's older citizens. It is driven both by the emergence of new consumers and by the need to improve the sustainability of age-related expenditures. It includes all the economic activities arising from public and consumer expenditure related to the rights, needs and demands of the (fast-growing) population of over-50s. This is a large section of the population that can be divided into three main groups, namely active, frail and dependent. Each group has specific needs, such as health and nutrition, leisure and well-being, finance and transport, housing, education and employment, and accordingly spending priorities. Essentially, the Council invited the Commission to consider working "on a horizontal basis, so that the possible contributions of all policy areas could be considered when developing options to act".[52]

In 2012, the OECD launched a Silver Economy Initiative[53] and Member States introduced several initiatives focused on national and local contexts. Against this backdrop, in 2015, the Commission published the background paper "Growing the European Silver Economy"[54] in which it explores the possible contributions of all policy areas with a view to develop options to act.[55] The European Commission is specifically focused on economic growth and jobs. Indeed, the Silver Economy is likely to result in the creation of jobs in the LTC sector and a wide range of older age related goods and services such as the development of new technologies.[56] It is important to maximise this potential of these measures.

The rationale for EU involvement

It follows from the above discussion that, either because there are challenges to address or opportunities to exploit, the EU needs to provide leadership in this area, as a matter of urgency. An EU position is also important because, given the cross-border element of care, it is necessary to avoid the fragmentation that

---

51 Resolution of the Council of the European Union of 22 February 2007, "Opportunities and Challenges of Demographic Change in Europe" (6226/07).
52 Ibid, 19.
53 Organisation for Economic Co-operation and Development (OECD) and Asia-Pacific Economic Cooperation (APEC), "Anticipating Special Needs of the 21st Century Silver Economy" (OECD-APEC Joint Workshop, Tokyo, September 2012) www.oecd.org/sti/silver-economy-facts-challenges-and-opportunities.htm. Accessed 25 July 2019.
54 European Commission, "Growing the European Silver Economy" (Background Paper, 23 February 2015) http://ec.europa.eu/research/innovation-union/pdf/active-healthy-ageing/silvereco.pdf. Accessed 25 July 2019.
55 Ibid, 6.
56 European Commission, "Proposal for Multi-annual Programme of Action for Health (2014–2020)", COM(2011) 709 final.

different national initiatives might bring.[57] In other words, the EU needs to take a proactive approach to LTC and develop suitable policies to guide the Member States in this area.

The economic rationale for the EU to develop a LTC strategy is clear. Numerous studies have analysed the potential impact of the Silver Economy and have estimated its value to be €7 trillion per year and it is projected to reach €15 trillion by 2020.[58] Thus, simply put, an ageing population challenges the traditional EU way "to do business".

At the same time, LTC is not only a way "to do business" but is also a form of social capital that should be constructed as a moral obligation to provide for people who cannot support themselves any longer. An EU LTC strategy cannot merely focus on economic concerns to the expense of emotional/human ones. This will likely lead to solutions which merely seek to ensure that some form of care is provided. In turn, this increases the risk that any legislative proposals developed on the basis of economic concerns alone, may be insufficiently sensitive to the needs of those involved and reductive in choices of both care givers and care recipients with regard to care arrangements. Such policy direction would go against the very essence of the notion of care.

Furthermore, as previously discussed, the very value of care goes beyond its economic currency and the economic argument cannot be "decoupled" from other considerations.[59] Care is the foundation of society, a part of human life, a most basic human need that all at some stage are likely to encounter. To ignore the emotional component of care is to ignore the very essence of care. In particular, without carefully developed LTC policies guided by the ethic of care, individuals' well-being risks being severely compromised.

LTC policy development in the EU and in the Member States

Despite acknowledging that LTC is an issue of public interest,[60] the EU has rarely and only very recently intervened on this topic. To date, the EU's intervention in LTC remains scarce and often fragmented and until recently there has been no effort to develop a normative framework in this area. Thus, the intervention has

---

57 See Annick Masselot, "Family Leave: Enforcement of the Protection against Dismissal and Unfavourable Treatment" (European Union 2018).
58 Euromonitor International, "Boomers as Consumers" (October 2012) www.euromonitor.com/boomers-as-consumers/report. Accessed 25 July 2019 and Financial Times, "Silver Economy Series" (3 November 2014) www.ft.com/intl/topics/themes/Ageing_populations. Accessed 25 July 2019.
59 See "Setting the scene: 'Everyone cares. Everyone is cared for'"; Grace James and Emma Spruce, "Workers with Elderly Dependants: Employment Law's Response to the Latest Caregiving Conundrum" (2015) 35 *Legal Studies* 463.
60 See for example: United Nations, 'Regional Implementation Strategy for the Madrid International Plan of Action on Ageing 2002' (ECE/AC.23/2002/2/Rev.6, 11 September 2002) www.unece.org/fileadmin/DAM/pau/RIS.pdf. Accessed 25 July 2019, that

been mainly limited to non-binding instruments and policy initiatives, which are at times ineffective and can have the undesired side effects of perpetuating gender stereotypes.

One of the main reasons for this limited approach is that LTC is not an express competence of the EU and remains predominantly the responsibility of the Member States, where methods and solutions provided vary widely.[61] It is at present difficult to have a clear picture of the overall state of LTC in the EU Member States because, for several reasons, information is patchy. For example, different definitions of LTC apply across Europe. While in some Member States LTC is part of health policy, in others it is considered to be part of the social care system.

As far as formal care is concerned, the range of services on offer varies considerably across countries: it includes home-care, semi-residential care and residential care.[62] Access and requirements for eligibility of care also differs across Member States. A report by the Social Protection Committee and the Commission acknowledged that "there are more pronounced differences between Member States in the way long-term care is provided than in any other aspect of social protection."[63] The different approaches reflect, among other things, differences in working patterns (in particular amongst women), societal attitudes

expresses a commitment "[t]o support families that provide care for older persons and promote intergenerational and intra-generational solidarity among their members". See also Recommendation of the Committee of Ministers to Member States on the Council of Europe Action Plan to promote the rights and full participation of people with disabilities in society: improving the quality of life of people with disabilities in Europe 2006–2015 Rec(2006) 5; United Nations Convention on the Rights of Persons with Disabilities, A/61/611 of 6 December 2006, Preamble: "Persons with disabilities and their family members should receive the necessary protection and assistance to enable families to contribute towards the full and equal enjoyment of the rights of persons with disabilities"; European Commission "Long-term care in European Union" (European Communities 2008): Within the Open Method of Coordination (OMC) related to the health and LTC agenda, informal care is recognised as a key factor in LTC system sustainability (art 3.3); Council Recommendation CM/Rec (2009) 6 on ageing and disability in the 21st century: sustainable frameworks to enable greater quality of life in an inclusive society, 8 July 2009 https://rm.coe.int/CoERMPublicCommonSearchServices/DisplayDCTMContent?documentId=09000016806992fc. Accessed 25 July 2019.

61 Francesca Bettio and Alina Verashchagina, "Long-Term Care for the Elderly: Provisions and Providers in 33 Countries" (Publication Office of the European Union 2013); Spasova Slavinia, and others, "Challenges in Long-Term Care in Europe. A Study of National Policies" (European Commission 2018).
62 Ibid.
63 Social Protection Committee and the European Commission, "Adequate Social Protection for Long-Term Care Needs in an Aging Society" 18 June 2014, 10,406/14 ADD 1; SOC 403 ECOFIN 525, 8. Perhaps the only common element that these different approaches share is that "non-professional family care plays a major role" although even in this case "the extent to which this is complemented by formal, publicly provided care varies widely." See further the discussion in Chapter 4.

to care, the country's perceived needs as well as different levels of financial resources provided.[64]

The wide variety of approaches to the delivery of LTC across Member States has both negative and positive elements. On the one hand, it can mean that standards are not consistent and this can impact on social justice. On the other hand, it means that there is a wealth of experience and ideas to refer to as the Member States seek to modernise, expand and improve services in response to demographic ageing and other challenges.

For its part, the EU has not developed as a rights-based cohesive strategy on LTC. The EU has mainly acted as a facilitator that provides "policy support" and "information sharing". In other words, the EU has limited its action to the promotion of cooperation between Member States in this field without providing active leadership. It has done so mainly through the Open Method of Coordination (OMC)[65] and the European Semester,[66] in particular, by exploring how to extend or restore older people's autonomy and capacity to live independently. Nevertheless, it should be highlighted that the lack of EU leadership has not necessarily resulted in inaction. In particular, within the OMC framework, Member States have agreed upon important principles, focusing in particular on access, quality and sustainability.[67] Three broad principles have been agreed upon.[68]

First, all individuals must be guaranteed access to adequate health and LTC. Member States have further agreed to explore inequities in access to care and in

---

[64] Caroline Glendinning and others, "Care Provision within Families and its Socio-Economic Impact on Care Providers across the European Union" (Social Policy Research Unit University of York, Working Paper No. EU 2342, May 2009). See also, Tine Rostgaard, "Caring for Children and Older People in Europe – A Comparison of European Policies and Practice" (2002) 32 *Policy Studies* 51. Furthermore, the differences are emphasised by the fact that comparative information is currently patchy and does not provide a clear picture of the situation. See Social Protection Committee and the European Commission, "Adequate Social Protection for Long-Term Care Needs in An Aging Society" 10,406/14 ADD 1; SOC 403 ECOFIN 525. See also Annick Masselot, "Family Leave: Enforcement of the Protection against Dismissal and Unfavourable Treatment" (European Union 2018), particularly 92–97.

[65] Communication from the Commission of 2 July 2008 "A Renewed Commitment to Social Europe: Reinforcing the Open Method of Coordination for Social Protection and Social Inclusion", COM(2008) 418 final. See also David Trubek and Louise Trubek, "Hard and Soft Law in the Construction of Social Europe Hard and Soft Law in the Construction of Social Europe: The Role of the Open Method of Co-ordination" (2005) 11 *European Law Journal* 343.

[66] Communication from the European Commission to support work-life balance for working parents and carers, 26 April 2017, COM(2017) 252 final, 14.

[67] E.g. see David Trubek and Louise Trubek, "Hard and Soft Law in the Construction of Social Europe Hard and Soft Law in the Construction of Social Europe: The Role of the Open Method of Co-ordination" (2005) 11 *European Law Journal* 343.

[68] European Commission, "Challenges in Long-term Care in Europe. A Study of National Policies" (2018).

health outcomes in order to ensure that the need for care does not lead to poverty and financial dependency.

Second, it is important to promote quality in health and LTC and to adapt care to the changing needs and preferences of society and individuals, notably by establishing quality standards reflecting best international practice and by strengthening the responsibility of health professionals and of patients and care recipients.

Third, Member States want to ensure that adequate and high quality health and LTC remains affordable and sustainable by promoting healthy and active life styles, good human resources for the care sector and a rational use of resources, notably through appropriate incentives for users and providers, good governance and coordination between care systems and institutions.

It follows from this last point that, as it is widely acknowledged that the main reason for the need of LTC is frailty, intervention concentrates on social protection against it, namely measures encouraging changes in lifestyle and improvement in the management of chronic disease and illness. A 2014 EU report,[69] for example, has identified possible steps to improve health amongst the older population. These are based around three main concepts: prevention, rehabilitation and re-enablement. The rationale behind prevention is that the care needed will depend on the overall physical conditions. Simply put, unless the prevalence of frailty and morbidity is reduced, the demand for LTC will increase. Prevention measures, thus, encourage people to remain active and healthy. They also include services for people with poor physical or mental health to help them to avoid unplanned or unnecessary admissions to hospital or residential settings and, in certain cases, it can include short-term emergency interventions as well as longer term low-level support. It is a low-cost but effective way to address some of the effects of LTC as it should decrease and postpone the onset of frailty. Across the EU, there are many examples highlighting how the Member States have implemented forms of prevention.[70] Rehabilitation services can play an important role in helping people with poor physical or mental health to get better. Finally, re-enablement is a more recent concept, which has been developed by policy makers especially in Denmark and in the UK. It aims to maximise independence and quality of life in older age, whilst at the same time reducing costs. It encourages individuals to do things themselves rather than having others do it for them. It focuses on real practical outcomes within a specified timeframe and is concerned with continuous rather than a one-off assessment of an individual's care needs.

Overall, these three concepts are aimed towards achieving a better management of disability and frailty; improving coordination between health and social care providers; and promoting a more effective deployment of technology to encourage

---

69 Social Protection Committee and the European Commission, "Adequate Social Protection for Long-Term Care Needs in an Aging Society" 18 June 2014, 10,406/14 ADD 1; SOC 403 ECOFIN 525.
70 See, for example, "The New Medicine Services" in the UK www.newdynamics.group.shef.ac.uk/map2030-modelling-ageing-populations-to-2030.html. Accessed 25 July 2019.

independent living among the older population. Yet such initiatives, however well intentioned, cannot and do not make up for a cohesive policy framework: they need to be complemented with measures aimed at recruitment and retention of formal care-givers as well as measures to support informal carers.

Recent policy development on long-term care

Although LTC is not an express EU competence, a commitment towards those in need of LTC is already enshrined in EU law. Such commitment is grounded in the fundamental and historical values of the EU, which was created as a tool for peace and European integration. In terms of primary legislation, the Article 2 Treaty on European Union (TEU) expressly refers, *inter alia*, to the respect for human dignity as one of the values on which the Union is based, and of the Article 3 TEU is committed to promote the well-being of its people as well as ensuring solidarity between generations. The Treaty on the Functioning of the European Union further provides a number of legal bases to act on issues indirectly connected to LTC including the provisions on gender equality,[71] age equality[72] and health and safety.[73] Furthermore the Charter, which is now primary legislation, specifically provides for the rights of the elderly and the disabled. In particular, Article 25 CFR states that "[t]he Union recognises and respects the rights of the elderly to lead a life of dignity and independence and to participate in social and cultural life" and Article 26 CFR aims to contribute toward the integration of persons with disabilities. These provisions contribute to ensure that relationships of care, love and solidarity are nurtured and valued. Nevertheless, they cannot, at least for the time being, be used as a direct legal base to enact specific EU legal measures on LTC.

The narrow approach limits the scope of the EU's action but does not prevent it. Recently, Principle 18 EPSR[74] by stating that "[e]veryone has the right to affordable long-term care services of good quality" has brought fresh impetus to this area. With this renewed commitment to social rights, the European Commission adopted the Communication on work-life balance for working parents and carers.[75] It sets out a comprehensive package of complementary and mutually reinforcing legal and policy measures designed to support Member States in achieving common goals on *inter alia* LTC. In particular, it states that the EU will endeavour to support Member States in addressing the lack of adequate care services for both children and adults. These measures further strive to improve the collection of data at EU level by Eurostat on the take up of family-related leaves and flexible

---

71 Article 157 TFEU.
72 Article 19 TFEU.
73 Articles 91, 114, 115, 151, 153 and 352 TFEU.
74 Interinstitutional Proclamation on the European Pillar of Social Rights, O.J. [2017] C428/10.
75 Communication from the European Commission to support work-life balance for working parents and carers, 26 April 2017, COM(2017) 252 final.

working arrangements by women and men. Moreover, the EU is committed to promoting the sharing of good practices with social partners and Member States by means, for example, of seminars under the Mutual Learning Programme. Finally, the EU pledges to make a range of funding available to develop LTC. In particular, some funding will be provided under the Programme for Employment and Social Innovation[76] that will fund new pilot schemes aimed at employers for the development of innovative working arrangements such as family leaves and flexible working arrangements.

The importance of the Commission's Communication[77] cannot be overstated: it is simply a game-changer and a turning point.[78] It expressly places LTC on the EU agenda and specifically sets strong foundations to build a relevant framework in this area. In doing so, it contributes to challenging the traditional public/private structure that underpins the relevant policy discourse. Furthermore, by raising awareness and encouraging the sharing of best practice it also contributes to shaping an environment where care, and in particular LTC, is seen as an integral element of everybody's life and a "normal" part of society. Such a policy development is therefore a welcome stepping-stone toward better recognition of LTC in EU policy.

Conclusion

Caring for the frailer members of society has become a key challenge for domestic governments. Across Europe, the organisation of LTC is fragmented and does not offer a comprehensive solution: an integrated LTC system of care is only just emerging in many Member States, let alone at EU level. This chapter has explored whether and to what extent the EU legislator and policy maker are – and can – further engage with this issue.

The EU intervention in this area remains minimal and recent. This is because the EU historically has had limited competences and can only address the issue indirectly on the basis of other competences such as gender equality and/or age discrimination. It is hoped that the adoption of the EPSR will strengthen the argument for EU intervention.

The development of LTC differs to the policy development in relation to childcare where the lack of express competence in relation to childcare has not prevented the EU from developing a set of policy provisions.[79]

---

76 EU Programme for Employment and Social Innovation (as for 23 June 2017). http://ec.europa.eu/social/main.jsp?catId=1081. Accessed 25 July 2019.
77 Communication from the European Commission to support work-life balance for working parents and carers, 26 April 2017, COM(2017) 252 final.
78 Denis Bouget, Chiara Saraceno and Slavina Spasova, "Towards New Work-Life Balance Policies for those Caring for Dependent Relatives?" in Bart Vanhercke, Sebastiano Sabato, Denis Bouget (eds), *Social Policy in the European Union: State of Play 2017* (ETUI 2017).
79 Annick Masselot, "The EU Childcare Strategy in Times of Austerity" (2015) 37 *Journal of Social Welfare & Family Law* 345.

Against this background, we contend that the EU should go further and take a proactive and leading role in *framing* the principles and the conditions under which LTC is organised. Even though LTC differs from childcare, the principles underpinning both strategy developments are similar. A reconceptualisation of the LTC policy would enable the development of structures, to better address the needs of recipients of LTC (older and frailer people) as well as those who provide care.

Although the development of a LTC strategy will not be an easy task, there is a strong argument to support the EU intervention in this area. It is true that, in light of the divergent LTC structures across the Member States, regulation of LTC is best addressed at national level and that the role of the EU should be (or remain) that of a facilitator. However, the EU should, at the very least, make sure that the basic values enshrined in the EU Treaty, in the Charter of Fundamental Rights and in European Pillar of Social Rights are upheld by the Member States. Finally, we remain aware that the current economic climate is likely to provide a strong counter argument to the improvement of social rights.[80] There is a widespread perception that social rights increase burdens on business: yet economic priorities should not be used to bypass fundamental rights.

---

80 Roberta Guerrina, "Socio Economic Challenges to Work Life Balance at Times of Crisis" (2015) 37 *Journal of Social Welfare & Family Law* 368.

4 The EU and carers

Introduction

In the previous chapters, we have discussed the EU's engagement with child and long-term care.[1] There is a further aspect to the care relationship, namely the position of carers.[2] It is estimated that at some point in their life most people will become carers, either as parents or for dependent adults.[3] In the EU, 51% of individuals aged 18–64 provide some form of care for an elderly or disabled relative,[4] and the statistics are higher when looking at childcare.[5] These figures might not be entirely accurate due to the fact that each Member State uses a range of different criteria for the purpose of defining who is a carer, and there is not enough data to provide a clear picture.[6] To understand the scale of the problem, it is sufficient to look at individual states: in the UK alone, for example, in 2012 there were 7.7 million families with dependent children, and it is estimated that the number of carers

---

1 See the discussion in Chapters 2 and 3.
2 This book addresses carers, regardless of whether they care for children or adults. See the discussion in "Setting the Scene: 'Everyone Cares. Everyone is Cared For'".
3 Office for National Statistics, "Working and Workless Households, 2013 – Statistical Bulletin" (Office of National Statistics 2013) www.ons.gov.uk/ons/dcp171778_325269.pdf. Accessed 25 July 2019.
4 Figures from the Eurofound, "Third European Quality of Life Survey (EQLS) 2011–2012" www.eurofound.europa.eu/surveys/european-quality-of-life-surveys/european-quality-of-life-survey-2012. Accessed 25 July 2019, reveal that 12% of men and 16% of women aged 18–64 in employment care for an elderly or disabled relative less than once a week, and 8% of men and 9% of women care for an elderly or disabled relative at least once or twice a week. Among workers aged 50–64, 18% of men and 22% of women provide care at least once a week. See also Eurofound, "European Quality of Life Survey (EQLS) 2016" (Publications Office of the European Union 2016) www.eurofound.europa.eu/sites/default/files/ef_publication/field_ef_document/ef1733en.pdf. Accessed 25 July 2019.
5 European Commission, *The Provision of Childcare Services* (Luxembourg Office for Official Publications 2009).
6 Joint Report by the Social Protection Committee and the European Commission Services, *Adequate Social Protection for Long-Term Care Needs in an Ageing Society* (European Union 2014) 12.

of adults will rise to 9 million by 2037.[7] It is undeniable that carers get a "raw deal"[8] from society. As carers in European countries cover between 50% and 90% of the overall cost of informal long-term care (LTC), not to mention childcare,[9] their role is therefore essential. Yet they are invisible to society and their needs are largely overlooked by the law. If carers are not engaged in paid employment, their "non-working status" contributes to their needs being underestimated, their availability being taken for granted and ultimately preventing them from accessing the labour market. If they are in paid employment, it is widely acknowledged that they face difficulties in combining their role as carers with their working responsibilities and, as a result, they are disadvantaged when compared to non-carers. Individuals who have caring responsibilities have, on average, a lower employment rate than the rest of the population.[10] They might not be able to work the same hours as someone who is free from caring responsibilities. Thus, they are more likely to enter contracts of employment which are non-standard and, often, precarious.[11] Such contracts are typically characterised by low levels of pay, limited legal protection, job insecurity, little possibility of advancement and reduced ability to support a household.[12] These characteristics are further accentuated in times of economic crisis and austerity.[13] In turn, a loose connection with the employment market

---

7 Carers UK, "Carers at a Breaking Point" (2014).
8 Jonathan Herring, "Caring" (2007) 89 *Law and Justice – Christian Law Review* 89.
9 European Commission, "Joint Report on Health Care and Long-Term Care Systems and Fiscal Sustainability", (European Commission Directorate-General for Economic and Financial Affairs, Institutional Paper 037, October 2016) https://ec.europa.eu/info/publications/economy-finance/joint-report-health-care-and-long-term-care-systems-fiscal-sustainability-0_en. Accessed 25 July 2019.
10 Sarah Cunningham-Burley, Kathryn Backett-Milburn, and Debbie Kemmer, "Constructing Health and Sickness in the Context of Motherhood and Paid Work" (2006) 28 *Sociology of Health & Illness* 385; European Commission, *Report on Progress on Equality between Women and Men in 2010: The Gender Balance in Business Leadership* (Publications Office of the European Union 2011); Eurofound, "European Quality of Life Survey (EQLS) 2016" (Publications Office of the European Union 2016).
11 Dirk Hofäcker and Stephanie König, "Flexibility and Work-life Conflict in Time of Crisis: A Gender Perspective" (2013) 33 *Intl Journal of Sociology and Social Policy* 613; Lindy Fursman and Nita Zodgekar, "Making It Work: The Impacts of Flexible Working Arrangements on New Zealand Families" (2009) 35 *Social Policy Journal of New Zealand* 43.
12 Judy Fudge and Rosemary Owens (eds), *Precarious Work, Women, and the New Economy: The Challenge to Legal Norms* (Hart Publishing 2006); Nicola Kountouris, "The Legal Determinants of Precariousness in Personal Work Relations: A European Perspective" (2012) 34 *Comparative Labour Law and Policy* 21.
13 Annick Masselot, "EU Childcare Strategy in Times of Austerity" (2015) 37 *Journal of Social Welfare & Family Law* 345; Johanna Kantola and Emanuela Lombardo (eds), *Gender and the Economic Crisis in Europe: Politics, Institutions and Intersectionality* (Palgrave 2017); Maria Karamessini and Jill Rubery (ed), *Women and Austerity: The Economic Crisis and the Future for Gender Equality* (Routledge 2014); European Parliament Resolution of 4 July 2013, "Impact of the crisis on access to care for vulnerable groups" (2013/2044(INI)).

will affect the possibility to accrue a pension. This has led Charlotte O'Brien to argue that, if not regulated, caring can become a "penalty".[14] In sum, carers are vulnerable.[15]

The strain that care responsibilities place on carers has long been acknowledged. In 1999, Advocate General Cosmas described carers as "unsung heroes" and urged that:

> measures should ... be taken to protect those persons because of the range of risks they run (psychological damage, social isolation, and so forth) as a result of being continually occupied in looking after someone reliant on care.[16]

In addition, the Court of Justice (CJEU or the Court) itself has contributed to highlighting the needs of carers. Its intervention is important not only because it has delivered individual justice in specific cases[17] helping to shape the relevant policies and legislation, but also because it has highlighted the value of care and the importance of carers for the well-being of society.[18]

How has the EU addressed this situation? Commissioner Tonio Borg has convincingly argued that:

> [o]ur common goals of smart, sustainable and inclusive growth – as defined in the Europe 2020 strategy – cannot be met if informal carers are left out of the labour market or overlooked by welfare systems.[19]

Is this vision within reach? In the past two decades, EU institutions have acknowledged that a competitive economy cannot be achieved without the development of a sustainable strategy to allow its citizens to care for their dependents and enable them to be employable.[20] Thus, in 2006 the European Commission advocated

---

14 Charlotte O'Brien, "Confronting the Care Penalty: The Cause for Extending Reasonable Adjustment Rights along the Disability/Care Continuum" (2012) 34(1) *Journal of Social Welfare & Family Law* 5.
15 See the discussion in "Setting the Scene: 'Everyone Cares. Everyone is Cared For'".
16 Case C-160/96 *M. Molenaar and B. Fath-Molenaar v Allgemeine Ortskrankenkasse Baden-Württember.* ECLI:EU:C:1998:84; Opinion of Advocate General Cosmas delivered on 9 December 1997, ECLI:EU:C:1997:599, fn 3.
17 Grace James, *The Legal Regulation of Pregnancy and Maternity in the Labour Market* (Routledge-Cavendish 2008).
18 See for example the seminal Case C-85/96 *María Martínez Sala v Freistaat Bayern.* ECLI:EU:C:1998:217.
19 Tonio Borg, European Commissioner, "Speech given to European Parliament Interest Group on Carers" (Brussels, Belgium, 9 April 2014).
20 European Council, "Lisbon European Council 23 and 24 March 2000 Presidency Conclusions" (23–24 March 2000) www.europarl.europa.eu/summits/lis1_en.htm. Accessed 25 July 2019.

The EU and carers 103

for the need to explore other reconciliation measures such as "leave to care for elderly parents or disabled family members."[21] In 2008, this intention was echoed in the comprehensive Work-Life Balance Package presented by the Commission.[22] Although this Package was only partially adopted,[23] it provided evidence of a new and emerging policy discourse in this area. In 2011, a consultation was initiated on possible EU measures in relation to carers' leave[24] and in 2013, the European Parliament passed a Resolution calling on the Commission and the Member States to "develop a coherent framework for all types of care leave" and to "propose a directive on carers' leave, in line with the subsidiarity principle as set out in the Treaties."[25] This was reiterated in the 2015 Commission Roadmap that called for initiatives "to allow for parents with children or those with dependent relatives to better balance caring and professional responsibilities."[26] Eventually, the Commission adopted the Communication on the New Start Initiative[27] in the context of the European Pillar of Social Rights (EPSR)[28] that expressly addresses

---

21 European Commission, "First-stage Consultation of European Social Partners on Reconciliation of Professional, Private and Family Life" 12 October 2006, SEC (2006) 1245, 10.
22 Communication from the Commission of 3 October 2008, "A Better Work-Life Balance: Stronger Support for Reconciling Professional, Private and Family Life" COM(2008) 635 final.
23 The European Commission's proposed Work-Life Package (MEMO/08/603 of 03 October 2008) was adopted a few weeks before the 2008 crisis engulfed the EU. It included a number of documents including two legislative proposals to revise existing directives: the Pregnant Workers Directive (Proposal for a Directive amending Council Directive 92/85/EEC on the introduction of measures to encourage improvements in the safety and health at work of pregnant workers and workers who have recently given birth or are breastfeeding, COM(2008) 637) and the Self-Employed Directive (Proposal for a Directive on the application of the principle of equal treatment between men and women engaged in an activity in a self-employed capacity and repealing Directive 86/613/EEC, COM(2008) 636). The Self-Employed Directive was amended but the proposed amendments to the Pregnant Workers Directive, was rejected by the Council in December 2010 and eventually axed by the Commission on 19 June 2014 because it was considered to be "red tape". See Petra Foubert and Šejla Imamović, "The Pregnant Workers Directive: Must Do Better – Lessons to be Learned from Strasbourg?" (2015) 37 *Journal of Social Welfare & Family Law* 309.
24 European Commission, "Public Consultation on Possible EU Measures in the Area of Carers' Leave or Leave to Care for Dependent Relatives" (August 2011).
25 European Parliament, Resolution of 4 July 2013, "Impact of the Crisis on Access to Care for Vulnerable Groups" (2013/2044(INI)), para 56.
26 European Commission, "ROADMAP: New Start to Address the Challenges of Work–Life Balance Faced by Working Families" (2015) http://ec.europa.eu/smart-regulation/roadmaps/docs/2015_just_012_new_initiative_replacing_maternity_leave_directive_en.pdf. Accessed 15 June 2019.
27 Communication from the Commission, "An Initiative to Support Work-Life Balance for Working Parents and Carers", COM(2017) 252 final.
28 Interinstitutional Proclamation on the European Pillar of Social Rights, O.J. [2017] C428/15; Mark Bell, "The Principle of equal treatment and the European Pillar of social Rights" (2018) 160 *Giornale di Diritto del Lavoro e di Relazioni Industriali* 783.

the position of carers. These efforts culminated in the adoption of the Work-Life Balance Directive in 2019 that provides a range of rights for carers and thus considerably strengthens their position under EU law.[29] The 2019 Directive represents a turning point as this is the first legislative initiative to "give teeth" to the policy approach towards carers. Until then the EU legislator had not developed a self-standing strategy to address the needs of all carers. This is not to say that up to that point there were no legislative instruments available to them. Indeed, the EU has been able to use existing provisions that, although not specifically directed at cares, have proven useful.

This chapter explores the EU relevant provisions and the way the legal framework has been used to cater for certain individuals with caring responsibilities. It is organised in two sections. The first section (Carers, non-discrimination and equality provisions) explores the existing legislation that can be applied to carers. The second section (Carers and the work-family reconciliation measures) discusses how the EU has developed a legal framework to support certain types of carers. Although this was developed with young children in mind, it can provide the basis for a framework for other caring responsibilities.[30] This section also assesses the potential of the Work-Life Balance Directive for all carers.

Carers, non-discrimination and equality provisions

Luke Clements asserts that:

> Carers should have the same as anyone else. The mere fact that they are providing care should not disentitle them to opportunities available to people who do not have caring responsibilities. To argue otherwise would be to suggest that it is legitimate to discriminate against carers in a way that would not be acceptable for any other group.[31]

As carers face discrimination and unfair treatment, the non-discrimination legislation appears to be the ideal framework to address their needs. The fight against discrimination has traditionally been acknowledged as "one of the central

---

29 Directive (EU) 2019/1158 of the European Parliament and of the Council of 20 June 2019 on work-life balance for parents and carers and repealing Council Directive 2010/18/EU, O.J. [2019] L188/79. After it was proposed by the Commission in April 2017, the Council adopted its position in June 2018 which formed the basis for the negotiation with the European Parliament. The presidency of the Council and the Parliament reached an agreement on January 2019, followed by a vote by the European Parliament on April of the same year. The Work-Life Balance Directive was eventually adopted by the Council in June 2019.
30 Denis Bouget, Chiara Saraceno and Slavina Spasova, "Towards New Work-Life Balance Policies for those Caring for Dependent Relatives?" in Bart Vanhercke, Sebastiano Sabato, Denis Bouget (eds), *Social Policy in the European Union: State of Play 2017* (ETUI 2017).
31 Luke Clements, *Carers and the Law* (Carers UK 2008).

missions and activities of the Union"[32] and is part of the EU's constitutional make-up.[33] Indeed, Article 2 of the Treaty on European Union (TEU) proclaims that equality is one of the values on which the Union is founded and the European Charter of Fundamental Rights (CFR or the Charter) has cemented its constitutional dimension.[34]

The EU has gradually created a framework, which has shifted from prohibiting discrimination to promoting equality,[35] moving beyond a formal understanding of the concept of equality as encapsulated in the Aristotelian mantra, "things that are alike must be treated alike, while things that are unalike should be treated in proportion to their unalikeness".[36] It has long been acknowledged that the main weakness of formal equality lies in its failure to consider the circumstances which make individuals different.[37] Today, the EU legislative framework is based on a substantive understanding of equality. This is a broader and more expansive concept that acknowledges the existence of social and material structural differences between people, and is partially based on a redistributive justice model, which suggests that measures must be taken to rectify past discrimination. Failure to do so would leave particular individuals and groups at different starting points.

The CJEU has been instrumental to the development of the EU legislation on equality and non-discrimination. In particular, it introduced the crucial distinction between direct and indirect discrimination.[38] Direct discrimination is a straightforward concept: it occurs when two individuals are treated differently because of a specific reason, such as gender or nationality. By contrast, indirect discrimination, which has been described as "the greatest achievement of the [Court of Justice] in its corpus of ... equality ... jurisprudence",[39] is a more nuanced concept that

---

32 Mark Bell, "The Principle of Equal Treatment: Widening and Deepening" in Paul Craig and Gráinne de Búrca (eds), *The Evolution of EU Law* (OUP 2012) 629.
33 Gillian More, "The Principle of Equal Treatment: From Market Unifier to Fundamental Right?" in Paul Craig and Gráinne de Búrca (eds), *The Evolution of EU Law* (OUP 1999); Sacha Prechal, "Equality of Treatment, Non-discrimination and Social Policy: Achievements in Three Themes" (2004) 41 *CML Rev* 533.
34 Article 20 CFR states that "Everyone is Equal before the Law".
35 Gilliam More, "The Principle of Equal Treatment: From Market Unifier to Fundamental Right?" in Paul Craig and Gráinne de Búrca (eds), *The Evolution of EU Law* (OUP 1999).
36 Aristotle, *Ethica Nicomachea* V. 3 1131a – 1131b (David Ross (tr), OUP 1925).
37 See Peter Westen, "The Empty Idea of Equality" (1982) 95 *Harv L Rev* 537; Catherine Barnard, "Gender Equality in the EU: A Balance Sheet" in Philip Alston (ed), *The EU and Human Rights* (OUP 1999).
38 See Case 43/75 *Defrenne v Société Anonyme Belge de Navigation Aérienne Sabena* (*Defrenne* no 2). ECLI:EU:C:1976:56, in particular at para 10. For a more recent analysis of the difference between direct and indirect discrimination see Case C-73/08 *Bressol v Gouvernement de la Communauté Française*, Opinion of Advocate General Sharpston delivered on 25 June 2009 ECLI:EU:C:2009:396, paras 43–57.
39 Claire Kilpatrick, "Community or Communities of Courts in European Integration? Sex Equality Dialogues Between UK Courts and the *European Law Journal*" (1998) 4 *European Law Journal* 121.

captures a variety of situations. Indirect discrimination is now codified in Article 2 of the Recast Directive, which defines it as:

> an apparently neutral provision, criterion or practice [that] would put persons of one sex at a particular disadvantage compared with persons of the other sex, unless that provision, criterion or practice is objectively justified by a legitimate aim, and the means of achieving that aim are appropriate and necessary.

As many carers are women, the concept of indirect discrimination is particularly apt to tackle this area.[40]

Importantly, discrimination, both direct and indirect, can only be justified if certain conditions are met. Justification for direct discrimination "is conceivable only in limited circumstances and has to be carefully reasoned."[41] It is often limited to circumstances specifically allowed by the legislation. By contrast, the test for indirect discrimination is less stringent. However, it must be objectively justified by a legitimate aim, which must be appropriate and necessary.[42]

Over the years, these important principles have been applied, developed and supported by a sophisticated array of policy initiatives and secondary legislation and, as a result, a robust EU non-discrimination and equality framework has emerged.[43] Despite the progress achieved, when it comes to carers, equality remains "elusive" and disadvantages persist. On a general level, EU equality law simply does not go far enough for carers. Sandra Fredman proposes to reconceptualise equality by using a four-dimensional approach aiming at redressing disadvantages, addressing stigma, stereotyping and violence, enhancing voice and participation and accommodating difference and structural changes.[44] This approach would benefit carers on many levels, in particular because it would increase the visibility of care and by doing so it is likely to make it accountable.[45] On a more specific level, carers face distinctive and practical obstacles when trying to rely on the non-discrimination legislation. EU law prohibits discrimination on

---

40 See the discussion in the "Setting the Scene: 'Everyone Cares. Everyone is Cared For'".
41 See the Opinion of Advocate General Kokott delivered on 30 September 2010 Case C-236/09 *Test-Achats*. ECLI:EU:C:2010:564.
42 Case 170/84 *Bilka Kaufhaus GmbH v Heber von Hartz*. ECLI:EU:C:1986:204.
43 Sacha Prechal, "Equality of Treatment, Non-discrimination and Social Policy: Achievements in Three Themes" (2004) 41 *CML Rev* 533; Mark Bell, "The Principle of Equal Treatment: Widening and Deepening" in Paul Craig and Gráinne de Búrca (eds), *The Evolution of EU Law* (OUP 2012).
44 Sandra Fredman, "Substantive Equality Revisited" (2016) 14 *ICON* 712.
45 See the discussion in Chapter 1.

a number of grounds: originally these were limited to gender[46] and nationality[47] but have since been expanded. Article 13 of the Amsterdam Treaty (now Article 19 Treaty on the Functioning of the European Union (TFEU)) has introduced other prohibited grounds for discrimination, namely racial or ethnic origin, religion or belief, disability, age or sexual orientation.[48] As EU law does not include caring responsibilities as grounds for discrimination, carers who experience discrimination can only be protected if they can establish a link between the disadvantages created by their caring responsibilities and one of the protected grounds.[49] The following sections explore how the existing prohibited grounds of discrimination, in particular discrimination on grounds of gender, have been used to protect carers.

Gender equality

The principle of gender equality represents an obvious starting point: we know that women are more likely than men to spend time caring, and therefore they are more likely to be discriminated against because of their caring commitment. For example, they might find it difficult to hold a traditional nine to five job. The requirement that they must conform with traditional working hours could arguably constitute a form of indirect sex discrimination. Although not *prima facie* directly discriminatory, as such requirement is not based on sex, it is likely to have a negative impact on women's ability to have a full-time traditional employment because they statistically are more likely than men to care for school-aged children and dependent relatives. The difficulties faced by women as carers were acknowledged by CJEU as early as in 1997 in the case of *Marshall*:

> [e]ven where male and female candidates are equally qualified, male candidates tend to be promoted in preference to female candidates particularly because of prejudices and stereotypes concerning the role and the capacities of women in working life and the fear, for example, that women will interrupt their careers more frequently, that owning to household and family duties they will be less flexible in their working hours, or that they will be absent from work more frequently because of pregnancy childbirth and breastfeeding.[50]

---

46 Article 119 Treaty of Rome.
47 Article 7 Treaty of Rome.
48 Article 19 TFEU. Note that under Article 14 of the European Convention of Human Rights, there are no restricted grounds of discrimination.
49 Eugenia Caracciolo di Torella, "Shaping and Re-shaping the Caring Relationship in European Law: A Catalogue of Rights for Informal Carers?" (2016) 28 *Child & Family LQ* 261.
50 Case C-409/95 *Hellmut Marschall v Land Nordrhein-Westfalen*. ECLI:EU:C:1997:533, para 29. See Federico Mancini and Siofra O'Leary, "The New Frontiers of Sex Equality Law in the European Union" (1999) 24 *ELR* 331.

Gender equality is one of the oldest and most sophisticated prohibited grounds of discrimination under EU law. Originally introduced by Article 119 of the Treaty establishing the European Economic Community (EEC) with a view to correcting competition distortions between the Member States,[51] it soon became clear that gender equality is much more than an economic tool. It is a value,[52] an objective,[53] a fundamental right,[54] a process,[55] as well as a positive duty[56] of EU law. The concepts of gender equality and non-discrimination on the grounds of sex have substantially been strengthened by the Treaty of Amsterdam in 1999[57] and, a decade later, by the Treaty of Lisbon.[58] Today's Article 157 TFEU reflects a wide understanding of gender equality, including specific reference to positive action acknowledging that historically caring responsibilities have been shouldered by women. Article 157(4) TFEU allows Member States to maintain or adopt measures "providing for specific advantages in order to make it easier for the under-represented sex to pursue a vocational activity or to prevent or compensate for disadvantages in professional career." Such provision could potentially be used to accommodate female workers with caring responsibilities to acknowledge that care responsibilities have historically been undertaken by women.

---

51 Bertil Ohlin, "Social Aspects of European Economic Co-operation", Report by the Group of Experts on Social Aspects of Problem of European Economic Co-operation, International Labour Office, Geneva, 1956. Reproduced in (1956) 74 *Intl Lab Rev* 99; Catherine Barnard, "The Economic Objectives of Article 119" in Tamara Hervey and David O'Keeffe (eds), *Sex Equality in the European Union* (Wiley 1996); Ruth Nielsen and Erika Szyszcsak, *The Social Dimension of the European Union* (Handelshøjskolens Forlag 1997); Wolfgang Streeck, "From Market Making to State Building? Reflections on the Political Economy of the European Social Policy" in Stephan Liebfried and Paul Pierson (eds), *European Social Policy: Between Fragmentation and Integration* (Brookings 1995); however, Catherine Hoskyns, *Integrating Gender: Women, Law and Politics in the European Union* (Verso 1996) suggests that non-economic factors also contributed to the inclusion of Article 119.
52 Article 2 TEU.
53 Article 3 TEU.
54 Case C-243/95 *Hill and Stapleton v The Revenue Commissioners and Department of Finance*. ECLI:EU:C:1998:298; Sophia Koukoulis-Spiliotopoulos, "The Lisbon Treaty and the Charter of Fundamental Rights: Maintaining and Developing the Acquis in Gender Equality" (2008) 1 *European Gender Equality L Rev* 15.
55 Article 8 TFEU provides that "[i]n all its activities, the Union shall aim to eliminate inequalities, and to promote equality, between men and women."
56 Sandra Fredman, "Changing the Norm: Positive Duties in Equal Treatment Legislation" (2005) 12 *MJ* 369.
57 Sally Langrish, "The Treaty of Amsterdam: Selected Highlight" (1998) 23 *ELR* 3; Jane Lewis, "Work/Family Reconciliation, Equal Opportunities and Social Policies: The Interpretation of Policy Trajectories at the EU Level and the Meaning of Gender Equality" (2006) 13 *J Public Policy* 420; Elizabeth Defeis, "Treaty of Amsterdam: The Next Step towards Gender Equality" (1999) 23 *Boston College Intl and Comparative L Rev* 1.
58 Evelyn Ellis, "The Impact of the Lisbon Treaty on Gender Equality" (2010) 1 *European Gender Equality L Rev* 7.

The primary legislation is complemented by a sophisticated array of secondary legislation developed over the years which covers many areas within and outside the employment relationship.[59] EU gender equality legislation has also served to inform and support policies on reconciliation between work and family life[60] and therefore, albeit indirectly, it has benefitted carers. However, to rely exclusively on (indirect) discrimination on grounds of gender in order to protect carers overlooks the fact that care is not and should not be construed as an inherent risk of either sex. Carers are not always women and should not always be assumed to be women. Indeed, to provide protection only to *women* carers is wrong as it ignores the disadvantages that men might endure. It also perpetuates the stereotype that

---

59 The Recast Directive (Directive 2006/54/EC of the European Parliament and of the Council of 5 July 2006 on the implementation of the principle of equal opportunities and equal treatment of men and women in matters of employment and occupation (recast), O.J. [2006] L204/23) incorporates and updates several existing Directives; the Equal Pay Directive 75/117/EEC (Council Directive 75/117/EEC of 10 February 1975 on the approximation of the laws of the Member States relating to the application of the principle of equal pay for men and women, O.J. [1975] L45/19), the Equal Treatment Directive 76/207/EEC (Council Directive 76/207/EEC of 9 February 1976 on the implementation of the principle of equal treatment for men and women as regards access to employment, vocational training and promotion, and working conditions, O.J. [1976] L39/40) as amended by Directive 2002/73/EC (Directive 2002/73/EC of the European Parliament and of the Council of 23 September 2002 amending Council Directive 76/207/EEC on the implementation of the principle of equal treatment for men and women as regards access to employment, vocational training and promotion, and working conditions, O.J. [2002] L269/15); the Occupational Social Security Directive 86/378/EEC (Directive 86/613/EEC of 11 December 1986 on the application of the principle of equal treatment between men and women engaged in an activity, including agriculture, in a self-employed capacity, and on the protection of self-employed women during pregnancy and motherhood, O.J. [1986] L359/56) as amended by Directive 96/97/EC (Council Directive 96/97/EC of 20 December 1996 amending Directive 86/378/EEC on the implementation of the principle of equal treatment for men and women in occupational social security schemes, O.J. [1997] L46/20) and the Burden of Proof Directive 97/80/EC (Council Directive 97/80/EC of 15 December 1997 on the burden of proof in cases of discrimination based on sex, O.J. [1998] L14/6); Council Directive 92/85/EEC of 19 October 1992 on the introduction of measures to encourage improvements in the safety and health at work of pregnant workers and workers who have recently given birth or are breastfeeding (tenth individual Directive within the meaning of Article 16 (1) of Directive 89/391/EEC), O.J. [1992] L348/1.
60 See for example Case C-243/95 *Kathleen Hill and Ann Stapleton v the Revenue Commission and the Department of Finance.* ECLI:EU:C:1998:298, para 42: the Court held that "Community policy in this area is to encourage and, if possible, adapt working conditions to family responsibilities. Protection of women within family life and in the course of their professional activities is, in the same way as for men, a principle which is widely regarded in the legal systems of the Member States as being the natural corollary of the equality between men and women, and which is recognised by Community law." See also Case C-1/95 *Hellen Gerster v Freistaat Bayern.* ECLI:EU:C:1997:452. Susanne Burri, "Reconciliation of Work and Private Life in EU Law: State of Affaire" (2010) 11 *ERA Forum* 111; Eugenia Caracciolo di Torella and Annick Masselot, *Reconciling Work and Family Life in EU Law and Policy* (Palgrave Macmillan 2010).

caring is a woman's job.[61] In this context, male carers would find no protection if they needed to rely on the EU gender equality principle and this would further deter them from taking these responsibilities. In addition, neither men nor women might find any protection in areas where caring is gender-neutral. Statistics show, for example, that men and women are relatively equally represented when caring for a dependent spouse.[62] In this case, it would therefore be difficult for women to argue indirect discrimination on the ground of sex.

Other grounds for discrimination

The insertion of Article 13 (now Article 19 TFEU) in the 1999 Amsterdam Treaty has been a welcome addition to the EU non-discrimination canon. It states that:

> without prejudice to the other provisions of the Treaties and within the limits of the powers conferred by them upon the Union, the Council, acting unanimously in accordance with a special legislative procedure and after obtaining the consent of the European Parliament, may take appropriate action to combat discrimination based on sex, racial or ethnic origin, religion or belief, disability, age or sexual orientation.

This provision is important in two respects: it extends the grounds for discrimination and it provides the possibility of going beyond the strict confines of the workplace. Indeed, Article 19 TFEU has quickly proved to be a useful tool in the fight against discrimination. Within a year of being adopted, it provided the legal basis for the adoption of the Race Directive[63] and the Framework Directive.[64] Both Directives address some forms of vulnerability, which is a constitutive element of the caring relationship. People are likely to need care and/or provide care because

---

61 Case C-366/99 *Joseph Griesmar v Ministre de l'Économie, des Finances et de l'Industrie, Ministre de la Fonction publique, de la Réforme de l'État et de la Décentralisation.* ECLI:EU:C:2001:648; and more recently Case C-572/10 *Maurice Leone and Blandine Leone v Garde des Sceaux, ministre de la Justice and Caisse nationale de retraite des agents des collectivités locales.* ECLI:EU:C:2014:117.
62 Louise Ackers and Peter Dwyer, *Senior Citizenship? Retirement, Migration and Welfare in the European Union* (Policy Press 2002); Ariane Bertogg and Susanne Strauss, "Spousal Care Giving Arrangements in Europe: The Role of Gender, Socio-economic Status and the Welfare State" (2018) *Ageing & Society* 1. However, Bertogg and Strauss show that if informal care for old age spouses is provided by both sexes and across all socio-economic backgrounds and welfare policy contexts, there are gender differences with regards to whether spouses care alone, receive informal support from other family members or formal support from professional helpers, or outsource the care of their spouse completely.
63 Council Directive 2000/43/EC of 29 June 2000 implementing the principle of equal treatment between persons irrespective of racial or ethnic origin, O.J. [2000] L180/22.
64 Council Directive 2000/78/EC of 27 November 2000 establishing a general framework for equal treatment in employment and occupation, O.J. [2000] L303/16.

of their age (either because they are very young or old) and/or because of disability. The provisions under these Directives thus offer an additional potential avenue for carers to fight discrimination.

Whilst the expansion of the protected grounds represents a remarkable step forward, "care" remains noticeably absent from the list. Thus, unless a discrimination is based on one of the grounds expressly mentioned in Article 19, "[t]here is no clear, logical scheme to identify those grounds that are for discrimination that are morally reprehensible to be categorised as unlawful."[65] Regrettably, in the case of *Chacòn Navas*,[66] the CJEU confirmed that the list in Article 19 TFEU is exhaustive.

The CFR and the EPSR have not modified the situation. Article 21 CFR also provides a list of prohibited discrimination, which largely mirrors Article 19 TFEU, but expands this position as it contains a non-exhaustive list. However, on at least two occasions the CJEU has clarified that Article 21(1) CFR does not create any legal competence to act to combat discrimination beyond that conferred in the Treaties.[67]

In the same vein, the newly adopted Principle 3 EPSR starts by reiterating that discrimination is prohibited on specific grounds and it then proceeds to replicate the list in Article 19 TFEU. However, it refers to gender, rather than sex. Mark Bell highlights the long-standing academic debate surrounding the interpretation of these terms.[68] Whilst "sex" is traditionally associated with a binary, biological understanding of the characteristic, "gender" typically indicates the social constructions of how "men" and "women" are expected to behave and the roles that they are expected to perform. The express reference to gender therefore could potentially be more helpful in relation to the protection of carers. Unfortunately, on this point the CJEU has not always sent a clear message. Whilst in some decisions it has referred to sex discrimination in a way that includes gender-based stereotypes that hinder women's participation in the labour market,[69] in others it has failed to acknowledge such connection. On one occasion, for example, it did not acknowledge the link between the disadvantageous treatment connected to taking parental leave and gender discrimination.[70]

---

65 Charlotte O'Brien, "Confronting the Care Penalty: The Cause for Extending Reasonable Adjustment Rights along the Disability/Care Continuum" (2012) 34(1) *Journal of Social Welfare & Family Law* 5, 9.
66 Case C-13/05 *Chacòn Navas v Eurest Colectividades* SA. ECLI:EU:C:2006:456.
67 Case C-354/13 *FOA, acting on behalf of Karsten Kaltoft v KL, acting on behalf of the Municipality of Billund.* EU:C:2014:2463; Case C-363/12 *Z v A Government Department, The Board of Management of a Community School.* EU:C:2014:159.
68 Mark Bell, "The Principle of Equal Treatment and the European Pillar of Social Rights" (2018) 160 *Giornale di Diritto del Lavoro e di Relazioni Industriali* 783.
69 C-409/95 *Hellmut Marschall v Land Nordrhein-Westfalen.* ECLI:EU:C:1997:533, para 29, discussed above.
70 Case C-220/02 *Österreichischer Gewerkschaftsbund, Gewerkschaft der Privatangestellten v Wirtschaftskammer Österreich.* EU:C:2004:334.

Discrimination by association

Against this background, the Court has made a valuable contribution in attempting to broaden the boundaries of the concept of discrimination, by introducing the concept of discrimination by association. In the seminal case of *Coleman*,[71] it considered whether non-discrimination law could include those individuals who suffer discrimination because they are related, connected or care for people who have specific protected characteristics. In this specific case, Mrs Coleman, a legal secretary, was the primary carer of her disabled son who needed specialised care. She was forced to resign after being harassed by her employer and refused flexible working arrangements, which were offered to some of her colleagues who had healthy children.

In his opinion, Advocate General Maduro supported an inclusive approach to disability discrimination as discussed in the Framework Directive.[72] Citing Dworkin,[73] Raz[74] and Gardner,[75] he argued that discrimination law should combat all forms of discrimination, including those associated with protected groups of people. He argued that discrimination by association:

> is a subtler form of discrimination [that] undermines the ability of persons who have a suspect characteristic to exercise their autonomy ... People belonging to certain groups are often more vulnerable than the average person, so they have come to rely on individuals with whom they are closely associated for help in their effort to lead a life according to the fundamental choices they have made. When the discriminator deprives an individual of valuable options in areas which are of fundamental importance to our lives because that individual is associated with a person having a suspect characteristic then it also deprives that person of valuable options and prevents him from exercising this autonomy.[76]

The Court followed the Advocate General's opinion and recognised that, in order to be effective, the protections against discrimination must extend not only to those having "protected characteristics" themselves, but also to those who are

---

71 Case C-303/06 *Coleman v Attridge Law*. ECLI:EU:C:2008:415.
72 Case C-303/06 *Coleman v Attridge Law*, Opinion of Advocate general Maduro, ECLI:EU:C:2008:61, 16, as noted by Tim Connor, "Discrimination by Association: A Step in the Right Direction" (2010) 32 *Journal of Social Welfare & Family Law* 59; Simon Honeyball, "Discrimination by Association" [2007] 4 Web JCLI http://webjcli.ncl.ac.uk/2007/issue4/honeyball4.html. Accessed 25 July 2019; Jonathan Herring, *Caring and the Law* (Hart Publishing 2013) 240.
73 Ronald Dworkin, *Is Democracy Possible Here?: Principles for a New Political Debate* (Princeton University Press 2006) ch 1.
74 Joseph Raz, *The Morality of Freedom* (OUP 1986).
75 John Gardner, "Discrimination as Injustice" (1996) 16 *OJLS* 353, 355.
76 Case C-303/06 *Coleman v Attridge Law*, Opinion of Advocate General Maduro delivered on 31 January 2008, ECLI:EU:C:2008:61, para 14.

associated with them, which may include their carers.[77] Potentially, this is a significant judgement which could help carers to combat unfavourable treatment and discrimination based on their caring commitment.[78] Even though this decision does not address directly the issue of discrimination on grounds of caring, it provides guidance as to the treatment of carers. There is a clear connection between the need for care and the specific characteristics encapsulated in Article 19 TFEU such as age or disability. However, in order to unveil its full potential, the principle of discrimination by association requires to be further developed.

The opportunity arose in 2012, when a British court referred the case of *Kulikauskas* to the CJEU.[79] The Court was asked whether a man can bring a sex discrimination claim on the basis that he has been discriminated against on the ground of his association with a pregnant woman. Mr Kulikauskas and his partner Alisa Mihailova were employed in a fish factory. A supervisor noticed that Mr Kulikauskas was doing Ms Mihailova's heavy lifting. Mr Kulikauskas informed the supervisor that his partner was pregnant. On the same day, both workers received letters of dismissal for poor performance. Both brought unfair dismissal and sex discrimination claims. Mr Kulikauskas argued that following *Coleman*,[80] the Recast Directive[81] should be interpreted in a way to provide protection to those associated with pregnant women. The Employment Tribunal rejected this argument because it stated that protection against discrimination on grounds of pregnancy under EU law is based on health and safety concerns for the "biological condition" of the pregnant women and her unborn child. Thus, there are no wider policy reasons to extend this protection to those associated with pregnant women. Accordingly, pregnancy and maternity are not covered by "associative discrimination". The case was appealed to the Employment Appeal Tribunal which upheld the Tribunal's decision.[82] The case was then appealed to the Court of Session, which decided to refer it to the CJEU, asking whether the Recast Directive renders it unlawful to directly discriminate against a person on grounds of another person's pregnancy. This could have been an important test case but unfortunately, before the CJEU could consider the question, the case was withdrawn from the registry.[83]

---

77 Case C-303/06 *Coleman v Attridge Law and Steve Law*. ECLI:EU:C:2008:415, para 38. See more recently, *Truman v Bibby Distribution Ltd* ET/2404176/2014 where an employee with caring responsibilities who was performing satisfactorily was suddenly dismissed.
78 Tamara Hervey and others, "Case C-303/06 *Coleman* v. *Attridge Law and Steve Law* Judgment of the ECJ 17 July 2008" (2009) 31 *Journal of Social Welfare & Family Law* 309. See also Marcus Pilgerstorfer and Simon Forshaw, "Transferred Discrimination in European Law" (2008) 37 *Industrial Law Journal* 384.
79 C-44/12 *Kulikauskas*, application: O.J. [2012] C109/6.
80 Case C-303/06 *Coleman v Attridge Law*. ECLI:EU:C:2008:415.
81 Directive 2006/54/EC of the European Parliament and of the Council of 5 July 2006 on the implementation of the principle of equal opportunities and equal treatment of men and women in matters of employment and occupation (recast), O.J. [2006] L204/23.
82 *Kulikauskas v Macduff Shellfish* [2011] ICR 48.
83 C-44/12 Kulikauskas, removal from the register: O.J. [2013] C108/18.

The CJEU was able to further expand on the concept of discrimination by association in *CHEZ*.[84] On this occasion, it clarified that the concept can apply to both direct (as in *Coleman*) and indirect discrimination. The importance of this judgement, which was delivered by the Grand Chamber, cannot be underestimated.[85] An electricity supplier had installed an electricity meter six metres from the ground in a neighbourhood commonly populated by Roma in order to prevent tampering. This made it difficult for those, like the claimant, who lived or ran businesses in the district to monitor their electricity usage and check that they were not being overcharged. The claimant brought a claim alleging that the electricity supplier's actions were direct or indirect race discrimination.

The facts in this case showed strong grounds for asserting that the electricity supplier's action in fact amounted to *direct* discrimination. In particular, the company had only applied its six metre policy in this and other "Roma districts". This was the principal factor in applying the policy and it was clear that the company thought it was mainly Roma people who were making unlawful connections. However, it had failed to produce evidence of the alleged damage and tampering and had apparently carried out no objective analysis of the extent of the problem in the various districts to which it supplied electricity. Accordingly, there were quite strong indications that the company's approach was tainted by racial stereotyping, which would normally indicate direct discrimination. Therefore, unsurprisingly, the CJEU ruled that the claimant could complain of direct race discrimination even though the less favourable treatment did not come about because of her own ethnic origin.

The CJEU also stated that, had this been a case of indirect, rather than direct discrimination, the claimant could have brought a valid complaint, notwithstanding the fact that she did not share the same ethnic origin with those who were particularly disadvantaged by the practice.[86] This part of the CJEU's decision suggests that once discrimination is established on a protected ground, anyone who suffers that same disadvantage can bring a claim of indirect discrimination regardless of whether or they share the same protected characteristic of the disadvantaged group.

The Court ruled that Directive 2000/43/EC extends to persons who, although not themselves a member of the racial or ethnic group concerned, nevertheless suffer "less favourable treatment" (direct discrimination) or a "particular disadvantage" (indirect discrimination) on the grounds of that race or ethnic origin.

---

84 C-83/14 *CHEZ Razpredelenie Bulgaria AD v Komisia za zashtita ot diskriminatsia*. ECLI:EU:C:2015:480.
85 Rossen Grozev, "A Landmark Judgment of the Court of Justice of the EU – New Conceptual Contributions to the Legal Combat against Ethnic Discrimination" (2015) 15 *Equal Rights Rev* 168.
86 C-83/14 *CHEZ Razpredelenie Bulgaria AD v Komisia za zashtita ot diskriminatsia*. ECLI:EU:C:2015:480, paras 105–109.

The CJEU observed that the wording of the Directive permits this wide interpretation as it defines indirect discrimination as occurring where an apparently neutral provision, criterion or practice would put persons of a racial or ethnic origin at a particular disadvantage compared with other persons (unless that provision, criterion or practice is objectively justified by a legitimate aim and the means of achieving that aim are appropriate and necessary). There is nothing in this wording stating that a victim of indirect discrimination must share the race or ethnic origin of the protected group.

While *CHEZ* was concerned with Directive 2000/43/EC, a very similar definition of indirect discrimination is used in all the other EU equality directives. Accordingly, we suggest that it is very likely that the CJEU's judgement can apply in relation to other protected characteristics. This broad approach has, thus, the potential to extend the reach of indirect discrimination law in other areas covered by EU law. For instance, the unfavourable treatment of part-time work could lead to claims of indirect discrimination from female employees on the basis that such practice disadvantages women in particular because they are more likely to have primary caring responsibilities that make it more difficult to work full-time. The reasoning in *CHEZ* suggests that male employees with caring responsibilities could also bring claims of indirect discrimination without needing to show that men, as a group, are put at a particular disadvantage. It is therefore likely that the CJEU is far from finished in addressing the issue of discrimination by association.

The concept of discrimination by association has been successfully employed by domestic courts. In particular, British courts have used the concept of discrimination by association in the cases of the dismissal of an employee who could not work overtime after 5.30pm because she had to care for her disabled father,[87] and because she was absent for a certain period due to her husband's leukaemia.[88]

There have also been instances where the concept has not been successful, particularly when the concept was invoked against the failure to make reasonable adjustments in relation to a person for whom the employee has caring responsibilities. In the case of *Hainsworth v Ministry of Defence*,[89] for example, the claimant's daughter suffered from Down's syndrome and further education could not appropriately be provided in Germany where the claimant worked but would have

---

87 *MacDonald v Fylde Motor Co Ltd* [2011] EqLR 660.
88 *Price v Action-Tec Services* [2013] EqLR 429.
89 *Hainsworth v Ministry of Defence* UKEATPA/0227/13/GE; another example is *Perrot v Department for Work and Pensions* [2012] EqLR 90. However, an employee with caring responsibilities is entitled to make an application for flexible working arrangements. The employer is obliged to carefully consider the request but is not under an obligation to grant such request.

been facilitated had the claimant be permitted to move her place of work. The Tribunal rejected the argument that Article 5 of EU Directive 2000/78 extended to persons who were not in relationship with the employer. Moreover, it argued that Article 5 was insufficiently clear and precise in its language.[90] On appeal, the domestic court reiterated that EU law does not require employers to provide reasonable accommodation for employees who are not themselves disabled but who care for a disabled person.[91]

Carers and the work-family reconciliation provisions

If, broadly speaking, any carers can rely on non-discrimination and equality legislation, the rights of *certain* carers are further protected through a set of specific measures designed to facilitate the reconciliation between work and family responsibilities. Such measures can be divided in two categories: those granting employees periods of leave, normally around the birth of a child (leave measures) and those allowing them to organise their working responsibility in such a way to be able to fulfil their caring commitments (time measures). These are complemented by the less developed measures aimed at allowing individuals to work by providing them with care support (care strategy).[92] We refer to these measures as the EU reconciliation provisions. Article 33 CFR has given them a clear constitutional dimension.[93] It states that:

> [t]o reconcile family and professional life, everyone shall have the right to protection from dismissal for a reason connected with maternity and the right to paid maternity leave and to parental leave following the birth or adoption of a child.

Yet, however welcomed, by exclusively referring to paid maternity leave without mentioning paternity leave, Article 33 CFR reflects and promotes a model where rights are focused on mothers.[94]

---

90 *Hainsworth v Ministry of Defence* UKEATPA/0227/13/GE.
91 *Hainsworth v Ministry of Defence* [2014] EWCA Civ 763.
92 Eugenia Caracciolo di Torella and Annick Masselot, *Reconciling Work and Family Life in EU Law and* Policy (Palgrave Macmillan 2010).
93 See further Cathryn Costello, "Family and Professional Life" in Steve Peers, Tamara Harvey, Jeff Kenner and Angela Ward (eds), *The EU Charter of Fundamental Rights – A Commentary* (Hart Publishing 2014); Marzia Barbera, "The Unsolved Conflict: Reshaping Family Work and Market Work in the EU Legal Order" in Tamara Hervey and Jeff Kenner (eds), *Economic and Social Rights under the EU Charter of Fundamental Rights: A Legal Perspective* (Hart Publishing 2003).
94 Cathryn Costello, "Article 33" in Steve Peers, Tamara Harvey, Jeff Kenner and Angela Ward (eds), *The EU Charter of Fundamental Rights – A Commentary* (Hart Publishing 2014) 891, 893.

The visibility of working carers has been further improved by principle 9 EPSR:[95]

> [p]arents and people with caring responsibilities have the right to suitable leave, flexible working arrangements and access to care services. Women and men shall have equal access to special leaves of absence in order to fulfil their caring responsibilities and be encouraged to use them in a balanced way.

Specifically, the leave and time provisions have gradually developed over the years to cover an increasingly wide range of situations.[96] In addition, they have recently received new impetus following the adoption of the Work-Life Balance Directive[97] in the aftermath of the failed attempt to revise the 1992 Pregnant Workers Directive.[98]

The Work-Life Balance Directive represents a welcome addition to this area. It repeals the existing Parental Leave Directive and expands and builds upon existing rights. Specifically, it provides four individual rights: paternity leave, parental leave, carers' leave and the right to request flexible working arrangements. Ultimately, it aims to modernise a framework which was set up in the 1990s by acknowledging evolving needs as well as the diversity of care and carers, in line with today's fast changing society.[99] This is not to say that the Directive is above criticism. In certain respects, it falls short of the expectations of parents and carers: for example, it does not address maternity leave, and its final text is a watered-down version of the original proposal. Nevertheless, there is little doubt that the Work-Life Balance Directive represents a step towards a stronger recognition of carers' work.

Taking into account the adoption of this Directive, the next sections focus on the leave and the time provisions, as the care strategy has already been discussed.[100]

The leave provisions

The leave provisions mainly allow parents to take time off in connection with the birth of a child, and in restricted circumstances they can also be used by other carers. These provisions can be gender-specific, such as maternity and paternity leave, or gender-neutral, for example parental leave, right to take time off for emergencies

---

95 Interinstitutional Proclamation on the European Pillar of Social Rights, O.J. [2017] C428/10. See also the discussion in "Setting the scene: 'Everyone cares. Everyone is cared for'".
96 See the discussion in the next sections in this Chapter.
97 Directive (EU) 2019/1158 of the European Parliament and of the Council of 20 June 2019 on work-life balance for parents and carers and repealing Council Directive 2010/18/EU, O.J. [2019] L188/79.
98 See fn 23 in this chapter.
99 Eugenia Caracciolo di Torella, "An Emerging Right to Care in the EU: A 'New Start to Support Work-Life Balance for Parents and Carers'" (2017) 18 *ERA Forum* 187.
100 See Chapters 2 and 3 respectively.

and the freshly introduced carers' leave. The relevant legislative instruments are the Pregnant Workers,[101] the Parental Leave,[102] the Recast Directives,[103] and the recently adopted Work-Life Balance Directive.[104]

Maternity leave

Maternity leave was introduced in 1992 by the Pregnant Workers Directive.[105] It grants a period of 14 continuous weeks' leave (of which two weeks must occur before and/or after the birth) to pregnant workers and new mothers in connection with the birth of a child.[106] During maternity leave, maintenance of a payment, and/or entitlement to an adequate allowance must be ensured[107] and cannot be lower than the entitlement to sick leave.[108] The Directive also introduces other rights such as the duty to assess the workplace for specific risks to pregnant workers and new mothers and to make adjustments for those employees who are at risk of harm, the right to take time off to attend antenatal appointments, the prohibition on dismissal from the beginning of the pregnancy until the end of maternity leave, as well as the maintenance of terms and conditions of employment during the maternity leave.

It has been felt for some time that this Directive is dated and ill-equipped to address the reality of today's society. Criticisms range from the short duration of the leave to the low level of payment, the failure to consider new reproductive technology, such as IVF and surrogacy,[109] the weak protection against dismissal[110] and the lack of breastfeeding breaks and/or facilities.[111] The main criticism, however,

---

101 Council Directive 92/85/EEC, O.J. [1992] L348/1.
102 Council Directive 2010/18/EU, O.J. [2010] L68/13.
103 Council Directive 2006/54/EC, O.J. [2006] L204/23.
104 Directive 2019/1158 (EU) on Work-Life Balance, O.J. [2019] L188/79.
105 See also the Recast Directive that acknowledges the need "of protecting a woman's biological condition during pregnancy and maternity and of introducing maternity protection measures as a means to achieve substantive equality".
106 Article 8 of Council Directive 92/85/EEC.
107 Article 11(2)(b) of Council Directive 92/85/EEC.
108 Article 11(3) of Council Directive 92/85/EEC.
109 Eugenia Caracciolo di Torella and Petra Foubert, "Maternity Rights for Intended Mothers? Surrogacy Puts the EU Legal Framework to the Test" (2014) *European Gender Equality L Rev* 5.
110 Stronger protection against dismissals could have been achieved, by extending the period of dismissal protection for a period of time after the end of maternity leave; prohibiting not only dismissals during the protected period but also steps for dismissal, such as recruiting a replacement employee on a permanent base; introducing a right to written reasons for dismissals during the full period for which dismissal protection is available.
111 Indeed, breastfeeding facilities are essential if the aim is to encourage women to go back to work before the first year of the child.

is that it does not contemplate fathers, thus implying that mothers are the main carers.[112] Indeed, for political reasons, the Pregnant Workers Directive was not adopted on the basis of gender equality but on health and safety grounds.[113]

An attempt to address the Pregnant Workers Directive's shortcomings was put forward in 2008 in the context of the Work-Life Balance Package.[114] The Package contained a proposal to increase the minimum period of maternity leave from 14 to 18 weeks paid at 100% of the worker's salary. However, some Member States, in particular the UK,[115] considered this too burdensome for employers in the aftermath of the Global Financial Crisis and the proposed reform of the Directive was eventually shelved in July 2015.[116] The 2019 Work-Life Balance Directive represents an opportunity to address some of these shortcomings.[117]

Paternity leave

Traditionally, despite ongoing policy developments,[118] EU law has not contemplated an individual right to paternity leave.[119] Article 16 of the Recast Directive merely provides that, if the entitlement exists under domestic law, fathers taking paternity leave are to be protected under the same circumstances as mothers

---

112 See the discussion further in this chapter.
113 Eugenia Caracciolo di Torella and Annick Masselot, *Reconciling Work and Family Life in EU Law and Policy* (Palgrave Macmillan 2010).
114 Communication from the Commission, "A Better Work-Life Balance: Stronger Support for Reconciling Professional, Private and Family Life", COM(2008) 635. See also European Commission, "MEMO/08/603" (Brussels, 3 October 2008) available at http://europa.eu/rapid/press-release_MEMO-08-603_en.htm. Accessed 25 July 2019. See also fn 23 in this chapter.
115 On that occasion, Nigel Farage, the UK EMP, commented "[t]he European Parliament, in their foolishness, have voted for increased maternity pay. I'm off for a drink" (Nigel Farage (@Nigel_Farage) Twitter (Oct. 20, 2010). See Eugenia Caracciolo di Torella, "The Unintended Consequences of Brexit: The Case of Work-Life Balance" in Moira Dustin, Nuno Ferreira and Susan Millns (eds), *Gender and Queer Perspectives on Brexit* (Palgrave Macmillan 2019); Roberta Guerrina and Annick Masselot, "Walking into the Footprint of EU Law: Unpacking the Gendered Consequences of Brexit" (2018) 17 *Social Policy & Society* 319.
116 European Commission, "Delivering for Parents: Commission Withdraws Stalled Maternity Leave Proposal and Paves the Way for a Fresh Approach" (Brussels, 1 July 2015) available at http://europa.eu/rapid/press-release_IP-15-5287_en.htm. Accessed 30 July 2019.
117 Eugenia Caracciolo di Torella, "An Emerging Right to Care in the EU: A "New Start to Support Work-Life Balance for Parents and Carers'" (2017) 18 *ERA Forum* 187.
118 See, for example, the 1992 Council Recommendation on childcare that encourages the equal sharing of family responsibilities between men and women. The position of men as carers was also echoed in the Council Resolution of 29 June 2000 on the balanced participation of women and men in family and working life provides that the balanced participation of women and men in both the labour market and in family life is an essential aspect of the development of society, and that maternity and paternity rights as well as the rights of children are current social values to be protected by society, the Member States and the European Community.
119 Annick Masselot, Eugenia Caracciolo di Torella and Susanne Burri, "Thematic Report of the European Network of Legal Experts in the Field of Gender Equality, 'Fighting Discrimination on the Grounds of Pregnancy, Maternity and Parenthood – The application

taking maternity leave. In other words, paternity leave has been formulated as an "option" for Member States, rather than a legal entitlement for fathers.[120]

The 2019 Work-Life Balance Directive drastically changes this lukewarm approach. Article 4 creates an individual right to at least ten working days' leave for fathers or the equivalent second parents "when and in so far as recognised by national law", to be taken on the occasion of the birth of their child. Article 8a stipulates that those exercising such right will receive a payment or an allowance which guarantees an "income at least equivalent to that which the worker concerned would receive in the event of a break in their activities on grounds connected with their state of health, subject to any ceiling laid down under national legislation".

As in the case of maternity leave, no period of work qualification is necessary to access this right. However, Member States can make the right to a payment "subject to periods of previous employment which shall not exceed six months immediately prior to the presumed date of confinement." The Directive gives to the Member States the possibility of determining how the leave can be exercised and whether it can be taken partly before and/or after birth or flexibly.[121]

Overall, the measure is unlikely to dramatically alter the situation for many Member States.[122] Indeed, to insert the right to paternity leave will simply bring EU legislation in line with the legislation already existing in most Member States – as well as most of the case law of the CJEU.[123] Nevertheless, its political resonance cannot be underestimated. The Work-Life Balance Directive finally lays the foundations for a stronger legislative framework in relation to men and care. In practical terms, it represents a much more robust commitment to gender equality than what was envisaged under the Pregnant Workers and the Recast Directives. It signals that the principle of gender equality necessarily requires a legislative framework that makes it possible for men to contribute to unpaid care-work.[124]

of EU and national law in practice in 33 European countries'" (European Commission, 2012), and more recently Annick Masselot, "Family Leave: Enforcement of the Protection against Dismissal and Unfavourable Treatment" (European Union 2018).

120 Eugenia Caracciolo di Torella, "Brave New Fathers for a Brave New World? Fathers as Caregivers in an Evolving European Union" (2014) 20 *European Law Journal* 88; Colette Fagan, *Analysis Note – Men and Gender Equality tackling Gender Segregated Family Roles and Social Care Jobs* (European Union 2010).

121 Article 4, Directive (EU) 2019/1158 on Work-Life Balance.

122 Annick Masselot, "Family Leave: Enforcement of the Protection against Dismissal and Unfavourable Treatment" (European Union 2018).

123 Case C-104/09 *Roca Álvarez v Sesa Start España ETT SA*. ECLI:EU:C:2010:561 and Case C-222/14 *Konstantinos Maïstrellis v Ypourgos Dikaiosynis, Diafaneias kai Anthropinon Dikaiomaton*. ECLI:EU:C:2015:473. However, see Case C-5/12 *Betriu Montull v Instituto Nacional de la Seguridad Social (INSS)*. ECLI:EU:C:2013:571 and Case C-12/17 *Tribunalul Botoșani and Ministerul Justiției v DICU*. EU:C:2018:799.

124 Nicole Busby and Michelle Weldon-Johns, "Fathers as Carers in UK Law and Policy: Dominant Ideologies and Lived Experience" (2019) *Journal of Social Welfare & Family Law* DOI:10.1080/09649069.1627085 www.tandfonline.com/doi/abs/10.1080/09649069.2019.1627085. Accessed 25 July 2019.

Parental leave

The Parental Leave Directive[125] entitles working parents to at least four months' leave on the birth or adoption of a child.[126] Such leave may be taken until the child has reached an age determined by national law and/or collective agreements, but in any case, before the child reaches the age of eight.[127] The modalities of application are left with the Member States and this can restrict parents' flexibility.[128] It might be that parents are "forced"[129] to take the leave in blocks, rather than in more flexible ways (part-time or in individual days) that better suit their needs. Furthermore, the right to parental leave is unpaid. For all these reasons, the right is underused, especially by fathers.[130] This means that, *de facto*, this leave is taken by mothers, rather than by fathers, thus entrenching the stereotype that women are the main carers.[131]

The Work-Life Balance Directive repeals the Parental Leave Directive by building upon existing rights. It seeks to address the Parental Leave Directive's shortcomings with a view to increasing the fathers' take up of the leave. Article 5(1) establishes that:

> Member States shall take the necessary measures to ensure that workers have an individual right to parental leave of four months to be taken before the child reaches a given age up to eight to be defined by Member States and/or the social partners. This age shall be determined by Member States and/or the social partners *in a way that ensures that each parent can effectively exercise their right to parental leave on an equal basis*.[132]

---

125 Council Directive 2010/18/EU of 8 March 2010 implementing the revised Framework Agreement on parental leave concluded by BUSINESSEUROPE, UEAPME, CEEP and ETUC and repealing Directive 96/34/EC (Text with EEA relevance), O.J. [2010] L68/13.
126 Clause 2 of Directive 2010/18/EU.
127 Clause 2(1) of Directive 2010/18/EU.
128 E.g. Case C-12/17 *Ministerul Justiţiei and Tribunalul Botoşani v Maria Dicu*. ECLI:EU: C:2018:799.
129 There is evidence that this is more an issue for fathers; see Eurofound, *Promoting Uptake of Parental and Paternity Leave among Fathers in the European Union* (European Union 2015). Annick Masselot, "Family Leave: Enforcement of the Protection against Dismissal and Unfavourable Treatment" (European Union 2018).
130 Eurofound, *Promoting Uptake of Parental and Paternity Leave among Fathers in the European Union* (European Union 2015). See also case C-12/17 *Ministerul Justiţiei and Tribunalul Botoşani v Maria Dicu*. ECLI:EU:C:2018:799.
131 Linda Haas, "Parental Leave and Gender Equality: Lessons from the European Union" (2003) 20 *Rev Policy Research* 89; Stephen Hardy and Nick Adnett, "The Parental Leave Directive: Towards a Family-Friendly Social Europe?" (2002) 8 *European J Industrial Relations* 157; Annick Masselot, "Family Leave: Enforcement of the Protection against Dismissal and Unfavourable Treatment" (European Union 2018) and Eurofound, *Parental and Paternity Leave – Uptake by Fathers*" (Publications Office of the European Union 2019).
132 Our emphasis.

Article 5(2) requires Member States to ensure that two months of parental leave are not transferable. The final text of this provision differs from the original proposal, which suggested that the whole four-month period available to each parent was not transferable.[133] This step backwards, however, must be balanced with Article 8, which introduces a most welcome change that builds upon the original requirement of the proposal, namely that the leave should receive an adequate income, at least equivalent to sick pay level.[134] The final version of Article 8 establishes "a payment or allowance to be defined by the Member State and/or social partners. Such payment or allowance shall be set in such a way as *to facilitate the take up of parental leave by both parents.*"[135] It will be crucial to see how the CJEU interprets this requirement.

Time off from work on the grounds of *force majeure* and carers' leave

Two further rights are noteworthy, namely the right to take time off from work in case of *force majeure*, and the right to leave for carers. These rights have a broader scope of application than other existing leave: they can be granted not only to parents but also to other individuals with caring responsibilities. Whilst the right to take time off for emergency reasons was already present in the Parental Leave Directive,[136] carers' leave was introduced by the Work-Life Balance Directive.

The Parental Leave Directive confirms the possibility of taking leave "on grounds of *force majeure* for urgent family reasons in cases of sickness or accident making the immediate presence of the worker indispensable".[137] This provision is the first that goes beyond *parents*. Its potential has, in the past, been curtailed by the interpretation of the Member States. In the UK, for example, although the relevant legislation[138] theoretically makes possible a broad interpretation, the courts[139] have *de facto* limited its scope of application. The right is only available to make alternative short-term arrangements rather than to deal with an emergency. It is designed to address a sudden or unexpected event affecting dependents by allowing them to make any necessary long-term arrangements for their care.

---

133 Article 5(2), Proposal for a Directive on the EU Parliament and the Council on Work-Life Balance for Parents and Carers, COM(2017) 253 final, Preamble, Recital 5, see also Recitals 14 and 15.
134 Article 8, proposed Directive on Work-Life Balance for Parents and Carers, COM(2017) 253 final.
135 Emphasis added.
136 Clause 7 of Directive 2010/18/EC now Article 7 of Directive (EU) 2019/1158.
137 Ibid.
138 Section 57A Employment Relation Act 1996 as amended.
139 See for example, *Qua v John Ford Morrison Solicitors* [2003] ICR 482 EAT; *Darlington v Alders of Croydon* Case n° 2304217/01 unreported.

Whilst this provision may provide a safety net for employed carers, it is not useful with regards to meeting ongoing needs of care.[140] Furthermore, this construction reflects a traditional view of the family in which relatives live close by and are available to offer informal support.

Possibly more striking is the new minimum entitlement for carers to take leave from work. Article 6(1) of the Work-Life Balance Directive requires Member States to "take the necessary measures to ensure that workers have the right to carers' leave of five working days per year, per worker." Article 6(2) gives Member States the possibility of expanding on this: they "might allocate carers' leave on the basis of a reference period other than a year, per person in need of care or support, or per case". *Prima facie*, the entitlement seems rather modest: the leave is unpaid[141] and covers a very short period. Thus, it is clearly inadequate to meet the ongoing demands that many carers face. Rather than developing a much-needed normative framework to protect carers, this provision merely strengthens the existing "safety net" for emergencies. Nevertheless, and despite these shortcomings, it represents a significant improvement on existing rights. Until now, the EU legislation did not cater for the needs of working carers, other than parents. In other words, it is paradigm-changing and sends the message that caring commitments are not limited to childcare. Even if this provision is unlikely to introduce major changes in the majority of the Member States, it provides an opportunity for national legislators to rethink their domestic systems with a view to taking carers into account. Furthermore, the very introduction of such a provision means that the EU now can legislate in this area.

The time provisions

Apart from periods of leave, the reconciliation measures also provide specific provisions that make it possible to alter certain elements of the working relationship. Unsurprisingly, many carers who lack access to affordable and/or quality care services are unable to work in full-time employment or to hold paid jobs at all.[142] The time provisions seek to enable individuals to adjust their working hours so that

---

140 See Rachel Horton, "Care Giving and Reasonable Adjustment in the UK" in Nicole Busby and Grace James (eds), *Families Care Giving and Paid Work – Challenging Labour Law in the 21st Century* (Edward Elgar 2011).
141 The original proposal provided for payment during these days, see Proposal for a Directive on the EU Parliament and the Council on Work-Life Balance for Parents and Carers COM (2017) 253 final.
142 European Commission, "Report on Equality between Women and Men – 2010" (Publication Office of the European Union 2010); Fiona Carmichael and Susan Charles, "The Opportunity Costs of Informal Care: Does Gender Matter?" (2003) 22 *J Health Economics* 781; Mark Bell, "EU Equality Law and Precarious Work" in Uladzislau Belavusau and Kristin Henrard (eds), *EU Anti-Discrimination Law Beyond Gender* (Hart Publishing 2019) 75. See also the discussion in "Setting the Scene: 'Everyone Cares. Everyone is Cared For'".

they can fulfil their family-related responsibilities while also being able to remain in paid employment.

The EU has adopted a number of time provisions over the years. The main one is the Working Time Directive,[143] which is complemented by the so-called atypical workers directives; namely the Part-Time Work Directive,[144] the Fixed-Term Directive[145] and the Agency Work Directive.[146] Ania Zbyszewska highlights the importance of the Working Time Directive in the context of work-life balance.[147] The Working Time Directive is the key EU instrument that regulates "normal" working hours. However, what is considered to be "normal" continues to be based on male patterns of work in which men are more likely than women to engage in full-time work. Thus, she convincingly argues that, as working excessive hours interferes with caring responsibilities, it is important to challenge our perception of "normal".

Amongst carers and parents,[148] perhaps the most popular of the time provisions is the Part-Time Work Directive that aims to ensure that part-time workers are "not to be treated in a less favourable manner than comparable full-time workers solely because they work part-time unless different treatment is justified on objective grounds."[149] The introduction of this Directive in the 1980s represented a welcome step towards better work-life balance standards. It creates a specific legal remedy for discrimination based on part-time work, increasing the protection for workers who have caring responsibilities, irrespective of their gender. Prior to the introduction of the Directive, women who worked

---

143 Council Directive 2003/88/EC of the European Parliament and of the Council of 4 November 2003 concerning certain aspects of the organisation of working time, O.J. [2003] L299/9.
144 Council Directive 97/81/EC of 15 December 1997 concerning the Framework Agreement on part-time work concluded by UNICE, CEEP and the ETUC – Annex: Framework agreement on part-time work, O.J. [1998] L14/9.
145 Council Directive 99/70/EC of 28 June 1999 concerning the framework agreement on fixed-term work concluded by ETUC, UNICE and CEEP, O.J. [1999] L175/43, corrigendum at O.J. [1999] L244/64.
146 Council Directive 2008/104/EC of the European Parliament and of the Council of 19 November 2008 on temporary agency work, O.J. [2008] L327/9.
147 Ania Zbyszewska, "Reshaping EU Working-Time Regulation: Towards a More Sustainable Regime" (2016) 7 *ELLJ* 331.
148 Jerry Jacobs and Kathleen Gerson, *The Time Divide: Work, Family and Gender Inequalities* (Harvard University Press 2004); Dirk Hofäcker and Stephanie König, "Flexibility and Work-life Conflict in Time of Crisis: A Gender Perspective" (2013) 33 *Intl Journal of Sociology and Social Policy* 613; Annick Masselot, "Family Leave: Enforcement of the Protection against Dismissal and Unfavourable Treatment" (European Union 2018).
149 Clause 4(1) of the Framework Agreement attached to the Part-Time Work Directive 97/81 EC, O.J. [1998] L14/9. See also, European Foundation for the Improvement of Living and Working Conditions, "Part-Time Work in Europe" (2007). Mark Bell, "Achieving the objectives of the Part-Time Work Directive? Revisiting the Part-Time Workers Regulations" (2011) 40 *Industrial Law Journal* 254–279.

part-time were, sometimes, able to rely on the principle of indirect sex discrimination.[150] The situation was more complex for those men acting as carers who could not seek redress for potential discrimination and unfavourable treatment. Today, women and men carers can rely on the Part-Time Work Directive to claim protection against unfavourable treatment. Furthermore, the Directive contains a positive obligation for Member States to "identify and review obstacles to part-time work."[151] Indeed, it aims to improve the quality of part-time work, to promote the development of part-time work on a voluntary basis,[152] and "to contribute to the flexible organisation of working time in a manner which takes into account the needs of employers and workers."[153] Under Clause 5 of the Part-Time Work Directive, employers are also obliged, as far as possible, to consider the worker's request to transfer from full-time to part-time and vice-versa. Arguably this represents an "early form" of the right to request flexible working arrangements.

Despite its clear value for workers with caring responsibilities, the Part-Time Directive constitutes a relatively weak instrument. The positive elements of this Directive are overshadowed by a series of restrictions on the personal and material scope of the Directive. Most notable is the possibility for employers to justify alleged unfavourable treatments of part-time workers on objective grounds.[154] Justification for the differential treatment can be subject "to a period of service, time worked or earnings qualification".[155] This means that criteria such as seniority and qualifications represent valid justifications to differential treatment between full- and part-timers. It is, therefore, hardly surprising that part-time work carries a price. It is under-paid compared to full-time work and associated with low quality jobs.[156] Furthermore, this is a price that is in the main paid by women, who on average are more likely to work part-time than men and this leads to "17% lower

---

150 Case 170/84 *Bilka – Kaufhaus GmbH v Karin Weber von Hartz.* ECLI:EU:C:1986:204.
151 Clause 5 of the Framework Agreement attached to the Part-Time Work Directive 97/81/EC, O.J. [1998] L14/9.
152 Clause 1(a) of the Framework Agreement attached to the Part-Time Work Directive 97/81/EC, O.J. [1998] L14/9.
153 Clause 1(b) of the Framework Agreement attached to the Part-Time Work Directive 97/81/EC, O.J. [1998] L14/9.
154 Clause 4(1) of the Framework Agreement attached to the Part-Time Work Directive 97/81/EC, O.J. [1998] L14/9.
155 Clause 4(4) of the Framework Agreement attached to the Part-Time Work Directive 97/81/EC, O.J. [1998] L14/9.
156 Alan Manning and Barbara Petrongolo, "The Part-Time Pay Penalty for Women in Britain" (2008) 118 *Economic Journal* F28; Mark Jeffery, "Not Really Going to Work? On the Directive on Part-Time Work, 'Atypical Work' and Attempts to Regulate It", (1998) 27 *Industrial Law Journal* 193; Jonathan Herring, *Caring and the Law* (Hart Publishing 2013); Theo Sparreboom, "Gender Equality, Part-Time Work and Segregation" (2014) 153 *Intl Labour Rev* 245.

average weekly hours worked by women."[157] This represents 33.7 hours in paid employment for women as against 40.6 hours for men in 2011, falling to 40 for men and 33.7 for women in 2017.[158]

Moreover, whilst the Part-Time Work Directive has contributed to the flexibilisation of the labour market, it is questionable how far it has advanced the positions of parents and carers. This question was apparent in the case of *Mascellani*.[159] Mrs Mascellani had been working part-time (three days per week) since 2000 in order to be able to care for her family, including caring for a 90-year-old parent who lived with her, as well as pursuing a university degree. In 2011, she was informed that she would have to work full-time over six days per week. Such decision was made possible by domestic legislation, introduced because of specific economic circumstances, that aimed at ensuring sustainability of public finance.[160] Advocate General Wahl accepted that the Part-Time Work Directive permits Member States to "reduce the level of protection afforded under their rules on part-time work in times of turmoil".[161] The CJEU confirmed this interpretation and held that the Part-Time Directive does not preclude an employer requiring a part-time worker to change to full-time work, even without the worker's consent. This reasoning was based on the assumption that the "worker is always at liberty to end the employment relationship if he or she does not wish to work full-time".[162] This decision pays very little regard to the reality of choice for those with caring responsibilities. It highlights that the wishes or the necessities of individual workers are *de facto* a lower priority in times of economic crises. Thus, this case is a reminder that historically flexibility was not designed with parents and carers in mind.

The adoption of the Work-Life Balance Directive in 2019 challenges the EU's traditional approach to flexibility. Article 9 introduces a "right to request" flexible working arrangements for parents with children up to a given age, which should be at least the age of eight, and for carers with caring responsibilities. Needless to say, the gender-neutral nature of Article 9 holds considerable potential for carers and can potentially lead to a real culture change.

The right to request flexible working arrangements is further strengthened by the Directive on transparent and predictable working conditions in the EU[163]

---

157 Communication from the Commission to the European Parliament, the Council, the European Economic and Social Committee and the Committee of the Regions, "Towards Social Investment for Growth and Cohesion – including implementing the European Social Fund 2014–2020", COM(2013) 83, 7.
158 Eurofound, *Striking a Balance: Reconciling Work and Life in the EU* (Publications Office of the European Union 2018).
159 Case C-221/13 *Mascellani v Ministero della Giustizia*. EU:C:2014:2286.
160 Sentenza n. 224/2013 Corte Costituzionale.
161 Case C-221/13, Opinion of AG Wahl, para 54.
162 Ibid.
163 Directive (EU) 2019/1152 of the European Parliament and of the Council of 20 June 2019 on transparent and predictable working conditions in the European Union, O.J. [2019] L186/105.

adopted on the same day as the Work-Life Balance Directive. Both Directives are directly linked to the EPSR, which serves "as a compass for the renewed upwards convergence in social standards in the context of the changing realities of the world of work."[164] The Directive on Transparent and Predictable Working Conditions aims to create more secured work relations in the face of increased flexible forms of work. In other words, this Directive has a double aim: "to ensure that dynamic innovative labour markets underpinning EU's competitiveness are framed in a way that offers basic protection to all workers, longer-term productivity gains for employers and allows for convergence towards better living and working conditions across the EU."[165] Together, the Work-Life Balance Directive and the Directive on transparent and predictable working conditions are likely to provide an environment in which workers with caring responsibilities are better supported in the workplace. These legislative developments also build constructively on the 2000s concept of flexicurity, which has too often in the past disregarded the principle of gender equality.[166]

Conclusion

> As a society that enshrines the virtues of independence, defines instrumental work as superior to emotional work, seeks to distance itself from basic life events, and devaluates the actions of women, we have tended to ignore the experience of caregivers.[167]

In this chapter we have discussed the protection that is available under EU law for carers. Such protection is articulated in two sets of legislative measures: non-discrimination and equality provisions and the reconciliation provisions. The recently adopted Work-Life Balance Directive represents a promising development that has the potential to considerably strengthen the position of carers. The contribution of the CJEU has also been central to the process of valuing carers. Thus, *prima facie*, a tentative EU legal framework has slowly but steadily emerged. Whether this is enough to address the needs of carers and to provide them with specific rights is still questionable.

---

164 Directive (EU) 2019/1152 on transparent and predictable working conditions in the EU, Explanatory memorandum 1.
165 Ibid.
166 Sandra Fredman, "Women at Work: The Broken Promise of Flexicurity" (2004) 33 *Industrial Law Journal* 299; Lise Lotte Hansen, "From Flexicurity to Flexicarity? Gendered Perspectives on the Danish Model" (2017) 3(2) *Journal of Social Sciences* 88–93; Jane Lewis and Ania Plomien, "'Flexicurity' as a Policy Strategy: The Implications for Gender Equality" (2009) 38(3) *Economy and Society* 433–459.
167 Emily Abel and Margaret Nelson, "Circles of Care: An Introductory Essay" in Emily Abel and Margaret Nelson (eds), *Circles of Care: Work and Identity in Women"s Lives* (SUNY Press 1990).

On the one hand, although over the years the non-discrimination and equality provisions have become increasingly sophisticated, they are still ill-equipped to deal with discrimination on the ground of caring responsibilities.[168] In developing the concept of discrimination by association, the CJEU has opened some potential opportunities. In practice, however, the *dicta* in *Coleman* and *CHEZ* shows that discrimination by association remains limited in its ability to improve the lives of all working carers: it applies to those who care for disabled children but not for "ordinary day-to-day" care. Furthermore, despite the adoption of a Directive prohibiting discrimination in the access to and the supply of goods and services,[169] most EU anti-discrimination law applies to situations taking place within the labour market. Overall, rights for carers are framed as "workplace rights" and as such they can only represent a small part of the response to the challenges posed by the increasing demand for care for both children and adults. Although the focus of this book is on carers in employment, we remain acutely aware that there are other carers who are not in paid employment: this does not make them any less worthy of protection. Indeed, those individuals might be willing to become engaged in paid employment but simply do not have the support they need in order to do so. The EPSR challenges this idea but, as a non-binding instrument, it remains limited in its application.

On the other hand, the EU work-family reconciliation provisions, although representing a welcome development, are not suitable to address the needs of *all* carers. They have three main pitfalls. First, these provisions remain concerned with the labour market. Second, at the moment they are mainly geared towards young and healthy children rather than the more challenging care to older people or children with disabilities. The right to carers' leave in the 2019 Work-Life Balance Directive remains minimal and ill adapted to addressing the challenges of LTC. Third, the application of the provisions on work-life balance have traditionally been highly gendered and as such they have contributed to perpetuating the very stereotypes that they want to dismantle. As care is highly gendered, traditional legal protection, rooted in industrial modes of production and based on an outdated male bread winner/female caregiver social norm,[170] is often inadequate[171] and, even where

---

168 Eugenia Caracciolo di Torella and Annick Masselot, *Reconciling Work and Family Life in EU Law and Policy* (Palgrave Macmillan 2010).
169 Council Directive 2004/113/EC of 13 December 2004 implementing the principle of equal treatment between men and women in the access to and supply of goods and services, O.J. [2004] L373/37.
170 Stephanie Bornstein, "Work, Family, and Discrimination at the Bottom of the Ladder" (2012) 19 *Georgetown J Poverty L and Policy* 1; Rosemary Crompton, *Employment and the Family: The Reconfiguration of Work and Family Life in Contemporary Societies* (CUP 2006).

relevant, under-enforced.[172] Paradoxically, neoliberal reform, focused on gross domestic product, de-unionisation and de-regulation of labour standards have contributed to the increase, rather than the protection of precarious work.[173] This is because employers have traditionally valued reliable, timely and consistent workers; the so-called "unencumbered worker", not the one whose performance might be "disrupted" by other commitments.[174]

Against this backdrop, the 2019 Work-Life Balance Directive provides a welcome change of perspective, which it is hoped will contribute to a change in attitude on the ground.

EU law has certainly been more successful at addressing the situation of carers rather than that of care. Nevertheless, there is little doubt that, both as a society and as a legal order, "historically, we have tended to ignore the experience of caregivers".[175] Although carers have firmly been put on the EU agenda, their rights remain, by and large underbuilt and disjointed. If the existing rights have answered a number of *ad hoc* quests, they are not (yet) organised into a comprehensive framework, because there is still a lack of uniform underlying themes and principles.

---

171 Leah Vosko, *Managing the Margins* (OUP 2010); Mathew Forstater, "Working for a Better World Cataloguing Arguments for the Right to Employment" (2015) 41 *Philosophy and Social Criticism* 61; Eugenia Caracciolo di Torella and Annick Masselot, "Work and Family Life Balance in EU Law and Policy 40 Years On: Still Balancing, Still Struggling" (2013) 2 *European Gender Equality L Rev* 6; Annick Masselot, "The Rights and Realities of Balancing Work and Family Life in New Zealand" in Nicola Busby and Grace James (eds), *Families, Care-Giving and Paid Work: Challenging Labour Law in the 21st Century* (Edward Elgar 2010).

172 Leah Vosko, Martha MacDonald and Ian Campbell (eds), *Gender and the Contours of Precarious Employment* (Routledge 2010); Arne Kalleberg, "Nonstandard Employment Relations: Part-Time, Temporary and Contract Work" (2000) 26 *Annual Rev Sociology* 341; Arne Kalleberg, "Precarious Work, Insecure Workers: Employment Relations in Transition" (2009) 74 *Am Soc Rev* 1.

173 Michael Quinlan, "The 'Pre-invention' of Precarious Employment: The Changing World of Work in Context" (2012) 23 *The Economic and Labour Relations Review* 3.

174 Grace James, "Law's Response to Pregnancy/Workplace Conflicts: A Critique" (2007) 15 *Feminist Legal Studies* 167; Mary Daly, "What Adult Worker Model? A Critical Look at Recent Social Policy Reform in Europe from a Gender and Family Perspective" (2011) 18 *Social Politics: Intl Studies in Gender, State & Society* 1.

175 Emily Abel and Margaret Nelson, "Circles of Care: An Introductory Essay" in Emily Abel and Margaret Nelson (eds), *Circles of Care: Work and Identity in Women's Lives* (SUNY Press 1990).

5 Reframing the debate

Introduction

The previous chapters have analysed how the European Union (EU) policy maker and legislator have sought to engage with care (both child and long-term) and carers.[1] This analysis has highlighted that, at least in terms of legislation, it has been, and remains, easier and more practically feasible to engage with (certain types of) carers, rather than with the broader concept of care. Briefly, there are several explanations for the limited EU involvement with the notion of care. First, how care is performed and organised depends heavily on cultural and economic national contexts which differ widely from each other. Second, the EU lacks express competence to intervene in this area. Third, the complexity of the concept of care itself makes it problematic, and possibly even undesirable, for the EU to intervene.[2] In sum, as far as care is concerned, it is probably more appropriate for the EU to strengthen its role as a facilitator for the exchange of information and good practices. Even in this case, however, the EU should at least ensure that Member States' actions are in line with its general principles and fundamental values.

In contrast, when it comes to carers, EU intervention *is* possible. Indeed, a number of EU provisions are already used to regulate the legal status and rights of certain carers.[3] A uniform regulation of carers across the Member States is not only achievable; it is also highly desirable as different standards impact on social justice as well as on the EU's ability to tackle poverty and social exclusion. Furthermore, to regulate and improve the position of carers is likely, in turn, to positively affect those who are cared for.

Against this backdrop, we submit that the EU must take the lead and develop a clear normative framework to ensure that carers can thrive, rather than simply ensuring that they are not discriminated against. A vision for such framework has recently began to emerge in particular following the adoption of the European

---

1 Chapters 2 and 3, respectively.
2 See the discussion in "Setting the scene: 'Everyone cares, Everyone is cared for'" and in Chapter 1.
3 See Chapter 4.

Pillar on Social Rights (EPSR)[4] and the Commission's Communication on the New Start Initiative.[5] This new environment has made it possible to introduce the 2019 Work-Life Balance Directive,[6] which represents a remarkable shift towards valuing carers and the work that they perform.[7] It is now imperative not to lose momentum, to consolidate and build upon this emerging approach in order to develop a coherent EU legal framework for carers.[8] We argue for stronger rights in this area and for these rights to be mainstreamed. In other words, any policy or legislation should consider the impact of caring responsibilities on individuals. For example, in the specific context of this book, considerations should be raised with regards to how new measures that regulate aspects of employment law can accommodate the needs of carers.

This chapter explores the possibilities of developing a normative framework to enable individuals who care for dependants to be able to fulfil their working commitments. It is organised in two main sections. The first section (Using the EU fundamental principles and values to underpin a legal framework for care) analyses the principles and values that could underpin specific rights for carers. We maintain that these principles and values are *already* embedded in the EU policy and legal system and they now need to be "unlocked" and used for this purpose.[9] Against this background, the second section (A rights-based strategy for carers), using the Work-Life Balance Directive as a starting point, seeks to lay the foundations for a normative strategy. Such a strategy consists of three elements: a clear legal base to confer express competence to the EU legislator, the identification of who is entitled to those rights (the personal scope), as well as an outline of the rights entailed in the strategy (the material scope).

---

4 Interinstitutional Proclamation on the European Pillar of Social Rights, O.J. [2017] C428/10.
5 Communication from the Commission "An Initiative to Support Work-Life Balance for Working Parents and Carers", COM(2017) 252 final.
6 Directive (EU) 2019/1158 of the European Parliament and of the Council on work-life balance for parents and carers and repealing Council Directive 2010/18/EU, O.J. [2019] L188/79. For an overview of the Directive, see the discussion in Chapter 4.
7 Denis Bouget, Chiara Saraceno and Slavina Spasova, "Towards New Work-Life Balance Policies for those caring for Dependent Relatives?" in Bart Vanhercke, Sebastiano Sabato, Denis Bouget (eds), *Social Policy in the European Union: State of Play 2017* (ETUI 2017) 155–179 www.etui.org/Publications2/Books/Social-policy-in-the-European-Union-state-of-play-2017. Accessed 20 July 2019.
8 Eugenia Caracciolo di Torella, "Shaping and Re-Shaping the Caring Relationship in European Law: A Catalogue of Rights for Informal Carers?" (2016) 28 *Child and Family L Q* 261.
9 See the discussion in Chapter 1.

Using the EU fundamental principles and values to underpin a legal framework for care

Because of its inherent characteristics, it can be difficult to address the caring relationship with the language of rights.[10] Nevertheless, such language remains important as rights are ultimately instrumental in shaping the normative framework: they have a "transformative aspect" in so far as they have "the potential to reduce ... dependency by changing the rights holder into a powerful individual who commands the respect of those in the legal system".[11] Gender equality and non-discrimination rights have clearly shown both the potential and the limitations of using a rights-based strategy when trying to address the problems faced by carers. Those rights have indeed proved central to advance the quest of certain carers.[12] To go further, they require the support of other principles and values that actively promote the caring relationship, rather than merely trying to counterbalance its disadvantages. Indeed, carers can only be adequately protected in a context where relevant legal provisions emphasise the importance of relationships and responsibilities. In other words, we argue that rights should be interpreted through the lens of the ethic of care that is already present in EU law.[13] An ethic of care is reflected in the fundamental and historical values which have a strong potential to provide a basis for the EU's engagement in this area. Article 2 of the Treaty on European Union (TEU) sets a list of the values on which the Union is founded:

> [the] respect for human dignity, freedom, democracy, equality, the rule of law and respect for human rights, including the rights of persons belonging to minorities. These values are common to the Member States in a society in which pluralism, non-discrimination, tolerance, justice, solidarity and equality between women and men prevail.

Amongst these values, the contribution of equality and non-discrimination to the needs of carers has already been discussed in this book. As for the others, whilst they are all important and instrumental in developing an environment where carers are valued, particularly relevant for our purpose are the concepts of human dignity, solidarity and well-being.[14]

---

10 See the discussion in Chapter 1.
11 Katherine Federle, "Rights, Not Wrongs" (2009) 17 *Intl J Children's Rights* 321, emphasis added.
12 For example, Article 153 TFEU provides that the Union shall adopt minimum requirements, as well as support and complement the activities of the Member States in the area of working environment, working conditions, as well as equality between men and women with regard to labour market opportunities and treatment at work.
13 Eugenia Caracciolo di Torella, "Shaping and Re-shaping the Caring Relationship in European Law: A Catalogue of Rights for Informal Carers?" (2016) 28 *Child and Family L Q* 261; see further the discussion in Chapter 1.
14 See the discussion in Chapter 1.

Human dignity is not a new concept in EU law. Prior to its formal inclusion in the Treaty of Lisbon and in the Charter of Fundamental Rights (CFR or the Charter),[15] the Court of Justice of the European Union (CJEU or the Court) had qualified human dignity as a general principle of EU law. In *Konstantinidis*,[16] Advocate General Jacobs stated that:

> the constitutional traditions of the Member States in general allow for the conclusion that there exists a principle according to which the State must respect not only the individual's physical well-being, but also his dignity, moral integrity and sense of personal identity.[17]

Further, in *P v S*, in relation to the treatment of transgender people in the workplace, the Court held that "to tolerate such discrimination would be tantamount, as regards such a person, to a failure to respect the dignity and freedom to which he or she is entitled, and which the Court has a duty to safeguard".[18] In the case of *Omega*,[19] the CJEU defined the "respect for human dignity as a general principle of law".[20] It was, however, the case of *Coleman*[21] that highlighted the potential of the concept of dignity for carers. In his Opinion, Advocate General Maduro indicated that "at its bare minimum, human dignity entails the recognition of the equal worth of every individual".[22] He went further to indicate that "[o]ne's life is valuable by virtue of the mere fact that one is human, and no life is more or less valuable than another."[23] It is easy to see how it would be beneficial to extend this reasoning to the caring relationship: preserving the dignity of those in need of care as well as those who provide care – regardless of the economic contribution that an individual can make – represents a powerful argument. Individuals are not just a means of economic investment; there is value in human dignity whether they are economically productive or not.

---

15 Article 1 CFR simply states that "[h]uman dignity is inviolable. It must be respected and protected". In addition, the concept of dignity is contained in other CFR provisions: Articles 25 (Rights of the Elderly) and 31 (Fair and Just Working Conditions) CFR.
16 Case C-168/91 *Christos Konstantinidis v Stadt Altensteig–Standesamt and Landratsamt Calw–Ordnungsamt*. ECLI:EU:C:1993:115; Opinion of AG ECLI:EU:C:1992:504, para 39.
17 Case C-168/91. ECLI:EU:C:1992:504, para 39.
18 Case C-13/94 *P v S and Cornwall County Council*. ECLI:EU:C:1996:170, para 22.
19 Case C-36/02 *Omega Spielhallen-und Automatenaufstellungs-GmbH v Oberbürgermeisterin der Bundesstadt Bonn*. ECLI:EU:C:2004:614.
20 Ibid, para 34.
21 Case C-303/06 *Coleman* v *Attridge Law and Steve Law*. ECLI:EU:C:2008:415
22 Advocate General Maduro in Case C-303/06 *Coleman v Attridge Law*. ECLI:EU:C:2008:61, para 9. See also paras 8–10, 12–13, 15 and 22.
23 Ibid.

Solidarity, one of the values on which the Union is founded,[24] is also an important concept in this context. Article 3 TEU lists the promotion of "solidarity between generations",[25] as one of the EU goals. For the purpose of our argument, solidarity implies that care-work should not fall as a burden on the shoulder of a few, mainly women, but should be shared amongst men and women as a norm.[26] Seen in this light, the concept places emphasis on relationships and represents an expression of the principle that "providing care for people over the life cycle is a social responsibility, an obligation that reflects our ties to one another as a human community."[27] The concept of solidarity is further located in the title of Solidarity in the CFR, which includes the right to reconcile work and professional life. Other references to, and applications of, the concept of solidarity can be found in policy papers such as the Green Paper *Confronting demographic change: a new solidarity between the generations*,[28] with which the European Commission launched a debate on the role of technology and better work-life balance in tackling problems associated with demographic ageing. Overall, research shows that across the EU "[t]here is considerable evidence of solidarity actions and support for policies to assist the vulnerable in society". Yet the concept remains "nuanced, conditional and often fragile".[29] If anything, this emphasises the need for measures that can incapsulate and give substance to the notion of solidarity.

In addition, Article 3(1) TEU states that "[t]he Union's aim is to promote peace, its values and the well-being of its peoples". There is no definition of well-being, rather the EU has addressed it in terms of what is not conducive of someone's well-being. In a report discussing the gender difference in relation to care, the European Parliament states that "the well-being of women who have left the labour market is lower than those who have not".[30] The report also highlights how poor work-life balance measures impact on individuals' mental health. In other words, measures aiming at achieving work-life balance can decrease stress and prevent burnout.[31]

The values enshrined in Articles 2 and 3 TEU are not the only provisions showing the "human face" of the EU.[32] The EU architecture embraces other important

---

24 Article 2 TEU.
25 Article 3 TEU.
26 Martha Fineman, *The Autonomy Myth* (New Press 2004).
27 Johanna Brenner, "Democratizing Care" in Janet Gornick and Marcia Meyers (eds), *Gender Equality, Transforming Family Divisions of Labor* (Verso 2009) 189.
28 COM(2005) 94 final.
29 Yuri Borgmann-Prebil and Andreas Obermaier-Muresan, *Solidarity in Europe – Alive and Active* (European Commission 2018).
30 European Parliament FEMM Committee 2016, (PE 556.933) "Differences in in Men and Women's Work, Care and Leisure Time" 16.
31 Eurofound, "Burnout in the Workplace: A Review of Data and Policy Response in the EU" (Eurofound 2018).
32 Nuno Ferreira and Dora Kostakopoulou (eds), *The Human Face of the European Union* (Springer 2016); see the discussion in Chapter 1.

principles and values, which both provide evidence of the EU's ethical dimension and are crucial to carers. Such EU principles and values are contained in the CFR whose provisions contribute to reinforce the emerging EU support for carers. It does so by unambiguously reiterating specific principles, such as dignity, non-discrimination and equality. The Charter also contains provisions that emphasise the rights and the protection of vulnerable citizens, including children,[33] the elderly[34] and disabled people[35] as well as (certain) carers.[36]

The CFR, which now has the status of primary legislation, is legally binding and represents "an enormous transformative potential"[37] in particular for the development of an ethic of care within EU law. This potential, however, falls short of creating new competences for the EU: essentially it merely enhances the status of fundamental rights within the confines of EU competences. In other words, the Charter does not extend the EU competences into enacting care related measures beyond those already set out in the TEU and the TFEU. Nevertheless, it has become "a point of reference"[38] commonly used in the development of EU policies. Indeed, the Commission not only guarantees that its proposals are compatible with the Charter, it also ensures that the Charter is respected when Member States implement EU law.[39] Moreover, both Advocates General and the CJEU have increasingly referred to it. We argue that there is evidence that, taken together, these provisions contribute to support mutually interdependent connections, reflecting an emerging EU ethic of care.

Furthermore, although not expressly a value or a principle of EU law, the CJEU has, on many occasions relevant to this area, adopted an approach that denotes and promotes compassion. This has happened by generously extending social rights: for example, by allowing third country nationals to remain in the EU to be able to be part of a caring relationship,[40] or by stating that domestic legislation should be interpreted to give mothers and fathers the same rights in relation to caring for a young child.[41] At the very least, there is evidence that there is political will to engage with an ethic of care discourse. Such political will is also apparent in the recently proclaimed EPRS.

33 Article 24 CFR on the right of the children.
34 Article 25 CFR on the rights of the elderly.
35 Article 26 CFR on the rights of persons with disabilities.
36 Article 33 CFR on the right to reconciliation between work and family life.
37 Nicola Countouris and Mark Freedland, "Resocialising Europe – Looking Back and Thinking Forward" in Nicola Countouris and Mark Freedland (eds), *Resocialising Europe in a Time of Crisis* (CUP 2013) 496.
38 Report from the Commission on the Application of the EU Charter of Fundamental Rights Brussels, COM(2012) 169 final 2011.
39 Ibid.
40 See the discussion later in this chapter.
41 See Case C-104/09 *Roca Álvarez* v *Sesa Start España. ETT SA*. ECLI:EU:C:2010:561, para 24 and Case C-222/14 *Maistrellis*. ECLI:EU:C:2015:473, para 47.

This emerging ethic of care within the EU is further supported by powerful international instruments, such as European Convention of Human Rights (ECHR), and the International Labour Organisation (ILO), which are both important reference points for the CJEU.

Article 8 ECHR expressly refers to the protection of "family life".[42] Care, which often takes place within the family, is an integral part of the concept of family life. The European Court of Human Rights (ECtHR) has held that, even if Article 8 does not expressly mention care, family life does indeed depend on close, continuing and practical ties. Its case law not only appears to acknowledge the rights of carers, it also suggests that parents and children have a right to bond with one another, regardless of the way in which a family is created.[43] Thus, Article 8 ECHR opens up possibilities for a new discussion that emphasises the importance of the caring relationship and an alternative way of interpreting non-discrimination provisions and workplace rights. This provision contains both negative and positive aspects. Whilst the negative aspect, namely the principle of non-interference, is the most prominent, the positive aspect requires Member States to take reasonable steps to provide services or otherwise act to maintain the familial and caring relationship.

The ILO has also been pivotal in shaping both the EU and domestic legislation that addresses the situations of carers.[44] Over the years, it has adopted several conventions relevant to individuals with caring responsibilities. In particular, ILO Convention on Workers with Family Responsibilities (n. 165)[45] and the accompanying Recommendation (n. 165) offer evidence of the importance of providing rights for carers in the workplace.[46] Care-work is also at the heart of other ILO initiatives such as the Women at Work[47] and the Future of Work Centenary Initiatives.[48] Both of these initiatives emphasise that action to regulate care-work, and therefore to protect carers, is crucial for the future of decent work that benefits all.

---

42 The relevance of the ECHR is also evident in other relevant articles, such as Article 14 ECHR on the protection from discrimination.
43 Petra Foubert and Šejla Imamović, "The Pregnant Workers Directive: Must Do Better: Lessons to be Learned from Strasbourg?" (2015) 37 *Journal of Social Welfare & Family Law* 309.
44 Tamar Landau and Yves Beigbeder, *From ILO Standards to EU Law: The Case of Equality between Men and Women at Work* (Brill Nijhoff 2008); Lee Adams, "The Family Responsibilities Convention Reconsidered: The Work-Family Intersection in International Law Thirty Years On" (2013) 22 *Cardozo J of International and Comparative Law* 201.
45 Articles 1 and 5 of ILO Convention concerning Equal Opportunities and Equal Treatment for Men and Women Workers: Workers with Family Responsibilities, 1981 (n. 165) are pressingly relevant.
46 Margaret O'Brien, "Fitting Fathers into Work-family Policies: International Challenges in Turbulent Times" (2013) 33 *Intl Journal of Sociology and Social Policy* 542.
47 International Labour Organisation, Women at Work today, www.itcilo.org/en/supporting-initiatives/women-at-work-itcilo/#1. Accessed 20 July 2019.
48 International Labour Organisation, The future of work Centenary initiative, www.ilo.org/global/topics/future-of-work/WCMS_448448/lang–en/index.htm. Accessed 20 July 2019.

A rights-based strategy for carers

Although the provisions discussed above support a vision that ensures that relationships of care, love and solidarity are nurtured and valued, they cannot alone provide the legal base to enact specific rights. Simply put, the Treaty does not contain explicit rights for carers, who have found little legal support from the EU. In particular, carers who are employed, continue to be in a disadvantaged position and in many cases suffer discrimination. So far, the few attempts to address their situation have not led to convincing results. For example, traditional provisions, such as Article 157 TFEU on the principle of gender equality and Article 19 TFEU on a broader non-discrimination principle, taken in isolation have proven to have pitfalls with regards to carers.[49] Specific rights for carers cannot be devised exclusively within a traditional normative framework that values personal autonomy and free choice. Instead, they need to be grounded within values that acknowledge the interdependence of individuals and accommodate human diversity. The previous section has shown that such values are already embedded in the EU legal framework. The EU therefore has the required instruments to devise an agenda for carers, rather than merely addressing them as a by-product of the internal market, as it has been the case until now. The Work-Life Balance Directive represents a considerable shift in such direction. It is only a starting point, however. The task ahead is to explore how these principles and values can be used to enhance the existing (scant) provisions and to devise a more robust and effective set of EU rights for carers. The next sections explore what rights for carers should look like.

The legal base

Rights need to be supported by a legal base that gives the EU legislator precise competences in a given area.[50] As care was not originally contemplated by the EU Treaty, technically there is no express EU legal base to underpin legislation on carers' rights. Instead, secondary legislation has been stretched to support the rights of certain carers. These provisions vary considerably in terms of their legal basis and their objectives. For example, the Pregnant Workers Directive, adopted on the basis of Article 118a, has been framed as a health and safety measure, while other provisions such as the Parental Leave Directive or the Framework Agreement on Part-Time Work have been based on the principle of gender equality. This is also the case for the recently adopted Work-Life Balance Directive which is based on Article 153(1)(i) TFEU, Article 3 TEU and Articles 23 and 33 CFR.

The provisions of the Treaty and the CFR on gender equality have proved to be a useful starting point. Nevertheless, the shortcoming remains that such

---

49 See the discussion in Chapter 4.
50 Articles 4 and 5 TEU. In particular Article 4(1) specifies that "competences not conferred upon the Union in the Treaties remain with the Member States".

138 *Reframing the debate*

provisions do not have the protection of carers as their main aim. We submit that in order to move forward, it is desirable to provide the EU legislator with the specific competence to adopt legislation to protect carers. Ideally, a new provision could be inserted into the Treaty with a view to protect carers and individuals who have caring responsibilities. This is unlikely to happen, however. The best way to achieve carers' protection under EU law is therefore to campaign for the amendment of the existing Article 19 TFEU.

Indeed, the position of carers would be strengthened by including a reference to the "prohibition of discrimination on the grounds of caring responsibilities" in Article 19 TFEU. This way, the provision would offer ample protection. It would cover the cases of discrimination and unfavourable treatment against individual carers whether or not they are workers. It would expand the traditional boundaries of EU anti-discrimination law and challenge the way care-work is accounted for. In turn, this is likely to challenge the traditional understanding of paid and unpaid work and the way the market economy is valued. It would also send the message that it is not enough simply not to discriminate against individuals for using rights that allow them to care, but it is also vital not to discriminate against individuals for the very fact that they have caring responsibilities. Sending a clear message regarding the EU commitment to social values would be paradigm-changing.

To ensure that carers are protected under EU law requires such a bold intervention: the discussion in this chapter shows that the Work-Life Balance Directive, although a step in the right direction, is not comprehensive enough. A Treaty amendment is necessary as, according to the CJEU at the time of writing, the list of protected grounds under Article 19 TFEU remains exhaustive[51] and neither the CFR nor the EPSR have succeeded in changing this *status quo*.[52]

In search of the personal scope: who has caring responsibilities?

Aside from a legal basis, rights require to have clearly designated personal scope to be enforced. The question therefore is: "Who are the carers?" or "Who are the individuals with caring responsibilities?" Considering that EU intervention in this area has been scarce, it is perhaps unsurprising that EU law has only very recently sought to define who an individual with caring responsibilities is.

This enquiry can be deceptively simple:[53] in many cases, it might be obvious and perhaps this is the very reason why the legislator did not deem it necessary to clarify the term. An individual with caring responsibilities is like the proverbial duck – "when I see a bird that walks like a duck, swims like a duck and quacks

---

51 Case C-13/05 *Chacòn Navas v Eurest Colectividades* SA. ECLI:EU:C:2006:456. See the discussion in Chapter 4.
52 Mark Bell, "The Principle of Equal Treatment and the European Pillar of Social Rights" (2018) 160 *Giornale di Diritto del Lavoro e di Relazioni Industriali* 783–810. See also the discussion in Chapter 4.
53 Eugenia Caracciolo di Torella, "Shaping and Re-Shaping the Caring Relationship in European Law: A Catalogue of Rights for Informal Carers?" (2016) 28 *Child and Family L Q* 261.

like a duck, I call that bird a duck"[54] – or elephant – "it is difficult to describe, but you know it when you see it".[55] However, if we are to legislate on individuals with caring responsibilities, a definition is just as important as it was important to define workers in the context of the free movement of workers.[56] A definition would clarify who is entitled to certain rights as well as to ensure uniformity of application of the rules. At present, data suggests that Member States do not share the same definition of carer.[57] To allow Member States to have variable personal scope in relation to this concept is likely to lead to confusion and potentially discriminatory treatment, as a carer in one Member State might not be considered a carer in another. The UK Government, for example, defines carer as "someone who uses a significant proportion of their life providing unpaid support to family or possibly friends. This could be caring for a relative, partner or friend who is ill, frail, disabled or has mental health or substance misuse problems."[58] Notably, this definition neither includes parents nor those, such as grandparents, who may look after young children instead of parents. It is undeniable that all of these individuals have caring responsibilities and are equally deserving of protection.

Recently, the EU legislator, although indirectly, has sought to define those individuals who have caring responsibilities. Article 3(1) of the Work-Life Balance Directive contains several definitions that are useful in this context. It identifies "paternity leave" as leave from work for "fathers or, where and in so far as recognised by national law, for equivalent second parents, on the occasion of the birth of a child for the purposes of providing care." It also defines parental leave as the "the leave from work for parents on the grounds of the birth or adoption of a child to take care of that child". Thus, these definitions infer that fathers and parents have caring responsibilities. The Directive introduces the concepts of carers' leave as:

> leave from work for workers in order to provide personal care or support to a relative, or to a person who lives in the same household as the worker, and who is in need of significant care or support for a serious medical reason, as defined by each Member State.[59]

54 James Whitcomb Riley, *Poems & Prose Sketches* (Portable Poetry 2007) 68.
55 *Per* Lord Justice Stuart-Smith in *Cadogan Estates Ltd v Morris* [1999] L & TR 154.
56 For a definition of worker see the case law development, inter alia, Case 53/81 *Levin v Secretary of State for Justice*. ECLI:EU:C:1982:105; Case 139/85 *Kempf v Staatssecretaris van Justitie*. ECLI:EU:C:1986:223; Case 39/86 *Lair v Universität Hannover*. ECLI:EU:C:1988:322 and more recently Case C-507/12 *Jessy Saint Prix v Secretary of State for Work and Pensions*. ECLI:EU:C:2014:2007, as noted by Nicole Busby, "Crumbs of Comfort: Pregnancy and the Status of 'Worker' under EU Law's Free Movement Provisions" (2015) 44 *Industrial Law Journal* 134.
57 Annick Masselot, "Family Leave: Enforcement of the Protection against Dismissal and Unfavourable Treatment" (European Union 2018); Debbie Verbeek-Oudijk and others, "Who Cares in Europe? A comparison of Long-Term Care for the Over 50s in Sixteen European Countries" (Netherlands Institute for Social Research 2014).
58 HM Government, "Carers at the Heart of 21st Century Families and Communities" (The Stationary Office 2008) 18.
59 Article 3(1) of Directive (EU) 2019/1158 on work-life balance for parents and carers and repealing Council Directive 2010/18/EU, O.J. [2019] L188/79.

It also introduces the concept of carer as:

> a worker providing personal care or support to a relative, or to a person who lives in the same household as the worker, and who is in need of significant care or support for a serious medical reason, as defined by each Member State

and clarifies that the term relative "means a worker's son, daughter, mother, father, spouse or, where such partnerships are recognised by national law, partner in civil partnership".

This represents a welcome starting point because it fills a gap, as it puts fathers and parents on the same footing with other types of carers, and thus promotes a diverse and inclusive vision of individuals with caring responsibilities. The definitions remain narrow, however. Paternity and parental leave are expressly reserved to parents, and this ignores the reality of modern life. Changes in family formation mean that there are increasing situations where children are cared for by individuals who are neither their parent nor blood relatives. Similarly, the Work-Life Balance Directive seems to apply only to some first-degree relatives. This restriction does not take into account that today's increased geographical mobility makes it less likely for first-degree relatives to live close by and therefore to be able to provide the necessary care. Moreover, care implies a social and personal element and an adult with disabilities or an ageing person may prefer to choose a friend or a neighbour over a relative. Thus, these definitions should be expanded to include any other person who is *actually* providing care.

The Work-Life Balance Directive has only just been adopted, but the CJEU has had, over the years, the opportunity to address situations involving care. Although it has never defined who a carer is, its contribution has helped in identifying some of the features of individuals with caring responsibilities. In early cases, care was linked to an economic context, or at the very least to an employment connection.[60] In the seminal case of *Martínez Sala*,[61] the CJEU, for the first time, considered care outside the strict confine of the economic framework and in doing so, it acknowledged the value of the work performed by carers. In this case the applicant was a Spanish national, living in Germany. Because at the time of the application she was not working, she was refused a child raising allowance on the basis that she was neither German nor an EU worker. The Court, however, found there was no need for the individual to be economically active in order to qualify for the right if such EU citizen was a "primary carer".

The rights of carers have further been addressed in other cases, especially in the context of family reunification. The Court has confirmed the link between carer

---

60 Jo Shaw, "Citizenship of the Union: Towards Post-National Membership" in Academy of European Law (ed), *Collected Course of the Academy of European Law* vol VI Book I (Kluwer International Law 1998).
61 Case C- 85/96 *María Martínez Sala v Freistaat Bayern*. ECLI:EU:C:1998:217.

and citizenship. In *Carpenter*,[62] the Court considered the situation of a non-EU citizen allowed to remain based on the fact that she was the primary carer of her EU husband's young children. In a similar vein, in *Baumbast*,[63] the Court considered the situation of two female applicants (US citizens), divorced from EU nationals, residing in the UK together with their school-age children. In both cases, the CJEU found that the mothers should be granted a right of residence in the UK, on account of the fact that they were the "primary carers" of children who enjoyed their right to pursue studies in the host Member State. Although the cases concerned the right of residence of the mother, the CJEU's reasoning focused on the impact of the parent's right of residence on the care of children and thus on the right to family life, as established in Article 8 ECHR.

The CJEU confirmed these findings in *Ibrahim*[64] and *Teixeira*,[65] where it held that the applicants could invoke a right of residence in their capacity as the primary carer of school-age children of a former migrant worker. In *Chen*,[66] the Court went even further as it considered that to refuse a right of residence to a parent who was a third country national and the "primary carer" of a child entitled to reside in a Member State would curtail the child's right to free movement and residence in the EU. In doing so, the Court reiterated the essential role of caring responsibilities as linked to the exercise of the rights of the EU citizen. Finally, in a similar case, *Zambrano*,[67] the CJEU held that a Colombian national could invoke the right to residence in Belgium based on the fact that his two children had Belgian nationality. Although in this case the Court did not expressly rely on the concept of "primary carer", it explained that the children of Mr Zambrano could not reside in Belgium independently from their carer. In contrast in *Dereci*,[68] the Court limited the meaning of "primary carer". On this occasion, the CJEU considered that the children involved, with whom the litigants were family members, would not be deprived of their means of subsistence and would not need to leave the EU if the rights of residence of the litigants were not recognised.[69] In other words, in this case there was no "care dependence". This reasoning was further

---

62 Case C-60/00 *Mary Carpenter v Secretary of State for the Home Department.* ECLI:EU:C:2002:434.
63 Case C-413/99 *Baumbast and R. v Secretary of State for the Home Department.* ECLI:EU:C:2002:493.
64 Case C-310/08 *London Borough of Harrow v Nimco Hassan Ibrahim.* ECLI:EU:C:2010:80.
65 Case C-480/08 *Maria Teixeira v London Borough of Lambeth and Secretary of State for the Home Department.* ECLI:EU:C:2009:642.
66 Case C-200/02 *Kunqian Catherine Zhu, Man Lavette Chen v Secretary of State for the Home Department.* ECLI:EU:C:2004:639.
67 Case C-34/09 *Gerardo Ruiz Zambrano v Office national de l'emploi (ONEm).* ECLI:EU:C:2011:124.
68 Case C-256/11 *Murat Dereci and Others v Bundesministerium für Inneres.* ECLI:EU:C:2011:734.
69 Ibid, para 74.

developed in *Iida*,[70] where the Court held that whether or not residence rights need to be accorded to the primary carer of an EU child may not depend solely on whether a child would otherwise have to leave the EU. The Court considered that it was less imperative for Mr Iida to remain with his daughter as she was not "materially dependent" on him.[71] This disregarded the fact that care between a parent and a child goes beyond material aspects.

The concept of caring responsibilities has also appeared in the case law of the CJEU in the context of employment law. The case of *Coleman*,[72] involving a single mother being the main carer of a disabled child, has already been discussed in the previous section. In other cases concerning periods of leave to care for a child, the Court has held that "the position of a male and female worker, father and mother of a young child, are comparable with regard to their possible need ... to look after the child".[73]

This case law highlights the importance of caring and the role of carers in different context. Yet it raises more question that it answers. The concept of "primary carer" is recurrent but remains undefined.[74] Who is the primary carer? Is it *de facto* a parent? Although this seems to be the norm, there have been occasions where the Court has been prepared to construe the concept more broadly to include other family members. This was the case in *Carpenter*,[75] where the wife of a worker was the primary carer for his children. Could the concept refer to both parents or is it limited to one? This is unclear as the Court has systematically considered the question of one carer only. For example, in *Carpenter* and *Baumbast* the fathers were not considered. In *Zambrano*, the CJEU only addressed the issue of one parent (the father), despite the fact that both parents were in need of a residence permit. It is difficult to imagine why only one parent could derive a right of residence from the need to preserve the interests of a child. In *Dereci*,[76] the Court appears to infirm this option as the husband was refused a right to reside with his spouse.

If anything, these cases highlight the need for a clearer and uniform definition of carers and individuals with caring responsibilities. The inclusion of the concept of caring responsibilities in the Treaty would make it easier for the Court to judicially develop a definition of carers and individuals with caring responsibilities in the same way as it has developed the definition of workers as an EU concept.[77] To

---

70 Case C-40/11 *Yoshikazu Iida v Stadt Ulm*. ECLI:EU:C:2012:691.
71 Ibid, para 55.
72 Case C-303/06 *Coleman* v *Attridge Law and Steve Law*. ECLI:EU:C:2008:415.
73 Case C-104/09 *Roca Álvarez v Sesa Start España ETT SA*. ECLI:EU:C:2010:561, para 24.
74 Nathan Cambien, "EU Citizenship and ECJ: Why Care about Primary Carers?" (UACES Annual Conference, Passau, September 2012) https://papers.ssrn.com/sol3/papers.cfm?abstract_id=2167890. Accessed 25 July 2019.
75 Case C-60/00 *Mary Carpenter v Secretary of State for the Home Department*. ECLI:EU:C:2002:434.
76 Case C-256/11 *Murat Dereci and Others v Bundesministerium für Inneres*. ECLI:EU:C:2011:734.
77 Alina Tryfonidou, "In Search of the Aim of the EC Free Movement of Persons Provisions: Has the Court of Justice Missed the Point?" (2009) 46 *CML Rev* 1591.

Reframing the debate 143

begin, the CJEU has made it clear that the definition of workers is a matter for EU law alone in order to avoid the possibility "for each Member State to modify the meaning of the concept of migrant worker" and "frustrate the objective of the Treaty."[78] Following on from this, the concept of workers has been defined in relation to two main elements. On the one hand, it takes into account the very essence of work as an economic activity.[79] In the case of *Jundt*,[80] for instance, the work must be remunerated and "the activity must not be provided for nothing".[81] On the other hand, the Court considered the relationship between the workers and the employer, which must be subordinate.[82] The EU has remained in charge of the development of the concept of workers and as a result it has been able to give variable nuances to the definition depending on the context and the purpose for which the term was invoked.[83]

Drawing on this, a definition of individuals with caring relationships could be framed around the essence of the caring relationship as well as the relationship between the carer and the care recipient. These two elements can be developed using the markers of the caring relationship, identified earlier in this book.[84] Thus, the essence of a caring relationship is one that involves "constant and on-going responsibilities" and is characterised by an "absence of choice" regarding looking after a dependent, be this a child or an adult. This would have been the case in much of the case law examined above. For example, in *Baumbast* the applicant was entitled to remain because she had responsibilities towards school-aged children and did not have a choice as whether to care for them or not. Ms Coleman was in a similar situation: the child had on-going needs that required prompt intervention and might have died, had she not cared for him. When the Court held in *Roca Álvarez* that "mothers and fathers are in the same position with regard to their possible need ... to look after the child",[85] it referred to more than just material

---

78 Case 75/63 *Mrs M.K.H. Hoekstra (née Unger) v Bestuur der Bedrijfsvereniging voor Detailhandel en Ambachten (Administration of the Industrial Board for Retail Trades and Businesses)*. ECLI:EU:C:1964:19, paras 28–29.
79 Case 53/81 *D.M. Levin v Staatssecretaris van Justitie*. ECLI:EU:C:1982:105.
80 Case C-281/06 *Hans-Dieter Jundt and Hedwig Jundt v Finanzamt Offenburg*. ECLI:EU:C:2007:816, para. 32.
81 Ibid, para. 33. See in contrast the situation where economic activity was not found: Case 344/87 *I. Bettray v Staatssecretaris van Justitie*. ECLI:EU:C:1989:226.
82 Case C-268/99 *Aldona Malgorzata Jany and Others v Staatssecretaris van Justitie*. ECLI:EU:C:2001:616, para. 34.
83 Case C-256/01 *Debra Allonby v Accrington & Rossendale College, Education Lecturing Services, trading as Protocol Professional and Secretary of State for Education and Employment*. ECLI:EU:C:2004:18, para. 63; Case C-138/02 *Brian Francis Collins v Secretary of State for Work and Pensions*. ECLI:EU:C:2004:172.
84 See the discussion in 'Setting the Scene: "Everyone Cares. Everyone is Cared For"'.
85 Case C-104/09 *Roca Álvarez v Sesa Start España ETT SA*. ECLI:EU:C:2010:561, para 24; see also Case C-222/14 *Maistrellis*. ECLI:EU:C:2015:473.

circumstances. "Constant and on-going responsibilities" is a broader concept than the "material dependency" identified in *Dereci*. Therefore, had the Court used it, the outcome in *Dereci* might have been different.

To take this emerging concept further, the role of the ethic of care must become more prominent. Concepts such as compassion, dignity and well-being must be consistently applied and inform the definition of carer and individuals with caring responsibilities.

It is not uncommon that, due to their very essence, caring responsibilities interfere with the ability to fully function as an individual and as a worker. For example, Ms Coleman eventually had to leave her job, because of the stress and the pressure she was under as she was caring for her disabled child while at the same time working for an unsupportive employer. This is likely to result in "financial, physical and emotional costs."

The relationship between the carer and the one who is cared for is also important to determine who is an individual with caring responsibilities. This relationship is often defined as "a labour of love" where there is an "emotionally sensitive personal connection" between the carer and the care-recipient. This link appeared clearly in all the cases discussed above. Although the CJEU has been prepared to accept that this connection does not need to be based on blood, as demonstrated in *Baumbast* and *Carpenter*, this has not been done systematically. The Court should clarify categorically that once there is an "emotionally sensitive personal connection", there is likely to be a caring relationship. While these markers will need to be refined, we argue that they will help to provide some pointers to understand the complexities of being an individual with caring responsibilities.

The material scope: rights for carers

The idea that carers need specific rights is not new.[86] The EU provides limited employment-related rights, such as the right to request flexible working arrangements or the right to take periods of leave. These rights are available to *some* carers only, mostly parents.[87] Whilst valuable, these are not enough to offer *all* carers, be they parents or not, much needed assistance in managing the demands of juggling work and care.

O'Brien has suggested extending the model of "reasonable adjustments" currently provided to allow disabled people to participate in employment, and more

---

86 Most noticeably, see Charlotte O'Brien, "Confronting the Care Penalty: The Cause for Extending Reasonable Adjustment Rights along the Disability/Care Continuum" (2012) 34(1) *Journal of Social Welfare and Family Law* 5; Rachel Horton, "Care Giving and Reasonable Adjustment in the UK" in Nicole Busby and Grace James (eds), *Families Care Giving and Paid Work: Challenging Labour Law in the 21st Century* (Edward Elgar 2011).
87 See the discussion in Chapter 4.

Reframing the debate 145

generally society, to address the shortcomings experienced by carers.[88] This model requires that employers:

> shall take appropriate measures, where needed in a particular case, to enable a person with a disability to have access to, participate in, or advance in employment, or to undergo training, unless such measures would impose a disproportionate burden on the employer.[89]

Whilst there are benefits to supporting this approach, as it can certainly remedy specific shortcomings, this book maintains that it would be conceptually inappropriate to extend it to carers for two main reasons. First, it arguably makes an inappropriate link between being a carer and disability. Carers might be in a position of vulnerability,[90] but this does not mean they are either ill or disabled. Although ill and disabled people can and do provide care to others, the caring relationship is not characterised by disability but by the barriers resulting from providing care. For example, the CJEU has made clear that "pregnancy is not an illness"[91] and that it would thus be paradoxical to equate the very consequence of pregnancy, namely childcare, to illness and disability. Second, the reasonable adjustments connected with disability are constructed in a reactive and individualistic way. This means that the employer is required to make specific adjustments for the individual situation of a particular employee because what might be reasonable for one disabled employee is not necessarily reasonable for another. By contrast, care, far from being an individual problem, is widespread and any approach to deal with it should be proactive rather than reactive. In addition, reasonable adjustments, as opposed to the prohibition of indirect discrimination, do not apply across the board as they only apply to the individual case for which it has been decided that the adjustment is necessary.[92] Thus, reasonable adjustments are not adaptable instruments to create a general framework applicable to all carers. The concept of discrimination, direct and indirect together with the adoption of substantive rights offer a better alternative for carers.

---

88 Charlotte O'Brien, "Confronting the Care Penalty: The Cause for Extending Reasonable Adjustment Rights along the Disability/Care Continuum" (2012) 34(1) *Journal of Social Welfare and Family Law* 5.
89 Article 5 Council Directive 2000/78/EC of 27 November 2000 establishing a general framework for equal treatment in employment and occupation.
90 See the discussion in Chapter 1.
91 See in particular, Case 177/88 *Elisabeth Johanna Pacifica Dekker v Stichting Vormingscentrum voor Jong Volwassenen (VJV-Centrum) Plus.* ECLI:EU:C:1990:383; Case 179/88 *Handels- og Kontorfunktionaerernes Forbund i Danmark v Dansk Arbejdsgiverforening (Hertz).* ECLI:EU:C:1990:384.
92 Lisa Waddington and Aart Hendriks, "Expanding Concept of Employment Discrimination in Europe: From Direct and Indirect Discrimination to Reasonable Accommodation Discrimination" (2002) 18(4) *The International Journal of Comparative Labour Law & Industrial Relations* 403.

Simply put, carers, regardless of whether they care for young healthy children or frail adults, need a range of provisions to support them to combine paid work with their care responsibilities. These rights must be designed on a life cycle approach, contain a mixture of positive (proactive) and negative (reactive) obligations and reflect the fact that carers of adults and carers of children require specifically tailored measures.[93] Using the Work-Life Balance Directive as a starting point, the next sections explore how these rights could be constructed.

A comprehensive set of leave provisions

Individuals with caring responsibilities need to be able to take periods of leave from paid work in order to care for their dependents – be these children or dependent adults – without worrying about any consequences affecting their paid job. These periods of leave should include a combination of long-term, short-term and emergency leave.

The analysis carried out in Chapter 4 has revealed that, at present, the EU mainly caters for parents' needs. However, even the rights available to parents are far from perfect. They remain underpinned by the assumption that those who are caring for young children are either the parents or adoptive parents.[94] In doing so, they ignore the reality of today's society where grandparents, step-parents and/or friends might be heavily involved in looking after children. Moreover, the law fails to consider the diversity of families forms and the implications of new reproductive technology. This means that some carers such as surrogate parents are excluded from accessing such rights.[95] Finally, although aiming to serve both parents, these rights are disproportionality taken by women, who in turn, are singled out by employers as "at risk" of taking time off for care-related responsibilities.[96] Specific legislative measures aiming at a better repartition of unpaid care leave between carers and a focus on involving men will be instrumental in challenging traditional gender stereotypes and improve gender equality so that

---

93 Rachel Horton, "Caring for Adults in the EU: Work-Life Balance and Challenge for EU law" (2015) 37 *Journal of Social Welfare and Family Law* 356.
94 Directive 92/85/EEC (Pregnant Workers Directive), Council Directive 2010/18/EU (Parental Leave Directive); see the discussion in Chapters 2 and 4.
95 Eugenia Caracciolo di Torella and Petra Foubert, "Surrogacy, Pregnancy and Maternity Rights: a Missed Opportunity for a More Coherent Regime of Parental Rights in the EU?" (2015) 40 *ELR* 52.
96 Annick Masselot, Eugenia Caracciolo di Torella and Susanne Burri, "Thematic Report of the European Network of Legal Experts in the Field of Gender Equality 'Fighting Discrimination on the Grounds of Pregnancy, Maternity and Parenthood – The application of EU and national law in practice in 33 European countries'" (European Commission 2012) and Annick Masselot, "Family Leave: Enforcement of the Protection against Dismissal and Unfavourable Treatment" (Publication of the European Union 2018).

workers who have care responsibilities are able to make choices regarding work and family reconciliation.[97]

Whilst parents' right to access leave under EU law – although with the limitations highlighted above – is relatively developed, the rights available to other carers remain seriously underdeveloped. These carers can benefit from the right to take time off from work on grounds of *force majeure* for urgent family reasons.[98] However, such a right is unpaid and usually reserved for a very short and impromptu occasion, sometimes only covering a few hours. Needless to say, this right offers only a safety-net and is unsuitable to cater for the needs of long-term care (LTC).

The Work-Life Balance Directive has sought to build upon the current system by introducing a specific carers' leave that requires Member States to grant workers up to five working days per year specifically for reasons related to their caring responsibilities. In reality, this provision, despite being potentially very important, falls short of providing a real solution for individuals with caring responsibilities.

In order to ensure that the Work-Life Balance Directive offers an opportunity to develop a discourse around caring responsibilities and provides a strong commitment, not only to protecting carers but also to addressing the challenges that demographic changes and an ageing population bring, some changes are necessary. This necessity is indeed acknowledged by Recital 27 of the Preamble that predicts that an ageing population will lead to a "continued rise in care".

First, all carers need a clear commitment that they will be able to access a range of long as well as short-term period of leave capable to cater for different situations. The existing reconciliation measures represent a starting point, which could be built upon to provide a blue print for more realistic carers' rights.[99] One way to achieve this could be, for example, to give more prominence to Article 6(2) that contemplates the *possibility* for Member States to "allocate carers' leave on the basis of a reference period other than a year, per person in need of care or support, or per case". Second, in order to be effective, periods of leave should be

---

97 Jane Lewis and Mary Campbell, "UK Work/Family Balance Policies and Gender Equality, 1997–2005" (2007) 14 *Social Politics: Intl Studies in Gender, State & Society* 4; Ann Orloff, "Should Feminists aim for Gender Symmetry? Why the Dual-earner/Dual Care Model May not be Every Feminist's Utopia" in Janet Gornick and Marcia Meyers (eds), *Institutions for Gender Egalitarianism: Creating the Conditions for Egalitarian Dual Earner/Dual Caregiver Families* (Verso 2009).

98 Clause 7 of the Parental Leave Directive.

99 In this vein, in the UK the Disability Rights Commission had argued that that the existing provisions, adequately strengthen, could offer a better answers to the situation of carers and parents. Disability Rights Commission (2006) Initial Submission to the Discrimination Law Review. See also the work of Rachel Horton in particular, "Care Giving and Reasonable Adjustment in the UK" in Nicole Busby and Grace James (eds), *Families Care Giving and Paid Work: Challenging Labour Law in the 21st Century* (Edward Elgar 2011) and "Caring for Adults in the EU: Work-Life Balance and Challenge for EU Law" (2015) 37 *Journal of Social Welfare and Family Law* 356.

complemented with financial support, otherwise individuals are left to shoulder the financial burden of care. At the moment, parents are the only carers guaranteed to receive some sort of compensation during periods of leave. The lack of financial compensation for carers' leave will not only affect carers by increasing their vulnerability, it will also negatively influence men's take up of carers' leave.[100] In turn, this will entrench stereotypes around traditional caring roles. Recital 32 of the Preamble of the Work-Life Balance Directive acknowledges this issue and specifically encourages Member States to introduce a payment or an allowance "to guarantee the effective take-up of the right by carers, in particular by men". However, it would be advisable not to leave it to the Member State but to introduce a minimum level of compensation which could be equivalent to the sick pay rate, as is the case for pregnancy, paternity and parental leave.

Flexible working arrangements

In addition to a set of comprehensive paid leave provisions, individuals with caring responsibilities need to be able to introduce flexibility in their working arrangements. Flexibility is not a new concept. Indeed, it has been one of the EU employment law's buzzwords for some time. Time provisions allowing flexibility have not specifically been designed with carers in mind, but Chapter 4 has shown that carers have used them extensively.[101] This is because, flexibility can offer much needed support to workers with caring responsibilities: without such support they are likely to either drop out or to opt for long periods of leave, which are not necessarily beneficial for the individuals. For example, research suggests that workers who return from maternity leave or parental leave face increased levels of discrimination and high rates of dismissal. Long leave periods also increase the risk of disconnection from the labour market and the difficulty of returning to paid employment.[102] Ultimately, they contribute to reinforcing traditional gender roles and increase the risk of poverty in old age.[103]

---

100 Annick Masselot, Eugenia Caracciolo di Torella and Susanne Burri, "Thematic Report of the European Network of Legal Experts in the Field of Gender Equality" Fighting Discrimination on the Grounds of Pregnancy, Maternity and Parenthood – The application of EU and national law in practice in 33 European countries' (European Commission 2012); Rebecca Ray, Janet Gornick and John Schmitt, "Who Cares? Assessing Generosity and Gender Equality in parental Leave Policy Designs in 21 Countries" (2010) 20 *Journal of European Social Policy* 196.
101 Jane Lewis, "Flexible working arrangements: Implementation, outcomes, and management" (2003) 18 *Intl Rev Industrial and Organizational Psychology* 1.
102 Peter Moss and Freddy Deven (eds), *Parental Leave: Progress Or Pitfall?: Research and Policy Issues in Europe*, vol 35 (NIDI/CBGS Publications 1999).
103 Kimberly Morgan and Kathrin Zippel, "Paid to Care: The Origins and Effects of Care Leave Policies in Western Europe" (2003) 10 *Social Politics: Intl Studies in Gender, State & Society* 49; Judith Galtry and Paul Callister, "Assessing the Optimal Length of Parental Leave for Child and Parental Well-Being: How Can Research Inform Policy?" (2005) 26 *J Family Issues* 219.

Chapter 4 has discussed the main instruments that ensure flexibility, namely the atypical work Directives and how carers use them. The Parental Leave Directive acknowledges that flexibility can be useful in addressing caring responsibilities. It grants workers returning from maternity leave the right to request a modification of their employment relationships, for example to change their working hours from full- to part-time.[104] It should be noted that this is a right to request rather than a right to obtain flexibility. Further it implies that, if granted, the desired changes to the contract of employment become permanent. This means that if the worker wants to return to the previous working arrangement, they will need to make another request for a flexible working arrangement, which could be denied. Thus, paradoxically, this makes the right to request flexible working arrangements rather inflexible. In other words, it is designed to suit the needs of business rather than the needs of workers.[105] In addition, the right to flexible working arrangements is far from gender-neutral. Research shows that whilst women are more likely to choose flexible working arrangements to decrease their working hours in order to meet their care responsibilities, men are more likely to choose to work flexibly to increase their working hours through digital and remote access to work.[106] In turn, employers are more likely to offer flexible forms of reduced hours to female workers while proposing increased and remote work access to men, thus perpetuating traditional gender stereotypes and limiting men's availability for care-work. Thus, at the moment, the right to flexible working arrangements presents serious drawbacks.

By expressly linking flexibility to caring responsibilities, the Work-Life Balance Directive explicitly seeks to address these drawbacks. Article 9 requires Member States to "take the necessary measures to ensure that workers with children up to a specified age, which shall be at least eight years, and carers, have the right to request flexible working arrangements for caring purposes." Importantly, the right to flexible working arrangements can be exercised on a temporary basis.[107] In such cases, "the worker shall have the right to return to the original working pattern at the end of the agreed period"[108] or can make a request for an early return to the original condition of employment. However, if the request is made for permanent changes, once obtained, the contract of employment is modified and the right cannot be easily reversed or modified and this denies the very nature of care and its demands. It follows that the Work-Life Balance Directive has not substantially

---

104 Clause 6(1) Parental Leave Directive 2010/18/EU implementing the revised Framework Agreement on parental leave.
105 Case C-221/13 *Mascellani* v *Ministero della Giustizia*. EU:C:2014:2286.
106 Dirk Hofäcker and Stephanie König, "Flexibility and Work-Life Conflict in Time of Crisis: A Gender Perspective" (2013) 33(9) *Intl Journal of Sociology and Social Policy* 613; Annick Masselot, "Gender Implications of the Right to Request Flexible Working Arrangements: Raising Pigs and Children in New Zealand" (2015) 39(3) *New Zealand Journal of Employment Relations* 59.
107 Article 8(1) Directive (EU) 2019/1158 on Work-Life Balance.
108 Article 8(3) Directive (EU) 2019/1158 on Work-Life Balance.

changed the existing problematic situation. It remains a right to request rather than a right to obtain and it does not guarantee an unconditional right to revert the changes. In sum, the gender implications of the right to request flexible working persist.

In order to develop the concept of flexibility in a way that is useful to carers, we maintain that it should be underpinned by EU fundamental values and principles, particularly the principle of gender equality. In other words, flexibility should be read in light of the ethic of care. In this way, flexible working arrangements will be designed with a view to encouraging all workers, regardless of their gender, to better share unpaid care responsibilities. For example, adequately valued part-time work could contribute to a better gender share of this type of flexibility. Equally, employers who reduce access to digital remote work during night time and weekends contribute to a better work-life balance for all. The right to flexible working arrangements should moreover be redesigned with the specific needs of caregivers in mind, rather than prioritising the benefits for the economy and businesses. This means that flexible working arrangements should include considerations of the range and the evolving nature of the caring needs as well as the level of dependency involved in the caring relationship. Only in this way will flexibility work for all carers. In this context, the Work-Life Balance Directive represents a first step in the right direction.

Other initiatives

Finally, it must be noted that to strengthen the normative framework alone, namely to ensure the rights to leave and to flexible working arrangements, although important, is not enough to improve the position of carers. Evidence in other related areas has consistently demonstrated that even when legislation exists, individuals continue to be treated unfavourably and to be discriminated against.[109]

Deeply ingrained sociocultural behaviours represent strong factors that sometimes can be unreceptive to the letter of the law, especially when the process is imposed top-down.[110] Changing citizens' outlook on the perception of care-work and on gender roles requires more than the adoption of legislation. A cultural shift needs to take place in order for the normative framework to be effective. In other words, there must be a change in how carers and caring responsibilities are perceived in society. For this to happen, legislation must be accompanied by non-binding initiatives and adequate resources. The Communication from the

---

109 Annick Masselot, "Family Leave: Enforcement of the Protection against Dismissal and Unfavourable Treatment" (European Union 2018).
110 Annick Masselot, Eugenia Caracciolo di Torella and Susanne Burri, "Thematic Report of the European Network of Legal Experts in the Field of Gender Equality 'Fighting Discrimination on the Grounds of Pregnancy, Maternity and Parenthood – The application of EU and national law in practice in 33 European countries'" (European Commission 2012); Annick Masselot, "Family Leave: Enforcement of the Protection against Dismissal and Unfavourable Treatment" (European Union 2018).

Reframing the debate 151

Commission on the New Start Initiative[111] puts forward several such wide-ranging initiatives. Drawing on these, we suggest the following.

Following the implementation of the Work-Life Balance Directive and any other rights adopted in the future, it will be crucial to collect data relating to such rights' uptake in order to gain a clear understanding of the demographic of carers and the usage of leave and time provisions in relation to caring responsibilities. In other words: who is using the right to take periods of leave in order to look after dependents? What are the modalities of leave that are being requested? Who is changing their working hours to fulfil their caring responsibilities? What kind of flexibility is being offered and is being taken? Under which conditions are these working arrangements being used? Intersectional gender desegregated data must be collected on a longitudinal perspective in order to detect trends and evolutions. Should the picture continue to be gendered, measures should be adopted to tackle the issue and to improve equality.

Monitoring rights' uptake should go hand in hand with raising awareness. A range of initiatives have already been taken by the European Commission and by stakeholders at national level. Resources should be made available for civil societies to support a bottom-up, inclusive and culturally sensitive changes to the perception of traditional gender roles and care. The EU should support and encourage the diffusion of information, the organisation of seminars within the framework of EU policy initiatives and the collection and dissemination of good practices across Member States and stakeholders. At the same time, support, in the form of legal aid, should be made available to those who need legal advice and those who want or need to bring a legal claim. A number of services are already available in the Member States, although not always adequately resourced.[112] A number of national institutions such as the national equality bodies, the trade unions and the labour inspectorates are already active on the ground and could be brought into the implementation of such wide-ranging initiatives. Education in relation to gender equality remains an absolute necessity for all stakeholders, including the judiciary.

Conclusion

This chapter has illustrated that, despite the fact that carers are widely acknowledged and celebrated, *de facto* they continue to be disadvantaged in the workplace. In sum, legislation aimed at supporting carers is long overdue. In turn, such improvement will also benefit those who are cared for, the economy (as more individuals will be able to work), and more generally, society (as it will increase the visibility of the caring relationship). This chapter has argued that the EU must play a leading role in this context. For this purpose, it has suggested the development

---

111 Communication from the European Commission, An initiative to support work-life balance for working parents and carers, COM(2017) 252 final.
112 Annick Masselot, "Family Leave: Enforcement of the Protection against Dismissal and Unfavourable Treatment" (European Union 2018).

of a normative strategy. This can be achieved by amending the existing Article 19 TFEU to unequivocally acknowledge the vital importance of carers and protect their rights. Using this as a legal base, the EU legislator could advance a thorough understanding of the meaning of individuals with caring responsibilities as well as to develop a specific and comprehensive set of rights in accordance with the ethical values enshrined in the Treaty. We also argue that effective protection of carers requires not only substantial rights but also a range of non-legislative interventions.

Finally, challenges are to be expected, in particular in relation to costs. The question of cost is constantly asked, especially since the 2008 financial crisis. Although it is not within the scope of this book, the creation of a set of rights for individuals with caring responsibilities would necessarily involve a level of expenditure from the Member States. Are such measures financially feasible at a time when markets around the worlds are not particularly stable? This was indeed one of the main arguments that hampered the success of the Work-Life Balance Package in 2008. More than a decade later, the same concerns have led to the drop in the requirement to compensation for the carers' leave in the Work-Life Balance Directive.[113]

Yet, even if markets are experiencing instability, we maintain that this is not an argument to decrease the protection of human rights. Caring for the frailer members of society *is* an expression of human rights. If we are serious about the value and the benefit of the caring relationship for society, Member States should take responsibility for the costs associated with leave and flexible working arrangements.

Moreover, the cost of care, invisible to traditional accounting, is borne in the main by women, who perform it for free but at a personal cost.[114] This falls short of the Treaty's commitment to promote "its values and the well-being of its peoples."[115] Accordingly, the existing economic model fails to incorporate the values of the Treaty, particularly that of gender equality,[116] which is considered to be too pricey.[117] By contrast, fulfilling the EU Treaty promises requires a shift to an economic model which is guided by the values of the Treaty.

---

113 Article 8 Proposal for a Directive of the European Parliament and of the Council on work-life balance for parents and carers and repealing Council Directive 2010/18/EU, 26 April 2017, COM(2017) 253 final.
114 See Chapter 1.
115 Article 3(1) TEU.
116 Annick Masselot, "Visions for gender equality post-2020: How to improve the interaction between legal instruments (EU acquis) and policy-making (communication, funding programme, European semester)?" in Niall Crowley and Silvia Sansonetti (eds), *New Visions for Gender Equality 2019* (SAAGE – Scientific Analysis and Advice on Gender Equality in EU 2019).
117 Sophia Koukoulis-Spiliotopoulos, "Les institutions the l'Union ne peuvent échapper a la Charte, mais elles sont exonérées de leur responsabilité par des mécanismes externes – *Quid* alors de l'autonomie du droit de l'Union ?" in Etienne Pataut, Frank Petti, Sophie Robin-Olivier and Alain Supiot (eds), *Droit Social International et Européen en Mouvement – Liber Amicorum en hommage à Pierre Rodière* (LGDJ 2019).

Final remarks

It is impossible to emphasise enough the importance of caring. It is an essential part of life, crucial for both individuals and society and it is "central to our flourishing".[1] A life without care is a "shallow one (and) indeed it would be an impossible one".[2] As such, care should be expressly acknowledged, valued and regulated by legal orders to ensure not only that that the most vulnerable in society are cared for, but also that those who provide care are supported, have the possibility to make genuine choices and are not penalised for prioritising care.

Yet historically, care and carers have been ignored and undervalued by the law in general, and EU law is no exception. As Herring has remarked,[3] law schools are very good at teaching students about the well-dressed businessman entering a contract and expressing his autonomy, but they often forget the exhausted mother who has very little autonomy or freedom. Caring has a widespread impact on many areas of individuals' life, society and legislation that can no longer be ignored. Today, for a variety of reasons, ranging from an ageing society, to a decrease in fertility rates and the increased presence of women in the workplace, caring has become a pressing challenge for governments across Europe. In other words, we are experiencing a "care-crisis".[4] So far little has been done to address this crisis and, in the main, issues related to care remain undervalued in our society and ignored by the legislator.

Against this backdrop, we have argued that the EU must lead the way and play a pivotal role by setting principles and standards to help shape relevant legislation in this area. This book has identified three reasons for a stronger EU engagement.[5]

First, care creates challenges that cannot be addressed solely at national level. In the EU, the free movement provisions have highlighted the global dimension of care: for example, individuals routinely cross borders to provide care or to be

---

1 Eva Feder Kittay, *Love's Labor: Essays on Women, Equality and Dependency* (Routledge 1999) 11.
2 Jonathan Herring, *Caring and the Law* (Hart Publishing 2013) 11.
3 Ibid, 1.
4 See the discussion in "Setting the Scene: 'Everyone Cares. Everyone is Cared For'".
5 Ibid.

cared for. If Member States are allowed to take different approaches to tackle issues related to care, the situation might arise where carers have access to different levels of protection according to where they live. In turn, different approaches impact on standards of social justice. The EU must intervene to ensure a common position to tackle poverty, social exclusion and gender inequality across Europe.

Second, there is a clear business case for the EU to intervene in this area: care is instrumental to the success of many important EU policies, in particular full employment and gender equality. Simply put, if individuals are not supported in meeting their caring responsibilities, they will be less likely to participate in paid employment and will not be able to contribute to the economy.

Third, and perhaps most importantly, there is a pressing moral reason to acknowledge and promote care, caring relationships and the contribution of carers. Indeed, the very value of care goes well beyond its economic currency: it is essential to society. Accordingly, we have argued that it is the very value of caring that should lead the political and legislative response to this care-crisis.

In this book, we have explored how, over the years, the EU has incorporated the caring relationship into its policy and legislation. It has been a long and complex journey. Having traditionally had very few competences, the EU necessarily has had a constrained role. The recognition of the necessity of care, however, was recently acknowledged in the European Pillar of Social Rights (EPSR)[6] and has led to the adoption of the long-awaited Work-Life Balance Directive.[7] This journey has contributed to a better understanding of the challenges in this area and, ultimately, has led to proposals for a way forward.

Identifying the challenges

On the journey towards a recognition of care, the EU has encountered challenges that stem from an existing set of tensions which underpin any attempt to regulate the caring relationship.

To start with, there is a clear tension between types of caring relationships, namely childcare and Long-Term Care (LTC). These have traditionally been perceived, and thus regulated, differently. On the one hand, childcare has been seen as an investment for the future and therefore carries a clear economic value. On the other hand, LTC has been framed as a social issue, which thus depends upon on the availability of resources.

Further, there is a clear tension between the regulation of care and that of carers. Care is intended as the organisation and financing of the infrastructures that allow individuals to care and to be cared for. Generally speaking, the EU

---

6 Interinstitutional Proclamation on the European Pillar of Social Rights, O.J. [2017] C428/10 https://eur-lex.europa.eu/legal-content/EN/TXT/PDF/?uri=CELEX:32017C1213(01)&from=EN. Accessed 25 July 2019.
7 Directive (EU) 2019/1158 of the European Parliament and of the Council of 20 June 2019 on work-life balance for parents and carers and repealing Council Directive 2010/18/EU.

Final remarks 155

approach to care has been minimalistic and a relatively low priority. EU intervention has been predictably scarce, with only a few guiding principles and no binding legislation. To an extent, this is understandable because of the Member States' historical and cultural differences,[8] which we should respect. For example, would it be appropriate for the EU to decide how an elderly person should be looked after? Or does the EU have a business in deciding that a young child should be looked after in a nursery rather than at home even if the family is willing and able to care? The organisation of care is also constrained by Member States' variable access to financial resources. These reasons, coupled with the lack of EU express competence in this area, explain why the regulation of care of both children and frailer adults at EU level might be difficult, although arguably not impossible, but, more importantly, undesirable. In turn, they also explain why, over the years, the EU has made use of soft law, ranging from the Open Method of Coordination (OMC) to the European Semester, as a primary form of governance to intervene in the area of care. These forms of governance have encouraged, rather than prescribed, Member States to develop policies, as well as services and structures concerning care. In other words, the EU's essential role, in relation to care, has been to provide a forum for sharing information and good practices. We have argued that, in relation to supporting the caring relationship, this is the most suitable approach and that the EU should strengthen this model: it should act as a facilitator which provides policy support and promotes cooperation between Member States. At the same time, the EU should also ensure that Member States act in accordance with the values embedded in the EU Treaty, the Charter of Fundamental Rights (CFR), the EPSR as well as the EU general principles, in particular, gender equality, human dignity and solidarity.

Aside from the impact on care, the lack of regulation in this area has considerable socio-economic and legal consequences for carers.[9] Throughout this book, we have mainly discussed the situation of those carers who are engaged in the employment market; this is not to say that other carers do not deserve protection or are not in a vulnerable position. The EU has been able to intervene in relation to carers not only at policy level but also by using existing legislation and by developing an emerging set of measures, namely the reconciliation provisions which culminated with the 2019 Work-Life Balance Directive. However, these measures have pitfalls and carers continue to be disadvantaged

---

8 See for example, Spasova Slavinia and others, "Challenges in Long-Term Care in Europe: A Study of National Policies" (European Commission 2018).
9 Furthermore we argue in favour of women's emancipation through work and this aligns with the EU's policy, which is supporting women to access the labour market. Indeed, it is accepted that "[t]rue interdependence between individual men and women will not be possible so long as the economic power relationships underpinning their interdependence are so unequal"; see further Brid Featherstone, "Gender, Rights, Responsibilities and Social Policy" in Julie Wallbank, Shazia Choudhry and Jonathan Herring (eds), *Rights, Gender and Family Law* (Routledge 2010) 26 citing Ruth Lister, *Citizenship: Feminist Perspectives* (NYU Press 2003).

and discriminated against. Furthermore, carers are disproportionately women. This means that female access to the labour market, the mitigation of work-family conflicts and the realisation of gender equality objectives as a whole, are variable across the Member States depending on the availability of care services and the level of rights afforded to carers.

The future of care in the EU: towards a holistic approach?

This book has made a case for a stronger EU involvement in relation to carers' rights through policy initiatives and the development of specific legislation. In turn, the improvement of the situations of carers will also benefit those who are cared for. Yet how can the EU succeed where so many Member States are struggling to grapple with the challenges posed by the caring relationship? In this book we have put forward several initiatives that can be summed up as a "holistic approach to care".

A holistic approach means that all the different elements of the debate must be considered and must be connected. To address only some aspects of the caring relationship, with *ad hoc* interventions, is only likely to produce cosmetic results. In practice, a holistic approach involves rethinking care policies on three levels.

First, a holistic approach considers the ultimate aim of policies and legislation to not only allow individuals to work, but to also develop a legal system that acknowledges, promotes and protects the caring relationship in general and carers in particular. In other words, the aim is to make the law more "human" and to identify alternative "way[s] of 'doing' law and justice",[10] because ultimately the law should "exist for people [and] for the sake of people".[11] In order to do this, policies and legislation should be underpinned by the EU fundamental values and by the ethic of care that, as we have argued, is already embedded in EU law.

In this context, we maintain that the EU has an obligation to set up policies that challenge the gender division of paid and unpaid work and which ultimately improve gender equality. Caring responsibilities still contribute to large gender inequalities in terms of distribution of time: men prioritise paid work whilst care, mostly done by women, is not properly valued and accounted for under traditional accounting systems. This situation hinders the measurement of care-work in monetary terms and, specifically, the possibility of taking care-work into account in designing comprehensive social protection policies and contributes to gender inequality.

Second, a holistic approach must consider all types of care. Although caring for young children might be seen as a worthwhile investment, the ultimate aim is to

---

10 Nuno Ferreira, "The Human Face of the European Union: Are EU Law and Policy Humane Enough? An Introduction" in Nuno Ferreira and Dora Kostakopoulou (eds), *The Human Face of the European Union: Are EU Law and Policy Humane Enough?* (CUP 2016).
11 Ibid.

value the caring relationship, because human beings remain dependent on each other. Caring for older and frailer people is *per se* valuable and worthwhile for humanity. If all types of caring relationships are acknowledged and valued, in turn this means all carers will benefit.

Third, a holistic approach cannot exclusively be achieved through traditional legislative instruments. We have acknowledged that these are important because they confer rights and empower individuals. However, they have limits because traditionally the law focuses on justice, rights, autonomy and choice, rather than responsibilities and relationships. We have argued that to address these limits, rights should be read through the lens of the ethic of care. Taken together, the Treaty provisions, the doctrine of the general principle EU law and the powerful international and human rights mechanisms such as the core ILO conventions and the European Convention of Human Rights (ECHR), constitute a solid basis to argue that the ethic of care is already present within the EU legal architecture. However, an effective care strategy cannot be solely achieved by extending the parameters of the EU competences, but also through implementing a range of non-legislative mechanisms.[12]

It follows that the EU now has the tools to push forward an agenda to design a comprehensive normative and policy framework in the area of care, rather than merely constructing it as a by-product of the internal market – as has been the case until now. Thus, the task is to use these existing instruments to reshape the care discourse. In doing this, it is imperative that the EU's core values and principles are embedded in supporting the relevant legislation, policy and processes. Care and the rights of carers have finally found a place on the EU agenda, in particular with the adoption of the Work-Life Balance Directive. It is now important not to lose momentum: the EU must take the lead in this area because neither caring responsibilities nor the disadvantages created by ignoring and undervaluing care will go away. Furthermore, the Member States cannot continue to avoid regulating the caring relationship and carers by simply claiming that it is too complex or too expensive. The EU cannot afford – either financially or morally – a society that neglects its most vulnerable individuals, and where those who care for them are discriminated against and marginalised.

---

12 See Communication from the European Commission to support work-life balance for working parents and carers, COM(2017) 252 final and the discussion in Chapter 5.

Table of legislation

European Union

Directives

Council Directive 75/117/EEC of 10 February 1975 on the approximation of the laws of the Member States relating to the application of the principle of equal pay for men and women, O.J. [1975] L45/19

Council Directive 76/207/EEC of 9 February 1976 on the implementation of the principle of equal treatment for men and women as regards access to employment, vocational training and promotion, and working conditions, O.J. [1976] L39/40 as amended by Directive 2002/73/EC (Directive 2002/73/EC of the European Parliament and of the Council of 23 September 2002 amending Council Directive 76/207/EEC on the implementation of the principle of equal treatment for men and women as regards access to employment, vocational training and promotion, and working conditions, O.J. [2002] L269/15)

Directive 86/613/EEC of 11 December 1986 on the application of the principle of equal treatment between men and women engaged in an activity, including agriculture, in a self employed capacity, and on the protection of self-employed women during pregnancy and motherhood, O.J. [1986] L359/56

Council Directive 92/85/EEC of 19 October 1992 on the introduction of measures to encourage improvements in the safety and health at work of pregnant workers and workers who have recently given birth or are breastfeeding (tenth individual Directive within the meaning of Article 16 (1) of Directive 89/391/EEC), O.J. [1992] L348/1

Council Directive 96/34/EC of 3 June 1996 on the framework agreement on parental leave concluded by UNICE, CEEP and the ETUC, O.J. [1996] L145/4

Council Directive 96/97/EC of 20 December 1996 amending Directive 86/378/EEC on the implementation of the principle of equal treatment for men and women in occupational social security schemes, O.J. [1997] L46/20

Council Directive 97/80/EC of 15 December 1997 on the burden of proof in cases of discrimination based on sex, O.J. [1998] L14/6

Council Directive 97/81/EC of 15 December 1997 concerning the Framework Agreement on part-time work concluded by UNICE, CEEP and the ETUC - Annex: Framework agreement on part-time work, O.J. [1998] L14/9

Council Directive 99/70/EC of 28 June 1999 concerning the framework agreement on fixed-term work concluded by ETUC, UNICE and CEEP, O.J. [1999] L175/43, corrigendum at O.J. [1999] L244/64

Council Directive 2000/43/EC of 29 June 2000 implementing the principle of equal treatment between persons irrespective of racial or ethnic origin, O.J. [2000] L180/22

Council Directive 2000/78/EC of 27 November 2000 establishing a general framework for equal treatment in employment and occupation, O.J. [2000] L303/16

Directive 2002/73/EC of the European Parliament and of the Council of 23 September 2002 amending Council Directive 76/207/EEC on the implementation of the principle of equal treatment for men and women as regards access to employment, vocational training and promotion, and working conditions, O.J. [2002] L269/15

Directive 2003/88/EC of the European Parliament and of the Council of 4 November 2003 concerning certain aspects of the organisation of working time, O.J. [2003] L 299/9

Directive 2006/54/EC of the European Parliament and of the Council of 5 July 2006 on the implementation of the principle of equal opportunities and equal treatment of men and women in matters of employment and occupation (recast), O.J. [2006] L204/23

Council Directive 2008/104/EC of the European Parliament and of the Council of 19 November 2008 on temporary agency work, O.J. [2008] L327/9

Council Directive 2010/18/EU of 8 March 2010 implementing the revised Framework Agreement on parental leave concluded by BUSINESSEUROPE, UEAPME, CEEP and ETUC and repealing Directive 96/34/EC (Text with EEA relevance), O.J. [2010] L68/13

Directive (EU) 2019/1152 of the European Parliament and of the Council of 20 June 2019 on transparent and predictable working conditions in the European Union, O.J. [2019] L186/105

Directive (EU) 2019/1158 of the European Parliament and of the Council of 20 June 2019 on work-life balance for parents and carers and repealing Council Directive 2010/18/EU, O.J. [2019] L188/79

Proposed legislation

Proposal for a Directive on the application of the principle of equal treatment between men and women engaged in an activity in a self-employed capacity and repealing Directive 86/613/EEC, COM(2008) 636

Proposal for a Directive amending Council Directive 92/85/EEC on the introduction of measures to encourage improvements in the safety and health at work of pregnant workers and workers who have recently given birth or are breastfeeding, COM(2008) 637

Proposal for a Directive of the European Parliament and of the Council on work-life balance for parents and carers and repealing Council Directive 2010/18/EU, 26 April 2017, COM(2017) 253 final

European Commission, Proposal for a Council Decision on guidelines for the employment policies of the Member States, COM(2017) 677 final

Regulations

Regulation (EU) No 1303/2013 of the European Parliament and of the Council of 17 December 2013 laying down common provisions on the European Regional Development Fund, the European Social Fund, the Cohesion Fund, the European Agricultural Fund for Rural Development and the European Maritime and Fisheries Fund and laying down general provisions on the European Regional Development Fund, the European Social Fund, the Cohesion Fund and the European Maritime and Fisheries Fund and repealing Council Regulation (EC), O.J. [2013] L347/320

Council recommendations

Council Recommendation 92/241/EEC of 31 March 1992 on Child Care, O.J. [1992] L123/16

Council Recommendation CM/Rec(2009)6 on ageing and disability in the 21st century: sustainable frameworks to enable greater quality of life in an inclusive society, 8 July 2009 https://rm.coe.int/CoERMPublicCommonSearchServices/DisplayDCTMContent?documentId=09000016806992fc

Council resolutions

Council Resolution of 15 December 1997 on the 1998 Employment Guidelines, O.J [1998] C30/1

Council Resolution of 22 February 1999 on the 1999 Employment Guidelines, O.J. [1999] C69/2

Council Resolution of 22 February 2007, "Opportunities and Challenges of Demographic Change in Europe" (6226/07)

International law

United Nation Convention on the Rights of the Child, General Assembly resolution 44/25 of 20 November 1989

United Nations, "Regional Implementation Strategy for the Madrid International Plan of Action on Ageing 2002" (ECE/AC.23/2002/2/Rev.6, 11 September 2002) https://www.unece.org/fileadmin/DAM/pau/RIS.pdf

United Nations Convention on the Rights of Persons with Disabilities, A/61/611 of 6 December 2006

National law

Iceland

Icelandic Act No. 95/2000

Table of case law

Court of Justice of the European Union

Case 26/62 *Van Gend en Loos* v *Nederlandse Administratie der Belastingen* ECLI:EU:C:1963:1

Case 75/63 *Mrs M.K.H. Hoekstra (née Unger)* v *Bestuur der Bedrijfsvereniging voor Detailhandel en Ambachten (Administration of the Industrial Board for Retail Trades and Businesses)* ECLI:EU:C:1964:19

Case 43/75 *Defrenne* v *Société Anonyme Belge de Navigation Aérienne Sabena (Defrenne no 2)* ECLI:EU:C:1976:56

Case 149/77 *Gabrielle Defrenne* v *Société anonyme belge de navigation aérienne Sabena.* (no. 3) ECLI:EU:C:1978:130

Case 53/81 *D.M. Levin* v *Staatssecretaris van Justitie* ECLI:EU:C:1982:105

Joined Cases 75/82 and 117/82 *Razzouk and Beydoun* v *Commission* ECLI:EU:C:1984:116

Case 184/83 *Ulrich Hofman* v *Barmer Ersatzkasse* ECLI:EU:C:1984:273

Case 170/84 *Bilka Kaufhaus GmbH* v *Heber von Hartz* ECLI:EU:C:1986:204

Case 139/85 *Kempf* v *Staatssecretaris van Justitie* ECLI:EU:C:1986:223

Case 39/86 *Lair* v *Universität Hannover* ECLI:EU:C:1988:322

Case 344/87 *I. Bettray* v *Staatssecretaris van Justitie* ECLI:EU:C:1989:226

Case 44/88 *J. E. G. Achterberg-te Riele and others* v *Sociale Verzekeringsbank* ECLI:EU:C:1989:261

Case 177/88 *Elisabeth Johanna Pacifica Dekker* v *Stichting Vormingscentrum voor Jong Volwassenen (VJV-Centrum) Plus* ECLI:EU:C:1990:383

Case 179/88 *Handels- og Kontorfunktionaerernes Forbund i Danmark* v *Dansk Arbejdsgiverforening (Hertz)* ECLI:EU:C:1990:384

Case C-31/90 *Johnson* v *Chief Adjudication Officer* ECLI:EU:C:1991:311

Case C-168/91 *Christos Konstantinidis* v *Stadt Altensteig–Standesamt and Landratsamt Calw–Ordnungsamt* ECLI:EU:C:1993:115; Opinion of the Advocate General ECLI:EU:C:1992:504

Case C-13/94 *P* v *S and Cornwall County Council* ECLI:EU:C:1996:170

Case C-77/95 *Bruna-Alessandra Züchner* v *Handelskrankenkasse (Ersatzkasse) Bremen* ECLI:EU:C:1996:425

Case C-1/95 *Hellen Gerster* v *Freistaat Bayern* ECLI:EU:C:1997:452

Case C-136/95 *Caisse nationale d'assurance vieillesse des travailleurs salariés (CNAVTS)* v *Evelyne Thibault* ECLI:EU:C:1998:178

Case C-409/95 *Hellmut Marschall* v *Land Nordrhein-Westfalen* ECLI:EU:C:1997:533

Case C-243/95 *Hill and Stapleton v The Revenue Commissioners and Department of Finance* ECLI:EU:C:1998:298
Case C- 85/96 *María Martínez Sala v Freistaat Bayern* ECLI:EU:C:1998:217
Case C-160/96 *M. Molenaar and B. Fath-Molenaar v Allgemeine Ortskrankenkasse Baden-Württember* ECLI:EU:C:1998:84; Opinion of the Advocate General ECLI:EU:C:1997:599
Case C-270/97 *Deutsche Post AG v Elisabeth Sievers* ECLI:EU:C:2000:76
Case C-207/98 *Silke-Karin Mahlburg* v *Land Mecklenburg-Vorpommern* ECLI:EU:C:2000:64
Case C-268/99 *Aldona Malgorzata Jany and Others* v *Staatssecretaris van Justitie* ECLI:EU:C:2001:616
Case C-366/99 *Joseph Griesmar* v *Ministre de l'Économie, des Finances et de l'Industrie, Ministre de la Fonction publique, de la Réforme de l'État et de la Décentralisation* ECLI:EU:C:2001:648
Case C-413/99 *Baumbast and R.* v *Secretary of State for the Home Department* ECLI:EU:C:2002:493
Case C-476/99 *Lommers* v *Minister van Landbouw, Natuurbeheer en Visserij* ECLI:EU:C:2002:183
Case C-60/00 *Mary Carpenter* v *Secretary of State for the Home Department* ECLI:EU:C:2002:434
Case C-256/01 *Debra Allonby v Accrington & Rossendale College, Education Lecturing Services, trading as Protocol Professional and Secretary of State for Education and Employment* ECLI:EU:C:2004:18
Case C-413/01 *Franca Ninni-Orasche* v *Bundesminister für Wissenschaft, Verkehr und Kunst* ECLI:EU:C:2003:600
Case C-36/02 *Omega Spielhallen-und Automatenaufstellungs-GmbH* v *Oberbürgermeisterin der Bundesstadt Bonn* ECLI:EU:C:2004:614
Case C-138/02 *Brian Francis Collins* v *Secretary of State for Work and Pensions* ECLI:EU:C:2004:172
Case C-200/02 *Kunqian Catherine Zhu, Man Lavette Chen* v *Secretary of State for the Home Department* ECLI:EU:C:2004:639
Case C-220/02 *Österreichischer Gewerkschaftsbund, Gewerkschaft der Privatangestellten* v *Wirtschaftskammer Österreich* EU:C:2004:334
Case C-13/05 *Chacòn Navas* v *Eurest Colectividades SA* ECLI:EU:C:2006:456
Case C-303/06 *Coleman* v *Attridge Law and Steve Law* ECLI:EU:C:2008:415; Opinion of the Advocate General ECLI:EU:C:2008:61
Case C-281/06 *Hans-Dieter Jundt and Hedwig Jundt* v *Finanzamt Offenburg* ECLI:EU:C:2007:816
Case C-73/08 *Bressol* v *Gouvernement de la Communauté Française* ECLI:EU:C:2010:181; Opinion of the Advocate General ECLI:EU:C:2009:396
Case C-310/08 *London Borough of Harrow* v *Nimco Hassan Ibrahim* ECLI:EU:C:2010:80
Case C-480/08 *Maria Teixeira* v *London Borough of Lambeth and Secretary of State for the Home Department* ECLI:EU:C:2009:642
Case C-14/09 *Hava Genc* v *Land Berlin* ECLI:EU:C:2010:57
Case C-34/09 *Gerardo Ruiz Zambrano* v *Office national de l'emploi (ONEm)* ECLI:EU:C:2011:124
Case C-104/09 *Roca Álvarez* v *Sesa Start España ETT SA* ECLI:EU:C:2010:561

Case C-236/09 *Association Belge des Consommateurs Test-Achats ASBL and Others v Conseil des ministres* ECLI:EU:C:2011:100 Opinion of the Advocate General ECLI:EU:C:2010:564
Case C-325/09 *Secretary of State for Work and Pensions* v *Dias* ECLI:EU:C:2011:498
Case C-434/09 *Shirley McCarthy v Secretary of State for the Home Department* ECLI:EU:C:2011:277
Case C-572/10 *Maurice Leone and Blandine Leone* v *Garde des Sceaux, ministre de la Justice and Caisse nationale de retraite des agents des collectivités locale*s ECLI:EU:C:2014:117
Case C-40/11 *Yoshikazu Iida v Stadt Ulm* ECLI:EU:C:2012:691
Joined Cases C-147/11 and C-148/11 *Secretary of State for Work and Pensions* v *Lucja Czop and Margita Punakova* ECLI:EU:C:2012:538
Case C-256/11 *Murat Dereci and Others* v *Bundesministerium für Inneres* ECLI:EU:C:2011:734
Case C-335/11 *HK Danmark, acting on behalf of Jette Ring* v *Dansk almennyttigt Boligselskab* ECLI:EU:C:2013:222; Opinion of the Advocate General ECLI:EU:C:2012:775
Case C-337/11 *HK Danmark, acting on behalf of Lone Skouboe Werge* v *Dansk Arbejdsgiverforening, acting on behalf of Pro Display A/S* ECLI:EU:C:2013:222
Case C-529/11 *Olaitan Ajoke Alarape and Olukayode Azeez Tijani* v *Secretary of State for the Home Department* ECLI:EU:C:2013:290
Case C-44/12 *Order of the President of the Court of 16 November 2012 (request for a preliminary ruling from the Court of Session in Scotland — United Kingdom) — Andrius Kulikauskas* v *Macduff Shellfish Limited, Duncan Wat*t, application: O.J. 2012 C109/6; Removal from the register: O.J. [2013] C108/18
Case C-363/12 *Z* v *A Government Department, The Board of Management of a Community School* EU:C:2014:159
Case C-507/12 *Jessy Saint Prix* v *Secretary of State for Work and Pensions* ECLI:EU:C:2014:2007
Case C-221/13 *Mascellani* v *Ministero della Giustizia* ECLI:EU:C:2014:2286
Case C-354/13 *FOA, acting on behalf of Karsten Kaltoft* v *KL, acting on behalf of the Municipality of Billund* ECLI:EU:C:2014:2463
C-83/14 *CHEZ Razpredelenie Bulgaria AD* v *Komisia za zashtita ot diskriminatsia* ECLI:EU:C:2015:480
Case C-222/14 *Konstantinos Maïstrellis* v *Ypourgos Dikaiosynis, Diafaneias kai Anthropinon Dikaiomaton* ECLI:EU:C:2015:473
Case C-12/17 *Ministerul Justiţiei and Tribunalul Botoşani v Maria Dicu* ECLI:EU:C:2018:799
Case C-483/17 *Neculai Tarola* v *Minister for Social Protection* ECLI:EU:C:2018:919

European Court of Human Rights

Petrovic v Austria, Application n° 20458/92 (27 March 1998)
Al- Nashif v Bulgaria, Application n° 50963/99 (20 June 2002)
Pretty v United Kingdom [2002] ECHR 427
RR v Poland (2011) 53 EHRR 31
Konstantin Markin v Russia, Application n° 30078/06 (22 March 2012)
Topčić-Rosenberg v. *Croatia* Application n° 19391/11 (2013)

Iceland

Supreme Court judgment No. 11/2010

New Zealand

Terranova Homes & Care Ltd v Service and Food Workers Union Ringa Tota Inc (CA631/2013) [2014] NZCA 516

United Kingdom

Turley v Allders Department Stores [1980] IRLR 4
Hayes v Malleable Working Men's Club and Institute [1985] IRLR 367
Webb v EMO Cargo (UK) Ltd [1992] CML Rev 793
Cadogan Estates Ltd v Morris [1999] L & TR 154
R (on the application of Burke) v General Medical Council [2005] England and Wales Court of Appeal (EWCA) Civ 1003
Grant v Ministry of Justice [2011] EWHC 3379 (QB)
Kulikauskas v Macduff Shellfish UKEATS/62/09 [2011] ICT 48
MacDonald v Fylde Motor Co Ltd [2011] EqLR 660
Hall v Bull [2012] England and Wales Court of Appeal (EWCA) Civ 83
Nicklinson v Ministry of Justice [2012] EWHC 304 (QB)
NS v Secretary of State for the Home Department [2012] 2 CML Rev 9
Perrot v Department for Work and Pensions [2012] EqLR 90
R (on the Application of (HA) (Nigeria)) v Secretary of State for the Home Department [2012] EWHC 979 (Admin)
Hainsworth v Ministry of Defence UKEATPA/0227/13/GE [2013]
Price v Action-Tec Services [2013] EqLR 429
Truman v Bibby Distribution Ltd ET/2404176/2014
Alder Hey Children's NHS Foundation Trust v Evans [2018] EWHC 308 (Fam)

United States of America

Massachusetts Board of Retirement v Murgia (1976) 438 US 285

Bibliography

Abel E and Nelson M, "Circles of Care: An Introductory Essay" in Abel E and Nelson M (eds), *Circles of Care: Work Identity in Women's Lives* 4–34 (Albany, NY, USA: SUNY Press 1990).

AC D and Mira d'Ercole M, *Trends and Determinants of Fertility Rates in OECD Countries: The Role of Policies* (Paris: OECD Social Employment and Migration Working Paper No. 27 2005).

Ackers L and Dwyer P, *Senior Citizenship? Retirement, Migration and Welfare in the European Union* (Bristol: Policy Press 2002).

Ackers L and Stalford H, *A Community for Children? Children, Citizenship and Internal Migration in the EU* (Aldershot, England/Burlington, USA: Ashgate 2004).

Adams L, "The Family Responsibilities Convention Reconsidered: The Work-Family Intersection in International Law Thirty Years On" (2013) 22 *Cardozo J of International and Comparative Law* 201.

Albertini M and Saraceno C, "Intergenerational Contact and Support: The Long Term Effects of Marital Instability in Italy" in Saraceno C (ed), *Families Ageing and Social Policy, Intergeneration Solidarity in European Welfare States* 194 (Cheltenham, UK/Northampton, MA, USA: Edward Elgar 2008).

Anttonen A and Sipilä J, "European Social Care Services: Is It Possible to Identify Models?" (1996) 6 *Journal of European Social Policy* 87.

Aristotle, *Ethica Nicomachea* vol. 3 1131a–1131b (Oxford: David Ross (tr), OUP 1925).

Ashiagbor D, *The European Employment Strategy: Labour Market Regulation and New Governance* (Oxford: OUP 2005).

Bacchi CL, *Women, Policy and Politics: The Construction of Policy Problems* (London, UK/Thousand Oaks, California, USA/New Delhi, India: SAGE 1999).

Bakker I, *The Strategic Silence: Gender and Economic Policy* (London: Zed Books 1994).

Balakrishnan R, Elson D and Patel R, "Rethinking Macro Economic Strategies from a Human Rights Perspective" (2010) 53 *Development* 27.

Barbera M, "The Unsolved Conflict: Reshaping Family Work and Market Work in the EU Legal Order" in Hervey T and Kenner J (eds), *Economic and Social Rights under the EU Charter of Fundamental Rights: A Legal Perspective* 139–160 (Oxford, UK/Portland, Oregon, USA: Hart Publishing 2003).

Barnard C, "The Economic Objectives of Article 119" in Hervey T and O'Keeffe D (eds), *Sex Equality in the European Union* 321–334 (Chichester, United Kingdom: Wiley 1996).

Barnard C, "Gender Equality in the EU: A Balance Sheet" in Alston P (ed), *The EU and Human Rights* 215–279 (Oxford: OUP 1999).

Bassel L and Emejulu A, *Minority Women and Austerity: Survival and Resistance in France and Britain* (Bristol: Policy Press 2017).

Bassel L and Emejulu A, "Caring Subjects: Migrant Women and the Third Sector in England and Scotland" (2018) 41 *Ethnic and Racial Studies* 36.

Becker G, "An Economic Analysis of Fertility" in Becker G (ed), *Demographic and Economic Change in Developed Countries* 209–240 (New York: Columbia University Press 1960).

Becker G, *An Economic Analysis of Fertility: The Economic Approach to Human Behavior* (Chicago: University of Chicago Press 1993).

Bell M, "Achieving the Objectives of the Part-Time Work Directive? Revisiting the Part-Time Workers Regulations" (2011) 40 *Industrial Law Journal* 254.

Bell M, "The Principle of Equal Treatment: Widening and Deepening" in Craig P and de Búrca G (eds), *The Evolution of EU Law* 611–939 (Oxford: OUP 2012).

Bell M, "The Principle of Equal Treatment and the European Pillar of Social Rights" (2018) 160 *Giornale Di Diritto Del Lavoro E Di Relazioni Industriali* 783.

Bell M, "EU Equality Law and Precarious Work" in Uladzislau Belavusau and Kristin Henrard (eds), *EU Anti-Discrimination Law Beyond Gender* 75–94 (Oxford: Hart Publishing 2019).

Benelli N and Modak M, "Analyser Un Objet Invisible: Le Travail De Care" (2010) 51 *Revue Française De Sociologie* 39.

Bengtsson T and Saito O (ed), *Population and the Economy: From Hunger to Modern Economic Growth* (Oxford: OUP 2000).

Berns S, *Women Going Backwards: Law and Change in a Family-Unfriendly Society* (Aldershot, England/Burlington, USA: Ashgate 2002).

Bertogg A and Strauss S, "Spousal Care-giving Arrangements in Europe: The Role of Gender, Socio-economic Status and the Welfare State" (2018) *Ageing & Society* 1.

Bettio F and others, *The Impact of the Economic Crisis on the Situation of Women and Men and on Gender Equality Policies* (Luxembourg: Directorate-General for Justice, European Commission 2012).

Bettio F and Plantenga J, "Comparing Care Regimes in Europe" (2004) 10 *Feminist Economics* 85.

Bettio F, Simonazzi A and Villa P, "Change in Care Regimes and Female Migration: The 'Care Drain' in the Mediterranean" (2006) 16 *Journal of European Social Policy* 271.

Bettio F and Verashchagina A, *Long Term Care for the Elderly: Provisions and Providers in 33 Countries* (Luxembourg: European Union 2013) https://publications.europa.eu/en/publication-detail/-/publication/6f79fa54-1199-45e0-bbf3-2619c21b299a/language-en.

Bielby W and Baron J, "Men and Women at Work: Sex Segregation and Statistical Discrimination" (1986) 91 *Am J Sociology* 759.

Björnberg U, "Ideology and Choice between Work and Care: Swedish Family Policy for Working Parents" (2002) 22 *Critical Social Policy* 33.

Blau F and Kahn L, "The Gender Pay Gap: Have Women Gone as Far as They Can?" (2007) 21 *Academy of Management Perspectives* 7.

Bonoli G, "The Politics of the New Social Policies: Providing Coverage against New Social Risks in Mature Welfare States" (2005) 33 *Policy and Politics* 431.

Borg T, *Speech Given to European Parliament Interest Group on Carers* (Brussels, Belgium 9 April 2014). http://ec.europa.eu/dgs/health_consumer/dyna/borg/speeches_en.cfm.
Borgmann-Prebil Y and Obermaier-Muresan A, *Solidarity in Europe – Alive and Active* (Luxembourg: European Commission 2018).
Bornstein S, "Work, Family, and Discrimination at the Bottom of the Ladder" (2012) 19 *Georgetown J Poverty L and Policy* 1.
Bouget D, Saraceno C and Spasova S, "Towards New Work-Life Balance Policies for Those Caring for Dependent Relatives?" in Vanhercke B, Sabato S and Bouget D (eds), 155–179 *Social Policy in the European Union: State of Play 2017* (Brussels: ETUI 2017) www.etui.org/Publications2/Books/Social-policy-in-the-European-Union-state-of-play-2017.
Bowden P, *Caring: Gender Sensitive Ethics* (London/New York: Routledge 1997).
Boyd S (ed), *Challenging the Public/Private Divide: Feminism, Law and Public Policy* (Toronto: Toronto University Press 1997).
Brenner J, "Democratizing Care" in Gornick G and Meyers M (eds), *Gender Equality, Transforming Family Divisions of Labor* 177–192 (London, UK/Brooklyn, NY, USA: Verso 2009).
Bubeck D, *Care, Gender and Justice* (Oxford: Clarendon Press 1995).
Bukner L and Yeandle S, *Valuing Carers – Calculating the Value of Carers' Support* (Leeds: CIRCLE, University of Leeds 2011).
Bukner L and Yeandle S, *Valuing Carers: The Rising Value of Carers Support* (London: Carers UK 2015) https://www.carersuk.org/for-professionals/policy/policy-library/valuing-carers-2015.
Bullock J and Masselot A, "Multiple Discrimination and Intersectional Disadvantages: Challenges and Opportunities in the EU Legal Framework" (2013) 19 *Columbia J European L* 55.
Burri S, "Reconciliation of Work and Private Life in EU Law: State of Affaire" (2010) 11 *ERA Forum* 111.
Busby N, "Only a Matter of Time" (2001) 64 *MLR* 489.
Busby N, *A Right to Care?: Unpaid Care Work in European Employment Law* (Oxford: OUP 2011).
Busby N, "Unpaid Care-Giving and Paid Work within a Rights Framework" in Busby N and James G (eds), *Families, Care-Giving and Paid Work: Challenging Labour Law in the 21st Century* 189–203 (Cheltenham, UK/Northampton, MA, USA: Edward Elgar 2011).
Busby N, "Labour Law, Family Law and Care: A Plea for Convergence" in Wallbank J and Herring J (eds), *Vulnerability Care and Family Law* 181–198 (London/New York: Routledge 2014).
Busby N, "Crumbs of Comfort: Pregnancy and the Status of 'Worker' under EU Law's Free Movement Provisions" (2015) 44 *Industrial Law Journal* 134.
Busby N and Weldon-Johns M, "Fathers as Carers in UK Law and Policy: Dominant Ideologies and Lived Experience" (2019) DOI:10.1080/09649069.1627085 https://tandfonline.com/doi/abs/10.1080/09649069.2019.1627085.
Butler R, *The Longevity Revolution: The Benefits and the Challenges of Living a Long Life* (New York: Public Affairs 2008).
Callister P and Galtry J, "'Baby Bonus' or Paid Parental Leave – Which One Is Better?" (2009) 34 *Social Policy Journal of New Zealand* 1.

Cambien N, "EU Citizenship and ECJ: Why Care about Primary Carers?" (UACES Annual Conference, Passau, September 2012) https://papers.ssrn.com/sol3/papers.cfm?abstract_id=2167890.

Cameron W, *Informal Sociology, A Casual Introduction to Sociological Thinking* (New York: Random House 1963).

Campbell-Brown L, "The Ethic of Care" (1997) 4 *UCL Jurisprudence Review* 272.

Caracciolo di Torella E, "Brave New Fathers for a Brave New World? Fathers as Caregivers in an Evolving European Union" (2014) 20 *European Law Journal* 88.

Caracciolo di Torella E, "Shaping and Re-Shaping the Caring Relationship in European Law: A Catalogue of Rights for Informal Carers?" (2016) 28 *Child and Family L Q* 261.

Caracciolo di Torella E, "An Emerging Right to Care in the EU: A 'New Start to Support Work-Life Balance for Parents and Carers'" (2017) 18 *ERA Forum* 187.

Caracciolo di Torella E, "The Unintended Consequences of Brexit: The Case of Work-Life Balance" in Dustin M, Ferreira N and Millns S (eds), *Gender and Queer Perspectives on Brexit* 61–91 (Cham, Switzerland: Palgrave Macmillan 2019).

Caracciolo di Torella E and Foubert P, "Maternity Rights for Intended Mothers? Surrogacy Puts the EU Legal Framework to the Test" 2(2014) *European Gender Equality L Rev* 5.

Caracciolo di Torella E and Foubert P, "Surrogacy, Pregnancy and Maternity Rights: A Missed Opportunity for a More Coherent Regime of Parental Rights in the EU?" (2015) 40 *ELR* 52.

Caracciolo di Torella E and Masselot A, "The ECJ Case Law on Issues Related to Pregnancy, Maternity and the Organisation of Family Life: An Attempt at Classification" (2001) 26 *ELR* 239.

Caracciolo di Torella E and Masselot A, *Reconciling Work and Family Life in EU Law and Policy* (London: Palgrave Macmillan 2010).

Caracciolo di Torella E and Masselot A, "Work and Family Life Balance in the EU Law and Policy 40 Years On: Still Balancing, Still Struggling" (2013) 2 *European Gender Equality L Rev* 6.

Carers UK, "Carers at Breaking Point" (London: Carers UK 2014).

Carmichael F and Charles S, "The Opportunity Costs of Informal Care: Does Gender Matter?" (2003) 22 *J Health Economics* 781.

Cavaghan R, "The Gender Politics of EU Economic Policy: Policy Shifts and Contestations Before and After the Crisis" in Kantola J and Lombardo E (eds), *Gender and the Economic Crisis in Europe: Politics, Institutions and Intersectionality* 49–71 (Cham, Switzerland: Springer 2017).

Cavaghan R and O'Dwyer M, "European Economic Governance in 2017: A Recovery for Whom?" (2018) 56 *JCMS* 96.

Challis D and others, "Care Management, Dementia Care and Specialist Mental Health Services: An Evaluation" (2002) 17 *Intl J Geriatric Psychiatry* 315.

Chan W, "Mothers, Equality and Labour Market Opportunities" (2013) 42 *Industrial Law Journal* 224.

Choudhry S and Herring J, *European Human Rights and Family Law* (Oxford, UK/Portland, Oregon, USA: Hart Publishing 2010).

Choudhry S, Herring J and Wallbank J, "Welfare, Rights, Care and Gender in Family Law" in Wallbank J, Choudhry S and Herinng J (eds), *Rights, Gender and Family Law* 1–25 (London/New York: Routledge 2010).

Clements L, *Carers and Their Rights: The Law Relating to Carers* (London: Carers UK 2007).
Clough B, "What about Us? A Case for Legal Recognition of Interdependence in Informal Care Relationships" (2014) 36 *Journal of Social Welfare & Family Law* 129.
Cohen B and Frazer N, *Childcare in a Modern Welfare System* (London: Institute of Public Policy Research 1991).
Collins Dictionaries, *Collins English Dictionary Complete and Unabridged* (Glasgow: Collins 2018).
Coltrane S, "Research on Household Labour: Modelling and Measuring the Social Embeddedness of Routine Family Work" (2000) 62 *J Marriage and Family* 1208.
Commission Staff Working Document, "Evidence on Demographic and Social Trends Social Policies' Contribution to Inclusion, Employment and the Economy" Brussels, 20.2.2013, SWD(2013) 38 final (Part of the Social Investment package 2013).
Communication European Commission of 9 February 2005, "The EU Social Agenda 2005–2010", COM(2005) 33 final
Communication from the Commission of 10 May 2007, "Promoting Solidarity between the Generations", COM(2007) 244.
Communication from the Commission of 13 November 2002, "Draft Joint Employment Report 2002", COM(2002) 621 final.
Communication from the Commission of 19 December 1985, "Equal Opportunities for Women. Medium-term Community Programme (1986–1990)", COM(1985) 801 final and final/2.
Communication from the Commission of 2 July 2008, "A Renewed Commitment to Social Europe: Reinforcing the Open Method of Coordination for Social Protection and Social Inclusion", COM(2008) 418 final.
Communication from the Commission of 21 September 2010, "Strategy for Equality Between Women and Men 2010–2015", COM(2010) 491 final.
Communication from the Commission of 3 January 2003, "Health Care and Care for the Elderly: Supporting National Strategies for Ensuring a High Level of Social Protection", COM(2002) 774.
Communication from the Commission of 3 March 2010, "Europe 2020 Strategy: A Strategy for Smart, Sustainable and Inclusive Growth", COM(2010) 2020.
Communication from the Commission of 3 October 2008, "A Better Work-Life Balance: Stronger Support for Reconciling Professional, Private and Family Life", COM(2008) 635 final.
Communication from the Commission of 5 December 2001, "The Future of Health Care and Care for the Elderly: Guaranteeing Accessibility, Quality and Financial Viability", COM(2001) 723.
Communication from the Commission of 9 December 1981, "A New Community Action Programme on the Promotion of Equal Opportunity for Women", COM (1981) 758.
Communication from the Commission to the European Parliament, the Council, the European Economic and Social Committee and the Committee of the Regions, "Towards Social Investment for Growth and Cohesion – Including Implementing the European Social Fund 2014–2020" 20 February 2013, COM(2013) 83.
Communication from the Commission to the European Parliament, the Council, the European Economic and Social Committee and the Committee of the Regions, "Launching a Consultation on a European Pillar of Social Rights", COM(2016) 127 final.

Bibliography

Communication from the Commission, Green Paper, "Confronting Demographic Change: A New Solidarity between Generations", COM(2005) 94 .

Communication from the European Commission of 1 March 2006, "A Roadmap for Equality between Women and Men (2006–2010)", COM(2006) 92 final.

Communication from the European Commission to support work-life balance for working parents and carers, 26 April 2017, COM(2017) 252 final.

Communication to the Spring European Council from President Barroso in agreement with Vice-President Verheugen, "Working Together for Growth and Jobs: A New Start for the Lisbon Strategy", COM(2005) 24.

Connor T, "Discrimination by Association: A Step in the Right Direction" (2010) 32 *Journal of Social Welfare & Family Law* 59.

Cook R and Cusak S, *Gender Stereotyping Transnational Legal Perspectives* (Philadelphia: University of Pennsylvania Press 2010).

Cory G and Stirling A, *Pay and Parenthood: An Analysis of Wage Inequality between Mums and Dads* (London: Touchstone Extra 2016).

Costello C, "Article 33" in Peers S, Harvey T, Kenner J and Ward A (eds), *The EU Charter of Fundamental Rights: A Commentary* (Oxford: Hart Publishing 2014).

Costello C, "Family and Professional Life" in Peers S, Harvey T, Kenner J and Ward A (eds), *The EU Charter of Fundamental Rights: A Commentary* (Oxford: Hart Publishing 2014).

Countouris N and Freedland M, "Resocialising Europe – Looking Back and Thinking Forward" in Countouris N and Freedland M (eds), *Resocialising Europe in a Time of Crisis* (Cambridge: CUP 2013).

Council of the European Union, "Joint Employment Report 2003/2004" 5 March 2004 (7069/04).

Council, Employment Guideline 7, Council document 10907/10, 9 June 2010.

Council of the European Union, Council conclusions of 7 March 2011 on European Pact for Gender Equality (2011–2020), (2011/C 155/02), O.J. [2011] C155/10.

Crimman A, Wiener F and Bellman L, "The German Work-sharing Scheme: An Instrument for the Crisis", (*International Labour Organization, Conditions of Work and Employment Series No. 25* 2010).

Crompton R, *Employment and the Family: The Reconfiguration of Work and Family Life in Contemporary Societies* (Cambridge: CUP 2006).

Crompton R, Lewis S and Lyonette C, "Introduction: The Unravelling of the Male Breadwinner Model – And Some of Its Consequences" in Crompton R, Lewis S and Lyonette C (eds), *Women, Men, Work and Family in Europe* 1–16 (Basingstoke, UK: Palgrave Macmillan 2007).

Crompton Rosemary C and Lyonette C, "Who Does the Housework? The Division of Labour within the House" in Park A, Curtice J, Thomson K, Philipps M, Johnson M and Clery E (eds), *British Social Attitudes: The 24th Report* 53–81 (London, UK/Thousand Oaks, California, USA/New Delhi, India: Sage 2008).

Cunningham-Burley S, Backett-Milburn K and Kemmer D, "Constructing Health and Sickness in the Context of Motherhood and Paid Work" (2006) 28 *Sociology of Health & Illness* 385.

Dahlby B, *Adverse Selection and Statistical Discrimination* (Dordrecht: Springer 1992).

Daly M, "A Fine Balance Women's Labour Market Participation in International Comparison" in FW S and VE S (eds), *Welfare and Work in the Open Economy, Vol II Diverse Responses to Common Challenges* 467–510 (Oxford: OUP 2000).

Daly M, "Caring in the Third Way: The Relationship between Obligation, Responsibility and Care in Third Way Discourse" (2000) 20 *Critical Social Policy* 5.
Daly M, "Care as a Good for Social Policy" (2002) 21 *Journal of Social Policy* 251.
Daly M, "What Adult Worker Model? A Critical Look at Recent Social Policy Reform in Europe from A Gender and Family Perspective" (2011) 18 *Social Politics: Intl Studies in Gender, State & Society* 1.
Daly M and Lewis J, "The Concept of Social Care and the Analysis of Contemporary Welfare States" (2000) 51 *British Journal of Sociology* 281.
Daly M and Scheiwe K, "Individualisation and Personal Obligations: Social Policy, Family Policy and Law Reform in Germany and the UK" (2010) 24 *Intl J L, Policy and the Family* 177.
Danzinger S and Walfogel J, "Investing in Children: What Do We Know? What Should We Do?" (Centre for the Analysis of Social Exclusion, London School of Economics, Case Paper 34, 2000).
de Beauvoir S, *Le Deuxième Sexe* (Paris: Gallimard 1949).
Defeis E, "Treaty of Amsterdam: The Next Step Towards Gender Equality" (1999) 23 *Boston College Intl and Comparative L Rev* 1.
Dejours C, "Intelligence Ouvrière Et Organisation Du Travail (À Propos Du Modèle Japonais De production)" in Hirata HS (ed), *Autour Du 'Modèle' Japonais – Automatisation, Nouvelles Formes D'organisation Et De Relations De Travail* 275–303 (Paris: L'Harmattan 1992).
Den Exter A and Hervey T (eds), *European Union Health Law: Treaties and Legislation* (Apeldoorn-Antwerpen: Maklu 2012).
Department of Health (UK), "Caring about Carers: A National Strategy for Carers" (London: Department of Health 1999).
Department of Health (UK), *Carers at the Heart of 21st Century Families and Communities: A Caring System on Your Side, A Life of Your Own* (London: Department of Health Stationary Office 2008).
Department of Health, "The Report of the Commission on Funding of Care and Support" (London: Department of Health 2011) www.ilis.co.uk/uploaded_files/dilnott_report_the_future_of_funding_social_care_july_2011.pdf.
Department of Work and Pensions (DWP), "Ready for Work: Full Employment in Our Generation" (London: Department of Work and Pensions 2007).
Dermott E, *Intimate Fatherhood: A Sociological Analysis* (Oxon, UK/New York, USA: Routledge 2014).
Deutsch F, *Halving It All: How Equally Shared Parenting Works* (Cambridge, Massachusetts, USA: Harvard University Press 1999).
Di Rosa M and others, "The Impact of Migrant Work in the Elder Care Sector: Recent Trends and Empirical Evidence in Italy" (2012) 15 *European J Social Care* 9.
Diduck A, "Autonomy and Vulnerability in Family Law: The Missing Link" in Wallbank J and Herring J (eds), *Vulnerabilities, Care and Family Law* 95–114 (Oxon, UK/New York, USA: Routledge 2013).
Diduck A and O'Donnovan K, "Feminism and Families: Plus Ça Change?" in Diduck A and O'Donnovan K (eds), *Feminist Perspectives on Family Law* 13–32 (Oxon, UK/New York, USA: Routledge-Cavendish 2006).
Dodds S, "Depending on Care: Recognition of Vulnerability and the Social Contribution of Care Provisions" (2007) 21 *Bioethics* 500.

Douglas G, "Marriage, Cohabitation and Parenthood: From Contract to Status?" in Katz S, Eekelaar J and Maclean M (eds), *Cross Currents: Family Law and Policy in the United States and England* 211–233 (Oxford: OUP 2000).

Douglas G, *Obligation and Commitment in Family Law* (Oxford, UK/Portland, Oregon, USA: Hart 2018).

Doyle M and Timonen V, "The Different Faces of Care Work: Understanding the Experiences of the Multi-cultural Care Workforce" (2009) 29 *Ageing and Society* 337.

Duncan S and Edwards R, *Lone Mothers, Paid Work and Gendered Moral Rationalities* (London: Palgrave Macmillan 1999).

Dupré C, "Article 1: Dignity" in Peers S, Harvey T, Kenner J and Ward A (eds), *The EU Charter of Fundamental Rights: A Commentary* (Oxford, UK/Portland, Oregon, USA: Hart 2014).

Dworkin R, *Taking Rights Seriously* (Cambridge, Massachusetts, USA: Harvard University Press 1978).

Dworkin R, *Life's Dominion* (Oxford: OUP 1993).

Dworkin R, *Is Democracy Possible Here?: Principles for a New Political Debate* (Princeton: Princeton University Press 2006).

Ellis E, "The Impact of the Lisbon Treaty on Gender Equality" (2010) 1 *European Gender Equality L Rev* 7.

Equality and Human Right Commission (EHRC), "Working Better: Fathers, Family and Work: Contemporary Perspectives" (London, EHRC 2009).

Ermisch J, "Purchased Child Care, Optimal Family Size and Mother's Employment Theory and Econometric Analysis" (1989) 2 *J Population Economics* 79.

Esping-Andersen G, "A Child-Centred Social Investment Strategy" in Esping-Andersen G (ed), *Why We Need a New Welfare State* 26–67 (Oxford: OUP 2002).

Eurochild, "A Child Rights Approach to Child Poverty – Discussion Paper" (September 2007) www.eurochild.org/fileadmin/public/05_Library/Thematic_priorities/01_Childrens_Rights/Eurochild/Eurochild_discussion_paper_child_rights_ poverty.pdf.

Eurofond, "Burnout in the Workplace: A Review of Data and Policy Response in the EU" (Luxembourg: Publications Office of the European Union 2018).

Eurofound, "Promoting Uptake of Parental and Paternity Leave among Fathers in the European Union" (Luxembourg: European Union 2015).

Eurofound, "European Quality of Life Survey (EQLS) 2016" (Luxembourg: Publications Office of the European Union 2016) www.eurofound.europa.eu/sites/default/files/ef_publication/field_ef_document/ef1733en.pdf.

Eurofound, "Striking a Balance: Reconciling Work and Life in the EU" (Luxembourg: Publications Office of the European Union 2018).

Eurofound, "Parental and Paternity Leave – Uptake by Fathers" (Luxembourg: Publications Office of the European Union 2019).

Eurofound, "Third European Quality of Life Survey (EQLS) 2011–2012" www.eurofound.europa.eu/surveys/european-quality-of-life-surveys/european-quality-of-life-survey-2012.

Euromonitor International, "Boomers as Consumers" (October 2012) www.euromonitor.com/boomers-as-consumers/report.

European Commission, "Increasing Labour Force Participation and Promoting Active Ageing", COM(2002) 9 (Luxembourg: Publications Office of the European Union 2002).

European Commission, "Health and Long-Term Care in the European Union" (Special Eurobarometer 283, Luxembourg: European Union 2007) http://ec.europa.eu/public_opinion/archives/ebs/ebs_283_en.pdf.

European Commission, *Long-term Care in the European Union* (Luxembourg: European Communities 2008).

European Commission, "Public Consultation on Possible EU Measures in the Area of carers' Leave or Leave to Care for Dependent Relatives" (August 2011).

European Commission, *Report on Progress on Equality between Women and Men in 2010: The Gender Balance in Business Leadership* (Luxembourg: Publications Office of the European Union 2011).

European Commission, Report on the Application of the EU Charter of Fundamental Rights Brussels, COM(2012) 169 final.

European Commission Report, "Implementation of the Barcelona Objectives Concerning Facilities for Pre-School-Age Children", 3 October 2008, COM(2008) 638.

European Commission, "Demography Report 2010 – Older, More Numerous and Diverse Europeans" (2011) http://senas.lnb.lt/stotisFiles/uploadedAttachments/es320111028114623.pdf.

European Commission, "Proposal for Multi-annual Programme of Action for Health", COM(2014–2020) (2011) 709 final.

European Commission, *2011 Report on the Application of the EU Charter of Fundamental Rights*, COM(2012) 169 final (Publications Office of the European Union 2012).

European Commission, "Barcelona Objectives: The Development of Childcare Facilities for Young Children in Europe with a View to Sustainable and Inclusive Growth" (Publications Office of the European Union 2013).

European Commission, "Social Investment Package: Key Facts and Figures" (Publications Office of the European Union 2013).

European Commission, Commission Staff Working Document of 20 February 2013, "Long Term Care in an Ageing Society – Challenges and Policy Options" SWD(2013) 41 final.

European Commission, "Growing the European Silver Economy" (*Background Paper*, 23 February 2015) http://ec.europa.eu/research/innovation-union/pdf/active-healthy-ageing/silvereco.pdf.

European Commission, "Report on Equality between Women and Men 2014" (Luxembourg: Publications Office of the European Union 2015) http://ec.europa.eu/justice/gender-equality/files/annual_reports/150304_annual_report_2014_web_en.pdf.

European Commission, "ROADMAP: New Start to Address the Challenges of Work–Life Balance Faced by Working Families" (2015) http://ec.europa.eu/smart-regulation/roadmaps/docs/2015_just_012_new_initiative_replacing_maternity_leave_directive_en.pdf.

European Commission, "The 2015 Ageing Report" (Luxembourg: European Union 2015), http://ec.europa.eu/economy_finance/publications/european_economy/2015/pdf/ee3_en.pdf.

European Commission, "Strategic Engagement for Gender Equality 2016–2019" (Luxembourg: European Union 2015) https://ec.europa.eu/anti-trafficking/sites/antitrafficking/files/strategic_engagement_for_gender_equality_en.pdf.

European Commission, "Joint Report on Health Care and Long-Term Care Systems and Fiscal Sustainability" (European Commission Directorate-General for Economic

and Financial Affairs, Institutional Paper 037, October 2016) https://ec.europa.eu/info/publications/economy-finance/joint-report-health-care-and-long-term-care-systems-fiscal-sustainability-0_en.
European Commission, "2013 Report on the Application of the EU Charter of Fundamental Rights" COM(2014) 224 final http://ec.europa.eu/justice/fundamental-rights/files/com_2014_224_en.pdf.
European Commission and Economic Policy Committee, "The 2012 Ageing Report Economic and Budgetary Projections for the 27 EU Member States (2010–2060)" (European Economy 2/2012, European Union 2012) http://ec.europa.eu/economy_finance/publications/european_economy/2012/pdf/ee-2012-2_en.pdf.
European Commission Childcare Network, "Childcare and Equality of Opportunity" (Luxembourg: European Commission 1988).
European Commission Childcare Network, "Paper 3: Quality Targets in Services for Young Children" (European Commission Equal Opportunities Unit, January 1996) http://childcarecanada.org/sites/default/files/Qualitypaperthree.pdf.
European Commission Childcare Network, "Reconciling Employment and Caring for Children: What Information Is Needed for an Effective Policy?" (Luxembourg: European Commission - DG V, 1996).
European Commission Recommendation 2013/112/EU of 20 February 2013, Investing in Children: Breaking the Cycle of Disadvantage, COM(2013) 778, O.J. [2013] L59/5.
European Commission Report, "The Development of Childcare Facilities for Young Children with a View to Increase Female Labour Participation, Strike a Work-life Balance for Working Parents and Bring about Sustainable and Inclusive Growth in Europe (The Barcelona Objectives)", COM(2018) 273 final.
European Commission Report on, 'Implementation of the Barcelona Objectives Concerning Facilities for Pre-School-Age Children', COM(2008) 638.
European Commission Staff Working Document, Analytical Document Accompanying the Consultation Document Second-stage Consultation of the Social Partners at European Level under Article 154 TFEU on Possible Action Addressing the Challenges of Work-life Balance Faced by Working Parents and Caregivers, 12 July 2016, SWD(2016) 145 final.
European Commission, "First-stage Consultation of European Social Partners on Reconciliation of Professional, Private and Family Life" 12 October 2006, SEC(2006) 1245.
European Council, "Extraordinary European Council Meeting on Employment, Luxembourg, 20 and 21 November 1997, Presidency Conclusions" (20–21 November 1997 www.consilium.europa.eu/uedocs/cms_data/docs/pressdata/en/ec/00300.htm.
European Council, "Lisbon European Council 23 and 24 March 2000 Presidency Conclusions" (23–24 March 2000) http://europarl.europa.eu/summits/lis1_en.htm.
European Council, "Presidency Conclusions, Barcelona European Council" 15 and 16 March 2002 (SN 100/1/02 REV 1) http://ec.europa.eu/invest-in-research/pdf/download_en/barcelona_european_council.pdf (Barcelona targets).
European Council, "Council conclusions of 17 June 2010 – A new European Strategy for jobs and growth', (EUCO 13/10) http://ec.europa.eu/eu2020/pdf/council_conclusion_17_june_en.pdf.

European Foundation for the Improvement of Living and Working Conditions, "Part-Time Work in Europe" (2007).

European Institute for Gender Equality (EIGE), "Gender Equality Index 2017: Measuring Gender Equality in the European Union 2005–2015" (2017).

European Network of Equality Bodies (Equinet), "In Focus Brief, Work-Life Balance" (May 2018).

European Parliament Resolution of 4 July 2013, Impact of the Crisis on Access to Care for Vulnerable Groups (2013/2044 (INI)).

European Parliament, "European Parliament resolution of 13 September 2016 on creating labour market conditions favourable for work-life balance (2016/2017(INI))" (13 September 2016) http://www.europarl.europa.eu/sides/getDoc.do?type=TA&reference=P8-TA-2016-0338&language=EN.

European Parliament FEMM Committee, "Differences in men and women's work, care and leisure time" (PE 556.933) (2016).

European Women's Lobby, *The Price of Austerity – The Impact of Gender Equality in Europe* (Brussels: EWL 2012).

European Union Presidency Conclusions of March 2006, "European Pact for Gender Equality" 7775/1/06/REV 1.

Eurostat, "Gender Pay Gap Statistics" (2014) http://ec.europa.eu/eurostat/statistics-explained/index.php/Gender_pay_gap_statistics#cite_note-1.

Eurostat, "Fertility Statistics" (11 March 2019) https://ec.europa.eu/eurostat/statistics-explained/index.php/Fertility_statistics.

Evans J, *Feminist Theory Today: An Introduction to Second-Wave Feminism* (London: Sage 1995).

Fagan C and others, "Gender Mainstreaming in the Enlarged European Union: Recent Developments in the European Employment Strategy and Social Inclusion Process" (2005) 36 *Industrial Relations J* 568.

Fagan C, "Analysis Note – Men and Gender Equality Tackling Gender Segregated Family Roles and Social Care Jobs" (Luxembourg: European Union 2010).

Fagan C and Norman H, "Men and Gender Equality: Tackling Gender Segregation in Family Roles and in Social Care Jobs" in Bettio F, Plantenga J and Smith M (eds), *Gender and the European Labour Market* 215–239 (London: Routledge 2013).

Featherstone B, "Gender, Rights, Responsibilities and Social Policy" in Wallbank J, Choudhry S and Herring J (eds), *Rights, Gender and Family Law* 34–50 (London: Routledge 2010).

Feder K, *Love's Labour: Essays on Women, Equality and Dependency* (New York: Routledge 1999).

Federle K, "Rights, Not Wrongs" (2009) 17 *Intl J Children's Rights* 321.

Ferreira N, "Putting the Age of Criminal and Tort Liability into Context: A Dialogue between Law and Psychology" (2008) 16 *Intl J Children's Rights* 29.

Ferreira N, "The Human Face of the European Union: Are EU Law and Policy Humane Enough? An Introduction" in Ferreira N and Kostakopoulou D (eds), *The Human Face of the European Union: Are EU Law and Policy Humane Enough?* 1–14 (Cambridge: CUP 2016).

Ferreira N, Hemerijck A and Rhodes M, *The Future of Social Europe: Recasting Work and Welfare in the New Economy* (Oeiras: Celta Editora 2000).

Ferreira N and Kostakopoulou D (eds), *The Human Face of the European Union: Are EU Law and Policy Humane Enough?* (Cambridge: CUP 2016).

Financial Times, "Silver Economy Series" (3 November 2014) www.ft.com/intl/topics/themes/Ageing_populations.
Finch J and Groves D (eds), *A Labour of Love: Women, Work and Caring* (Henley on Thames: Routledge 1983).
Fineman M, *The Neutered Mother, the Sexual Family and Other Twentieth Century Tragedies* (Oxon/New York: Routledge 1995).
Fineman M, *The Autonomy Myth: A Theory of Dependency* (New York: New Press 2004).
Fineman M, "The Vulnerable Subject: Anchoring Equality in the Human Conditions" (2008) 20 *Yale J L & Feminism* 1.
Fineman M, "Responsibility, Family and the Limits of Equality: An American Perspective" in Lind C, Keating H and Bridgeman J (eds), *Taking Responsibility, Law and the Changing Family* 37–49 (Aldershot, England/Burlington, USA: Ashgate 2011).
Finley L, "Transcending Equality Theory: A Way Out of the Maternity and the Workplace Debate?" (1986) 86 *Colum L Rev* 1118.
Fisher B and Tronto J, "Toward a Feminist Theory of Caring" in Abel E and Nelson M (eds), *Circles of Care: Work and Identity in Women's Lives* 35–62 (New York: SUNY Press 1990).
Folbre N, "Reforming Care" in Gornick J and Meyers M (eds), *Gender Equality, Transforming Family Divisions of Labor* 111–128 (London, UK/Brooklyn, NY, USA: Verso 2009).
Folgueras MD, "L'inégal Partage Des Responsabilités Familiales Et Domestiques Est Toujours d'Actualité" (2014) 2 *Regards Croisés Sur l'Economie* 183.
Forstater M, "Working for a Better World: Cataloguing Arguments for the Right to Employment" (2015) 41 *Philosophy and Social Criticism* 61.
Foubert P and Imamović S, "The Pregnant Workers Directive: Must Do Better: Lessons to Be Learned from Strasbourg?" (2015) 37 *Journal of Social Welfare & Family Law* 309.
Foucault M, "La Philosophy Analytique De La Politique" (1978) in *Dits et écrits, 1976–1988* (Gallimard 2001).
Fraser N, "After the Family Wage: Gender Equity and the Welfare State" (1994) 22 *Political Theory* 591.
Fredman S, *Women and the Law* (Oxford: Clarendon Press 1997).
Fredman S, "Women at Work: The Broken Promise of Flexicurity" (2004) 33 *Industrial Law Journal* 299.
Fredman S, "Changing the Norm: Positive Duties in Equal Treatment Legislation" (2005) *MJ* 12 369.
Fredman S, "Reversing Roles: Bringing Men into the Frame" (2014) 10 *Intl J L Context* 442.
Fredman S, "Substantive Equality Revisited" (2016) 14 *ICON* 712.
Freeman M, "The Human Rights of Children" (2010) 63 *Current Legal Problems* 1.
Fudge J and Owens R (eds), *Precarious Work, Women, and the New Economy: The Challenge to Legal Norms* (Oxford, UK/Portland, Oregon, USA: Hart Publishing 2006).
Fursman L and Zodgekar N, "Making It Work: The Impacts of Flexible Working Arrangements on New Zealand Families" (2009) 35 *Social Policy Journal of New Zealand* 43.
Galtry J and Callister P, "Assessing the Optimal Length of Parental Leave for Child and Parental Well-Being How Can Research Inform Policy?" (2005) 26 *J Family Issues* 219.

Gardner J, "Discrimination as Injustice" (1996) 16 *OJLS* 353.

Gaymu J and others, "Who Will Be Caring for Europe's Dependent Elders in 2030?" (2007) 62 *Population* 675.

Gerstel N, "The Third Shift: Gender and Care Work Outside the Home" (2000) 23 *Qualitative Sociology* 467.

Gilbert N, *A Mother's Work: How Feminism, the Market and Policy Shape Family Life* (New Haven, CT, USA: Yale University Press 2008).

Gillespie G and Khan U, "Integrating Economic and Social Policy: Childcare a Transformational Policy?" in Campbell J and Gillespie M (eds), *Feminist Economics and Public Policy* 94–100 (London/New York: Routledge 2016).

Gilligan C, *In a Different Voice: Psychological Theory and Women's Development* (Cambridge, Massachusetts, USA: Harvard University Press 1982).

Gilligan C, "Reply" in "On in a Different Voice: An Interdisciplinary Forum" (1986) 11 *Signs: J Women in Culture and Society* 324.

Glaser K and others, *Grandparenting in Europe: Family Policy and Grandparents' Role in Providing Childcare* (London: Grandparents plus 2013).

Glendinning C and others, "Care Provision within Families and Its Socio-Economic Impact on Care Providers across the European Union" (Social Policy Research Unit University of York, Working Paper No. EU 2342, May 2009).

Glucksmann M, "Why 'work'? Gender and the 'total Social Organisation of Labour'" (1995) 2 *Gender, Work and Organisation* 63.

Gornick J and Meyers M, *Families that Work: Policy for Reconciling Parenthood and Employment* (New York: Russell Sage Foundation 2003).

Gornick J and Meyers M (eds), *Gender Equality, Transforming Family Divisions of Labor* (London, UK/Brooklyn, NY, USA: Verso 2010).

Gornick J and Meyers M, "Institutions that Support Gender Equality in Parenthood and Employment" in Gornick J and Meyers M (eds), 3–64 *Gender Equality, Transforming Family Divisions of Labor* (London, UK/Brooklyn, NY, USA: Verso 2010).

Greeno C and Maccoby E, "How Different Is the 'Different Voice'?" (1986) 11 *Signs: J Women in Culture and Society* 310.

Greenstein T, "Economic Dependence, Gender, and the Division of Labor in the Home: A Replication and Extension" (2000) 62 *J Marriage and Family* 322.

Gregory A, Milner S and Windebank J, "Guest Editorial: Work-Life Balance in Times of Economic Crisis and Austerity" (2013) 33 *Intl Journal of Sociology and Social Policy* 528.

Grimley EJ, "Age Discrimination: Implications of the Ageing Process" in Fredman S and Spencer S (eds), *Age as an Equality Issue: Legal and Policy Perspectives* 11–20 (Oxford, UK/Portland, Oregon, USA: Hart Publishing 2003).

Gronden J and others (eds), *Health Care and EU Law* (The Hague: Springer 2011).

Grozev R, "A Landmark Judgment of the Court of Justice of the EU – New Conceptual Contributions to the Legal Combat against Ethnic Discrimination" (2015) 15 *Equal Rights Rev* 168.

Guerrina R, "Socio Economic Challenges to Work Life Balance at Times of Crisis" (2015) 37 *Journal of Social Welfare & Family Law* 368.

Guerrina R and Masselot A, "Walking into the Footprint of EU Law: Unpacking the Gendered Consequences of Brexit" (2018) 17 *Social Policy & Society* 319.

Haas L, "Parental Leave and Gender Equality: Lessons from the European Union" (2003) 20 *Rev Policy Research* 89.

Bibliography

Habermas J, "Democracy in Europe: Why the Development of the EU into a Transnational Democracy Is Necessary and How It Is Possible" (2015) 21 *European Law Journal* 546.

Hakim C, "Lifestyle Preferences as Determinants of Women's Differentiated Labor Market Careers" (2002) 29 *Work and Occupations* 428.

Hamington M, *Embodied Care: Jane Addams, Maurice Merleau-Ponty and Feminist Ethics* (Urbana and Chicago: University of Illinois Press 2004).

Hansen L, "From Flexicurity to Flexicarity? Gendered Perspectives on the Danish Model" (2017) 3(2) *Journal of Social Sciences* 88.

Hardy S and Adnett N, "The Parental Leave Directive: Towards a Family-Friendly Social Europe?" (2002) 8 *European J Industrial Relations* 157.

Hart H, "Bentham on Legal Rights" in Simpson A (ed), *Oxford Essays in Jurisprudence* 171–201 (Oxford: OUP 1973).

Hart H, *Legal Rights* (Oxford: OUP 1982).

Held V, *The Ethic of Care: Personal, Political, and Global* (Oxford: OUP 2006).

Herring J, "Caring" (2007a) 89 *Law and Justice – Christian Law Review* 89.

Herring J, "Where are the Carers in Healthcare Law and Ethics?" (2007) 27 *Legal Studies* 51.

Herring J, *Older People in Law and Society* (Oxford: OUP 2009).

Herring J, *Caring and the Law* (Oxford, UK/Portland, Oregon, USA: Hart Publishing 2013).

Herring J, "Making Family Law More Careful" in Wallbank J and Herring J (eds), *Vulnerability Care and Family Law* (London/New York: Routledge 2014).

Herring J, *Relational Autonomy and Family Law* (Cham, Heidelberg, New York, Doredrecht, London: Springer 2014).

Herring J, *Vulnerable Adults and the Law* (Oxford: OUP 2016).

Herring J, "Compassion, Ethic of Care and Legal Rights" (2017) 13 *Intl J L Context* 158.

Herring J, *Family Law* (London: Pearson 2017).

Hervey T and others, "Case C-303/06 *Coleman V. Attridge Law and Steve Law* Judgment of the ECJ 17 July 2008" (2009) 31 *Journal of Social Welfare & Family Law* 309.

Hervey T and others, "Long Term Care for Older People and EU Law: The Position in England and Scotland" (2012) 34 *Journal of Social Welfare & Family Law* 105.

Hervey T and McHale J, *European Union Health Law: Themes and Implications* (Cambridge: CUP 2015).

Hervey T and Shaw J, "Women, Work and Care: Women's Dual Role and Double Burden in EC Sex Equality Law" (1998) 8 *Journal of European Social Policy* 43.

Heyes A, "The Economics of Vocation of 'Why Is a Badly Paid Nurse a Good Nurse?'" (2005) 24 *Journal of Health Economics* 561.

Himmelweit S, "Rethinking Care, Gender Inequality and Policies" (United Nations, Division for the Advancement of Women, EGM/ESOR/2008/EP.7, 25 September 2008).

HM Government, "Carers at the Heart of 21st Century Families and Communities" (London: The Stationary Office, 2008).

Hobson B, "The Individualised Worker, the Gender Participatory and the Gender Equity Models in Sweden" (2004) 3 *Social Policy & Society* 75.

Hobson B (ed), *Worklife Balance: The Agency and Capabilities Gap* (Oxford: OUP 2014).

Hochschild A and Machung A, *The Second Shift: Working Parents and the Revolution at Home* (New York: Viking Penguin 1989).
Hofäcker D and König S, "Flexibility and Work-life Conflict in Time of Crisis: A Gender Perspective" (2013) 33 *Intl Journal of Sociology and Social Policy* 613.
Honeyball S, "Discrimination by Association" [2007] 4 *Web JCLI* http://webjcli.ncl.ac.uk/2007/issue4/honeyball4.html.
Honneth A, *La Société Du Mépris: Vers Une Nouvelle Théorie Critique* (Paris: la Découverte 2008).
Horton R, "Care Giving and Reasonable Adjustment in the UK" in Busby N and James G (eds), *Families Care Giving and Paid Work: Challenging Labour Law in the 21st Century* 137–152 (Cheltenham, UK/Northampton, MA, USA: Edward Elgar 2011).
Horton R, "Caring for Adults in the EU: Work-Life Balance and Challenge for EU Law" (2015) 37 *Journal of Social Welfare & Family Law* 356.
Horton R, *Dignity and the Legal Justification of Age Discrimination in Health Care* (PhD thesis, Middlesex University 2016).
Hoskyns C, *Integrating Gender. Women, Law and Politics in the European Union* (London, UK/Brooklyn, NY, USA: Verso 1996).
Hoskyns C, "Mainstreaming Gender in the Macroeconomic Policies of the EU – Institutional and Conceptual Issues" (ECPR conference, Bologna, June 2004).
Hoskyns C, "Linking Gender and International Trade Policy: Is Interaction Possible?" (*Centre for the Study of Globalisation and Regionalisation, Working Paper 217/07*, February 2007).
Hughes B and others, "Love's Labour's Lost? Feminism, the Disabled People's Movement and the Ethic of Care" (2005) 39 *Sociology* 259.
Hurst S, "Vulnerability in Research and Health Care: Describing the Elephant in the Room" (2008) 22 *Bioethics* 191.
Ikegami N, Hirdes J and Carpenter I, "Long Term Care: A Complex Challenge" (2001) 229 *OECD Observer* 27.
Interinstitutional Proclamation on the European Pillar of Social Rights, O.J. 2017 C428/15, https://eur-lex.europa.eu/legalcontent/EN/TXT/PDF/?uri=CELEX:32017C1213(01)&from=EN.
International Labour Organisation (ILO), Women at Work Today https://itcilo.org/en/supporting-initiatives/women-at-work-itcilo/#1.
International Labour Organisation (ILO), The Future of Work Centenary Initiative https://ilo.org/global/topics/future-of-work/WCMS_448448/lang–en/index.htm.
International Labour Organisation (ILO), Care Work & Care Jobs for the Future of Work – Care Burden on Women https://ilo.org/global/publications/books/WCMS_633135/lang–en/index.htmf.
Jacobs J and Gerson K, *The Time Divide: Work, Family and Gender Inequalities* (Cambridge, Massachusetts, USA: Harvard University Press 2004).
James G, "Law's Response to Pregnancy/Workplace Conflicts: A Critique" (2007) 15 *Feminist Legal Studies* 167.
James G, "Mothers and Fathers as Parents and Workers: Family-friendly Employment Policies in an Era of Shifting Identities" (2009) 31 *Journal of Social Welfare & Family Law* 271.
James G, *The Legal Regulation of Pregnancy and Parenting in the Labour Market* (London/New York: Routledge-Cavendish 2009).

James G, "Forgotten Children: Work–Family Reconciliation in the EU" (2012) 34 *Journal of Social Welfare & Family Law* 363.
James G, "Family-friendly Employment Laws (Re) Assessed: The Potential of Care Ethics" (2016) 45 *Industrial Law Journal* 477.
James G and Spruce E, "Workers with Elderly Dependants: Employment Law's Response to the Latest Care-giving Conundrum" (2015) 35 *Legal Studies* 463.
Jane L, *Work-Family Balance, Gender and Policy* (Cheltenham: Edward Elgar 2010).
Janta B, *Caring for Children in Europe* (Luxembourg: European Union 2014).
Jappens M and Van Bavel J, "Regional Family Norms and Child Care by Grandparents in Europe" (2012) 27 *Demographic Research* 85.
Jay G and others, "Feminist Fallacies: A Reply to Hakim on Women's Employment" (1996) 47 *British Journal of Sociology* 167.
Jeffery M, "Not Really Going to Work? On the Directive on Part Time Work, 'Atypical Work' and Attempts to Regulate It" (1998) 27 *Industrial Law Journal* 193.
Jenson J, "Social Investment for New Social Risks: Consequences of the LEGO™ Paradigm for Children" in Lewis J (ed), *Children in Context: Changing Families and Welfare States* 27–50 (Cheltenham, UK/Northampton, MA, USA: Edward Elgar Publishing 2006).
Julén Votinius J, "Parenthood Meets Market-Functionalism: Parental Rights in the Labour Market and the Importance of Gender Dimension" in Numhausen-Henning A and Rönmar M (eds), *Normative Patterns and Legal Developments in the Social Dimension of the EU* (Oxford, UK/Portland, Oregon, USA: Hart Publishing 2013) 185.
Kaelin L, "Care Drain: The Political Making of Health Worker Migration" (2011) 32 *J Public Health Policy* 489.
Kaganas F, "Child Protection, Gender and Rights" in Wallbank J, Choudhry S and Herring J (eds), *Rights, Gender and Family Law* 43–69 (London/New York: Routledge 2010).
Kahu E and Morgan M, "A Critical Discourse Analysis of New Zealand Government Policy: Women as Mothers and Workers" (2007) 30 *Women's Studies Intl Forum* 134.
Kalleberg A, "Nonstandard Employment Relations: Part-Time, Temporary and Contract Work" (2000) 26 *Annual Rev Sociology* 341.
Kalleberg A, "Precarious Work, Insecure Workers: Employment Relations in Transition" (2009) 74 *Am Soc Rev* 1.
Kantola J and Lombardo E (eds), *Gender and the Economic Crisis in Europe: Politics, Institutions and Intersectionality* (Cham, Switzerland: Palgrave 2017).
Karamessini M and Rubery J, "The Challenge of Austerity for Equality. A Consideration of Eight European Countries in the Crisis" (2014) 2 *Revue De l'OFCE* 15.
Karamessini M and Rubery J (ed), *Women and Austerity: The Economic Crisis and the Future for Gender Equality* (London/New York: Routledge 2014).
Kelly F, "Conceptualising the Child through an 'Ethic of Care': Lessons for Family Law" (2005) 1 *Int JLC* 375.
Kerber L, "Some Cautionary Words for Historians" (1986) 11 *Signs: J Women in Culture and Society* 304.
Keywood K, "Gatekeepers, Proxies, Advocates? The Evolving Role of Carers under Mental Health and Mental Incapacity Law Reforms" (2003) 25 *Journal of Social Welfare & Family Law* 355.

Kilkey M and Bradshaw J, "Lone Mother, Economic Well-Being, and Policies" in Sainsbury D (ed), *Gender and Welfare State Regimes* 147–184 (Oxford: OUP 1999).

Kilpatrick C, "Community or Communities of Courts in European Integration? Sex Equality Dialogues between UK Courts and the ECJ" (1998) 4 *European Law Journal* 121.

Knijn T and Kremer M, "Gender and the Caring Dimension of Welfare State: Towards Inclusive Citizenship" (1997) 4 *Social Politics* 328.

Kohlberg L, *Essays in Moral Development Volume 1: The Philosophy of Moral Development* (San Francisco: Harper and Row 1981).

Kohlberg L, *Essays in Moral Development Volume 2: The Psychology of Moral Development* (San Francisco: Harper and Row 1984).

Koukoulis-Spiliotopoulos S, "The Lisbon Treaty and the Charter of Fundamental Rights: Maintaining and Developing the Acquis in Gender Equality" (2008) 1 *European Gender Equality L Rev* 15.

Koukoulis-Spiliotopoulos S, "Les institutions de l'Union ne peuvent échapper à la Charte, mais elles sont exonérées de leur responsabilité par des mécanismes externes. Quid alors de l'autonomie du droit de l'Union?" in Pataut E, Petti F, Robin-Olivier S and Supiot A (eds), *Droit Social International Et Européen En Mouvement – Liber Amicorum En Hommage À Pierre Rodière* 169–184 (Issy-les-Moulineaux: LGDJ 2019).

Kountouris N, "The Legal Determinants of Precariousness in Personal Work Relations: A European Perspective" (2012) 34 *Comparative Labour Law and Policy J* 21.

Kreyenfeld M, Andersson G and Pailhé A, "Economic Uncertainty and Family Dynamics in Europe: Introduction" (2012) 27 *Demographic Research* 835.

Kröger T and Yeandle S, *Combining Paid Work and Family Care* (Bristol: Policy Press 2013).

L'Heureux Dubè C, "Making a Difference: The Pursuit of a Compassionate Justice" (1997) 31 *UBC L Rev* 1.

Lacey N, "Legislation against Sex Discrimination: Questions from a Feminist Perspective" (1987) 14 *J L Society* 411.

Lafortune G and Balestrat G, "Trends in Severe Disability among Elderly People: Assessing the Evidence in 12 OECD Countries and the Future Implications" (*OECD Health Working Papers, No. 26, OECD Publishing*, 2007), doi: 10.1787/217072070078.

Landau T and Beigbeder Y, *From ILO Standards to EU Law: The Case of Equality between Men and Women at Work* (Leiden/Boston: Brill Nijhoff 2008).

Langrish S, "The Treaty of Amsterdam: Selected Highlights" (1998) 23 *ELR* 3.

Lareau A, "My Wife Can Tell Me Who I Know: Methodological and Conceptual Problems in Studying Fathers" (2000) 23 *Qualitative Sociology* 407.

Laugier S, "Le Sujet Du *Care*: Vulnérabilité Et Expression Ordinaires" in Molinier P, Laugier S and Paperman P (eds), *Qu'est-ce Que Le Care? Souci Des Autres, Sensibilité, Résponsibilité* 159–203 (Paris: Payot et Rivages 2009).

Leira A, *Welfare State and Working Mothers: The Scandinavian Experience* (Cambridge: CUP 1992).

Lesthaeghe R, "The Unfolding Story of the Second Demographic Transition" (2010) 36 *Population and Development Rev* 211.

Letablier M and Lanquetin M, *Concilier Travail Et Famille En France: Approches Socio-Juridiques* (Paris: Centre d'études de l'emploi 2005).

182 Bibliography

Lewis J, "Flexible Working Arrangements: Implementation, Outcomes, and Management" (2003) 18 *Intl Rev Industrial and Organizational Psychology* 1.

Lewis J, "Work/Family Reconciliation, Equal Opportunities and Social Policies: The Interpretation of Policy Trajectories at the EU Level and the Meaning of Gender Equality" (2006) 13 *J Public Policy* 420.

Lewis J, "Childcare Policies and the Politics of Choice" (2008) 79 *Political Q* 499.

Lewis J, *Work-Family Balance, Gender and Policy* (Cheltenham, UK/Northampton, MA, USA: Edward Elgar 2010).

Lewis J and Campbell M, "UK work/family Balance Policies and Gender Equality, 1997–2005" (2007) 14 *Social Politics: Intl Studies in Gender, State & Society* 4.

Lewis J and Giullari S, "The Adult Worker Model Family, Gender Equality and Care: The Search for New Policy Principles and the Possibilities and Problems of a Capabilities Approach" (2005) 34 *Economy and Society* 76–104.

Lister R, *Citizenship: Feminist Perspectives* (New York: NYU Press 1997).

Lister R, "Children (But Not Women) First: New Labour, Child Welfare and Gender" (2006) 26 *Critical Social Policy* 315.

Luria Z, "A Methodological Critique" (1986) 11 *Signs: J Women in Culture and Society* 316.

Lutz H and Palenga-Möllenbeck E, "Care Workers, Care Drain, and Care Chains: Reflections on Care, Migration, and Citizenship" (2012) 19 *Social Politics: Intl Studies in Gender, State & Society* 15.

Lynch K, "Affective Equality: Who Cares?" (2009) 52 *Development* 410.

Mackenzie C and Stoljar N (eds), *Relational Autonomy: Feminist Perspectives on Autonomy, Agency, and the Social Self* (Oxford: OUP 2000).

MacKinnon C, "Difference and Dominance: On Sex Discrimination" in Phillips A (ed), *Feminisms and Politics* 295–313 (Oxford: OUP 1998).

Mailand M, "The Uneven Impact of the European Employment Strategy on Member States' Employment Policies: A Comparative Analysis" (2008) 18 *Journal of European Social Policy* 353.

Mancini G and O'Leary S, "The New Frontiers of Sex Equality Law in the European Union" (1999) 24 *ELR* 331.

Mandel H and Semyonov M, "A Welfare State Paradox: State Interventions and Women's Employment Opportunities in 22 Countries" (2006) 111 *Am J Soc* 1910.

Manning A and Petrongolo B, "The Part-Time Pay Penalty for Women in Britain" (2008) 118 *Economic J* F28.

Masselot A, "The Rights and Realities of Balancing Work and Family Life in New Zealand" in Busby N and James G (eds), *Families, Care-Giving and Paid Work: Challenging Labour Law in the 21st Century* 69–85 (Cheltenham, UK/Northampton, MA, USA: Edward Elgar 2010).

Masselot A, "EU Childcare Strategy in Times of Austerity" (2015) 37 *Journal of Social Welfare & Family Law* 345.

Masselot A, "Gender Implications of the Right to Request Flexible Working Arrangements: Raising Pigs and Children in New Zealand" (2015) 39 *New Zealand Journal of Employment Relations* 59.

Masselot A, "Family Leave: Enforcement of the Protection against Dismissal and Unfavourable Treatment" (Luxembourg: European Union 2018) https://equalitylaw.eu/downloads/4808-family-leave-enforcement-of-the-protection-against-dismissal-and-unfavourable-treatment-pdf-962-kb.

Masselot A, "Visions for Gender Equality Post-2020: How to Improve the Interaction between Legal Instruments (EU acquis) and Policy-making (Communication, Funding Programme, European semester)?" in Niall Crowley and Silvia Sansonetti (eds), *New Visions for Gender Equality 2019* (Luxembourg: SAAGE –Scientific Analysis and Advice on Gender Equality in EU, 2019).

Masselot A, "Reformulating Gender Equality in the EU: Social Investment and Childcare as a Central Element of the Economic Recovery" in Canelas de Castro P (ed), *60 Years after the Treaties of Rome: What Is the Future for the European Union?* (Macau: University of Macau Publication, 2020).

Masselot A and Bullock J, "Intersectional Aspirations in the EU Anti-Discrimination Legal Framework" 1 and 2 (2012–2013) *Australian and New Zealand J European Studies* 3.

Masselot A, Caracciolo di Torella E and Burri S, *Thematic Report of the European Network of Legal Experts in the Field of Gender Equality "Fighting Discrimination on the Grounds of Pregnancy, Maternity and Parenthood – The Application of EU and National Law in Practice in 33 European countries"* (Luxembourg: European Commission 2012).

Masselot A and Maymont A, "Gendering Economic and Financial Governance through Positive Action Measures: Compatibility of the French Real Equality Measure under the European Union Framework" (2015) 22 *MJ* 57.

Mattson D and Clark S, "Human Dignity in Concept and Practice" (2011) 44 *Policy Sciences* 303.

Mayeroff M, *On Caring* (New York: HarperCollins Publishers 1972).

McGlynn C, "Ideologies of Motherhood in European Community Sex Discrimination" (2000) 6 *European Law Journal* 29.

Meszarors G and Moss P, *Employment and Family Life: A Review of Research in the UK (1980–1994)* (London: Employment Department 1994).

Meyers C, "Cruel Choices: Autonomy and Critical Care Decision-Making" (2004) 18 *Bioethics* 104.

Meyers M, Gornick J and Ross K, "Public Childcare, Parental Leave and Employment" in Sainsbury D (ed), *Gender and Welfare State Regimes* 117–147 (Oxford: OUP 1999).

Mills M and others, *Use of Childcare Services in the EU Member States and Progress Towards the Barcelona Targets (Short Statistical Report 1)* (Luxembourg: European Union 2014).

Miranda V, "Cooking, Caring and Volunteering: Unpaid Work around the World" *OECD Social, Employment and Migration Working Papers No. 116* (Geneva: OECD Publishing, 2011).

Miranda V, "*Unpaid Work of Older Adults in OECD Countries*" (Social Situation Observatory, 29 November 2011).

Moebius I and Szyszczack E, "Of Raising Pigs and Children" (1998) 18 *YEL* 125.

Molinier P, *L'Enigme De La Femme Active* (Paris: Payot 2003).

Molinier P, "Quel Est Le Bon Témoin Du *Care*?" in Molinier P, Laugier S and Paperman P (eds), *Qu'est-ce Que Le Care? Souci Des Autres, Sensibilité, Responsabilité* 233–251 (Paris: Petite Bibliothèque Payot 2009).

Molinier P, Laugier S and Paperman P, "Introduction: Qu'est-ce Que Le Care?" in Molinier P, Laugier S and Paperman P (eds), *Qu'est-ce Que Le Care? Souci Des Autres, Sensibilité, Résponsibilité* 7–34 (Paris: Payot et Rivages 2009).

Montanari I, Nelson K and Palme J, "Towards a European Social Model? Trends in Social Insurance among EU Countries 1980–2000" (2008) 10 *European Societies* 787.

184 Bibliography

Moon G and Allen R, "Dignity Discourse in Discrimination Law: A Better Route to Equality?" (2006) 6 *EHRLR* 610.

More G, "The Principle of Equal Treatment: From Market Unifier to Fundamental Right?" in Craig P and de Búrca G (eds), 517–553 *The Evolution of EU Law* (Oxford: OUP 1999).

Moreau, MP and Robertson M, "You Scratch My Back and I'll Scratch Yours'? Support to Academics Who Are Carers in Higher Education" (2019) 8(6) *Social Sciences* 164.

Morgan K and Zippel K, "Paid to Care: The Origins and Effects of Care Leave Policies in Western Europe" (2003) 10 *Social Politics: Intl Studies in Gender, State & Society* 49.

Morgan P and Berkowitz King R, "Why Have Children in the 21st Century? Biological Predisposition, Social Coercion, Rational Choice" (2001) 17 *European Journal of Population/Revue Européenne de Démographie* 3.

Mortari L, *Filosofia Della Cura* (Milan: Raffaello Cortina 2015).

Mosher J and Trubek D, "Alternative Approaches to Governance in the EU: EU Social Policy and the European Employment Strategy" (2003) 41 *J Common Market Studies* 63.

Moss P and Deven F (eds), *Parental Leave: Progress or Pitfall?: Research and Policy Issues in Europe* vol. 35 (Brussels: NIDI/CBGS Publications 1999).

Müller K, Neuman M and Wrohlich K, "The Family Working-Time Model: Towards More Gender Equality in Work and Care" (2018) 28 *Journal of European Social Policy* 471.

Mullin A, "Parents and Children: An Alternative to Selfless and Unconditional Love" (2006) 21 *Hypatia* 181.

Munro V, *Law and Politics and the Perimeter: Re-Evaluating Key Debates in Feminist Theory* (Oxford, UK/Portland, Oregon, USA: Hart Publishing 2007).

Nakano Glenn E, "From Servitude to Service Work: Historical Continuities in the Racial Division of Paid Reproductive Labor" (1992) 18 *Signs: J Women in Culture and Society* 1.

Naldini M and Saraceno C, *Conciliare Famiglia E Lavoro* (Bologna: Il Mulino 2011).

Nelson J, "Of Market and Martyrs: Is It OK to Pay Well for Care?" (1999) 5 *Feminist Economics* 43.

Nelson J and Folbre N, "Why a Well-paid Nurse Is a Better Nurse!" (2006) 24 *Journal of Nursing Economics* 127.

Nicole B and James G (eds), *Care Giving and Paid Work: Challenging Labour Law in the 21st Century* (Cheltenham, UK/Northampton, MA, USA: Edward Elgar 2011).

Nielsen R and Szyszcsak E, *The Social Dimension of the European Union* (Copenhagen: Handelshøjskolens Forlag 1997).

Noddings N, *Caring: A Feminine Approach to Ethics and Moral Education* (Berkley, Los Angeles, London: University of California Press 1984).

Nolan M, Grant G and Keady J, *Understanding Family Care: A Multidimensional Model of Caring and Coping* (Buckingham/Philadelphia: Open University Press 1996).

Numhauser-Henning A (ed), *Elder Law: Evolving European Perspectives* (Cheltenham: Edward Elgar 2017).

Numhauser-Henning A and Rönmar M (eds), *Normative Patterns and Legal Developments in the Social Dimension of the EU* (Oxford, UK/Portland, Oregon, USA: Hart Publishing 2013).

Nussbaum M, "Human Capabilities, Female Human Beings" in Nussbaum M and Glover J (eds), *Women, Culture and Development: A Study of Human Capabilities* 61–104 (Oxford: OUP 1995).

Nussbaum M, *Sex and Social Justice* (Oxford: OUP 1999).
Nussbaum M, *Upheavals of Thought: The Intelligence of Emotions* (Cambridge: CUP 2001a).
Nussbaum M, *Women and Human Development: The Capabilities Approach* vol. 3 (Cambridge: CUP 2001).
Nussbaum M, "Capabilities and Social Justice" (2002) 4 *Intl Studies Rev* 123.
Nussbaum M, "Capabilities as Fundamental Entitlements: Sen and Social Justice" (2003) 9 *Feminist Economics* 33.
Nussbaum M, "Care, Dependency, and Social Justice: A Challenge to Conventional Ideas of the Social Contract" in Lloyd-Sherlock P (ed), *Living Longer: Ageing, Development and Social Protection* 275–299 (London: Zed Books 2004).
O'Brien C, "Confronting the Care Penalty: The Cause for Extending Reasonable Adjustment Rights along the Disability/Care Continuum" (2012) 34 *Journal of Social Welfare & Family Law* 5.
O'Brien M, "Fitting Fathers into Work-family Policies: International Challenges in Turbulent Times" (2013) 33 *Intl Journal of Sociology and Social Policy* 542.
O'Donovan K, *Sexual Division in Law* (London: Weidenfield and Nicholson 1984).
Office for National Statistics, "Working and Workless Households, 2013 – Statistical Bulletin" (2013) http://ons.gov.uk/ons/dcp171778_325269.pdf.
Office for National Statistics, "Sustainable Development Indicators" (July 2015) https://ons.gov.uk/peoplepopulationandcommunity/wellbeing/datasets/sustainabledevelopmentindicators.
Ohlin B, "Social Aspects of European Economic Co-operation", Report by the Group of Experts on Social Aspects of Problem of European Economic Co-operation, International Labour Office, Geneva, 1956 Reproduced in (1956) 74 *Intl Lab Rev* 99.
Olsen F, "The Family and the Market: A Study on Ideology and Market Reform" (1993) 96 *Harv L Rev* 1497.
Organisation for Economic Co-Operation and Development (OECD), *Starting Strong: Childhood Education and Carer* (Paris: OECD 2001).
Organisation for Economic Co-Operation and Development (OECD), *Babies and Bosses – Reconciling Work and Family Life: A Synthesis of Findings for OECD Countries* (Paris: OECD 2007).
Organisation for Economic Co-Operation and Development (OECD), *Gender Equality in Education and Entrepreneurship: Final Report to the MCM 2012* (Paris: OECD 2012).
Organisation for Economic Co-Operation and Development (OECD), *Health at a Glance 2013: OECD Indicators* (Paris: OECD 2013).
Organisation for Economic Co-Operation and Development (OECD), *Balancing Paid Work, Unpaid Work and Leisure* (Paris: OECD 2018).
Organisation for Economic Co-Operation and Development (OECD), and Asia-Pacific Economic Cooperation (APEC), "Anticipating Special Needs of the 21st Century Silver Economy" (OECD-APEC Joint Workshop, Tokyo, September 2012) http://oecd.org/sti/silver-economy-facts-challenges-and-opportunities.htm.
Orloff A, "Should Feminists Aim for Gender Symmetry? Why the Dual-earner/Dual Care Model May Not Be Every Feminist's Utopia" in Gornick J and Meyers M (eds), *Institutions for Gender Egalitarianism: Creating the Conditions for Egalitarian Dual Earner/Dual Caregiver Families* 129–160 (London, UK/Brooklyn, NY, USA: Verso 2009).

Osborne G, "Women at Work and Childcare" (speech, 27 February 2006) http://toryspeeches.files.wordpress.com/2013/11/osborne-women-at-work-and-childcare.pdf.

Parreñas R, *Servants of Globalization: Women, Migration and Domestic Work* (Stanford: Stanford University Press 2001).

Parreñas R, "The Care Crisis in the Philippines: Children and Transnational Families in the New Global Economy" in Ehrenreich B and Hochschild A (eds), *Global Woman: Nannies, Maids, and Sex Workers in the New Economy* 39–54 (London: Macmillan 2003).

Pavolini E and others, "From Austerity to Permanent Strain? The EU and Welfare State Reform in Italy and Spain" (2015) 13 *Comparative European Politics* 56.

Pfau-Effinger B, "Socio Historical Paths of the Male Breadwinner Model – An Explanation of Cross National Differences" (2004) 55 *British Journal of Sociology* 377.

Pfau-Effinger B, "Welfare State Policies and the Development of Care Arrangements" (2005) 7 *European Societies* 321.

Pfau-Effinger B and Geissler B, *Care and Social Integration in European Societies* (Bristol: Policy Press 2005).

Pickard L, "A Growing Care Gap? The Supply of Unpaid Care for Older People by Their Adult Children in England to 2032" (2015) 35 *Ageing and Society* 96.

Pickard S and Glendinning C, "Comparing and Contrasting the Role of Family Carers and Nurses in the Domestic Health Care of Frail Older People" (2002) 10 *Health and Social Care in the Community* 144.

Pilgerstorfer M and Forshaw S, "Transferred Discrimination in European Law" (2008) 37 *Industrial Law Journal* 384.

Plantenga J and Remery C, *The Provision of Childcare Services: A Comparative Review of 30 European Countries* (Luxembourg: Office for Official Publications of the European Communities 2009).

Prechal S, "Equality of Treatment, Non-discrimination and Social Policy: Achievements in Three Themes" (2004) 41 *CML Rev* 533.

Quinlan M, "The 'Pre-invention' of Precarious Employment: The Changing World of Work in Context" (2012) 23 *Economic and Labour Relations Rev* 3.

Radulova E, "The Construction of EU's Childcare Policy through the Open Method of Coordination" in Kröger S (ed), *What We Have Learnt: Advances, Pitfalls and Remaining Questions in OMC Research* 1–20 (Vienna: EIOP 2009) vol. 13 http://eiop.or.at/eiop/texte/2009-013a.htm.

Ray R, Gornick J and Schmitt J, "Who Cares? Assessing Generosity and Gender Equality in Parental Leave Policy Designs in 21 Countries" (2010) 20 *Journal of European Social Policy* 196.

Raz J, "Legal Rights" (1984) 4 *Journal of Legal Studies* 1.

Raz J, *The Morality of Freedom* (Oxford: OUP 1986).

Recommendation of the Committee of Ministers to Member States on the Council of Europe Action Plan to promote the rights and full participation of people with disabilities in society: improving the quality of life of people with disabilities in Europe 2006–2015, Rec(2006) 5.

Reece H, *Divorcing Responsibilities* (Oxford, UK/Portland, Oregon, USA: Hart Publishing 2003).

Rhode D, *Justice and Gender* (Cambridge, Massachusetts, USA: Harvard University Press 1991).

Richardt N, "European Employment Strategy, Childcare, Welfare State Redesign: Germany and the United Kingdom Compared" (Conference of Europeanists, Chicago, March 2004) http://citeseerx.ist.psu.edu/viewdoc/download;jsessionid=5557F1338491134E9272F3C8FEEAD63A?doi=10.1.1.497.9971&rep=rep1&type=pdf.

Riley JW, *Poems & Prose Sketches* (Portable Poetry 2007).

Rindfuss R and others, "Child Care Availability and First-birth Timing in Norway" (2007) 44 *Demography* 345.

Robeyns I, "Sen's Capability Approach and Gender Inequality: Selecting Relevant Capabilities" (2003) 9 *Feminist Economics* 61.

Rodgers L, "Labour Law and Vulnerability" in Bedford D and Herring J (eds), *Embracing Vulnerability: The Implications and Challenges for Law* (London: Routledge 2020).

Rodrigues R, Huber M and Lamura G (eds), "Facts and Figures on Healthy Ageing and Long-term Care: Europe and North America" (European Centre for Social Welfare Policy and Research 2012).

Rostgaard T, "Caring for Children and Older People in Europe – A Comparison of European Policies and Practice" (2002) 32 *Policy Studies* 51.

Rubery J, "Gender Mainstreaming and Gender Equality in the EU: The Impact of the EU Employment Strategy" (2002) 33 *Industrial Relations J* 500.

Rubery J and Fagan C, "Equal Opportunities and Employment in the European Union" (Federal Ministry of Labour, Health and Social Affairs 1998).

Rubery J and Rafferty A, "Women and Recession Revisited" (2013) 27 *Work, Employment & Society* 414.

Rubio E, "A Policy in its Infancy: The Case for Strengthening and Rethinking EU Action on Childhood" (Brusssels: Notre Europe 2007).

Ruddick S, "Care as Labor and Relationship" in Haber J and Haflon M (eds), *Norms and Values: Essays on the Work of Virginia Held* 3–25 (Lanham, Maryland, USA/Oxford, UK: Rowman & Littlefield 1998).

Ruddick S, "Maternal Thinking" (1980) 6 *Feminist Studies* 342.

Ruth M, "Work-Life Balance: A Case of Technical Disempowerment?" (2009) 16 *Social Politics: Intl Studies in Gender, State and Society* 111.

Rutter J and Evans B, *Informal Childcare: Choice or Chance? A Literature Review* (London: Daycare Trust 2011).

Ryrstedt E, "Dementia and Autonomy" in Numhauser-Henning A (ed), *Elder Law: Evolving European Perspectives* 358–378 (Cheltenham, UK/Northampton, MA, USA: Edward Elgar 2017).

Saint-Exupéry A, *Le Petit Prince* (Paris: Gallimard 1946).

Sandler M, "The Procedural Republic and the Unencumbered Self" (1984) 12 *Political Theory* 81.

Saraceno C, "Childcare Needs and Childcare Policies: A Multidimensional Issue" (2011) 59 *Current Sociology* 78.

Saraceno C and Wolfgang K, "Can We Identify Intergenerational Policy Regimes in Europe?" (2010) 12 *European Societies* 675.

Schiek D and Chege V, *European Union Non-Discrimination Law: Comparative Perspectives on Multidimensional Equality Law* (London: Routledge Cavendish 2009).

Schiek D and Lawson A (eds), *European Union Non-Discrimination Law and Intersectionality: Investigating the Triangle of Racial, Gender and Disability Discrimination* (Aldershot, England/Burlington, USA: Ashgate Publishing 2013).

Schiek D, Waddington L and Bell M, *Cases, Materials and Text on National, Supranational and International Non Discrimination Law* (Oxford, UK/Portland, Oregon, USA: Hart Publishing 2007).

Schroeder M, "Compassion on Appeal" (1990) 22 *Ariz St L J* 45.

Schultz V, "Life's Work" (2000) 100 *Colum L Rev* 1881.

Scott J, "Family and Gender Roles: How Attitudes are Changing" (2006) 15 *Arxius De Ciències Socials* 143.

Seatzu F, "Reshaping EU Old Age Law in the Light of Normative Standards in International Human Rights Law in Relation to Older Person" in Ippolito F and Sánchez SI (eds), *Protecting Vulnerable Groups: The European Human Rights Framework* 49–70 (Oxford, UK/Portland, Oregon, USA: Hart Publishing 2015).

Sen A, *Commodities and Capabilities* (Oxford: OUP 1987).

Sen A, *Inequality Re-examined* (Cambridge, MA: Harvard University Press 1992).

Sen A, "Capability and Well-being" in Hausman M (ed), *The Philosophy of Economics* 30–53 (Cambridge: CUP 1993).

Sen A, "Gender Inequality and Theories of Justice" in Nussbaum M and Glover J (eds), *Women, Culture, and Development: A Study of Human Capabilities: A Study of Human Capabilities* 259–273 (Oxford: OUP 1995).

Sen A, *Development as Freedom* (Oxford/New York: Alfred Knopf 1999).

Sen A, "Human Rights and Capabilities" (2005) 6 *J Human Development* 151.

Sen A, "Equality of What?" in MacMurrin S (ed), *The Tanner Lectures on Human Values* 4 2nd edn 195–220 (Cambridge: CUP 2010).

Sen A, *The Idea of Justice* (Cambridge, MA: Harvard University Press 2011).

Sen A and Hawthorn G, *The Standard of Living* (Cambridge: CUP 1988).

Sevenhuijsen S, *Citizenship and the Ethics of Care: Feminist Considerations on Justice, Morality, and Politics* (Amsterdam: Psychology Press 1998).

Sevenhuijsen S, "Care as a Good for Social Policy" (2002) 31 *Journal of Social Policy* 251.

Sevenhuijsen S, "The Place of Care: The Relevance of the Feminist Ethic of Care for Social Policy" (2003) 4 *Feminist Theory* 179.

Shaw J, "Citizenship of the Union: Towards Post-National Membership" in Academy of European Law (ed), *Collected Course of the Academy of European Law* vol. VI Book I 237–387 (AH Alphen aan den Rijn: Kluwer International Law 1998).

Shortell S and Kaluzny A, *Health Care Management: Organization, Design and Behavior* (Clifton Park, NY, USA: Delmar Publishers 1994).

Simon G and others, "Randomised Trial of Monitoring, Feedback, and Management of Care by Telephone to Improve Treatment of Depression in Primary Care" (2000) 320 *BMJ* 550.

Slack K and Fraser M, "Husband, Partner, Dad, Son, Carer? – A Survey of the Experiences and Needs of Male Carers" (Carers Trust 2014).

Slavinia S and others, "*Challenges in Long-Term Care in Europe: A Study of National Policies*" (European Commission 2018).

Smart C, "The Legal and Moral Ordering of Child Custody" (1991) 18 *J L and Society* 485.

Smart C, "Losing the Struggle from Another Voice: The Case for Family Law" (1995) 15 *Dal L J* 173.

Bibliography 189

Smart C, *Personal Life: New Directions in Sociological Thinking* (Cambridge: Polity Press 2007).
Smith M and Villa P, "The Ever-Declining Role of Gender Equality in the European Employment Strategy" (2010) 41 *Industrial Relations J* 526.
Soares A, *Les (In)visibles De La Santé* (Montréal: Université du Québec à Montréal 2010).
Social Protection Committee and the European Commission Services, "Adequate Social Protection for Long Term Care Needs in an Ageing Society" (Luxembourg: European Union 2014).
Social Protection Committee and the European Commission, Adequate Social Protection for Long-Term Care Needs in an Aging Society, 18 June 2014, 10406/14 ADD 1; SOC 403 ECOFIN 525.
Social Protection Committee, "Social Europe – Aiming for inclusive growth – Annual report of the Social Protection Committee on the social situation in the European Union (2014)" (European Union, 10 March 2015), http://ec.europa.eu/social/main.jsp?catId=738&langId=en&pubId=7744.
Sohrab J, "Avoiding the 'Exquisite Trap': A Critical Look at the Equal Treatment/Special Treatment Debate in Law" (1993) 1 *Feminist Legal Studies* 141.
Solera C and Bettio F, "Women's Continuous Careers in Italy: The Education and Public Sector Divide" (2013) 52 *Population Rev* 129.
Sparreboom T, "Gender Equality, Part-time Work and Segregation in Europe" (2014) 153 *Intl Labour Review* 245.
Spitz L, "Grandparents: Their Role in the 21st Century Families" (2012) 42 *Family L* 1254.
Stack C, "The Culture of Gender: Women and Men of Color" (1986) 11 *Signs: J Women in Culture and Society* 321.
Stalford H and Drywood E, "Coming of Age? Children's Rights in the European Union" (2009) 46 *CML Rev* 143.
Stone D, "For Love nor Money: The Commodification of Care" in Ertman M and Williams J (eds), *Rethinking Commodification: Cases and Readings in Law and Culture* 271–290 (New York: NYU Press 2005).
Stratigaki M, "The European Union and the Equal Opportunities Process" in Hantrais L (ed), *Gendered Policies in Europe: Reconciling Employment and Family Life* 27–48 (London New York: Macmillan and St. Martin's Press 2000).
Streeck W, "From Market Making to State Building? Reflections on the Political Economy of the European Social Policy" in Liebfried S and Pierson P (eds), 389–430 *European Social Policy: Between Fragmentation and Integration* (Washington, DC, USA: Brookings 1995a).
Streeck W, "Neo-Voluntarism: A New Social Policy Regime" (1995) 1 *European Law Journal* 31.
Susan M-O, *Justice, Gender and the Family* (Princeton: Basic Books 1998).
Täht K and Mills M, "Nonstandard Work Schedules, Couple Desynchronization, and Parent–Child Interaction: A Mixed-methods Analysis" (2012) 33 *J Family Issues* 1054.
Taylor-Gooby P, "New Risks and Social Changes" in Taylor-Gooby P (ed), *New Risks, New Welfare; the Transformation of the European Welfare State* 1–28 (Oxford: OUP 2004).
Tempest M, "Tories Reach Out to Young Mothers" *The Guardian* (London, 27 February 2006) www.theguardian.com/politics/2006/feb/27/conservatives.gender.

Therborn G, *Between Sex and Power: Family in the World, 1900–2000* (London/New York: Routledge 2004).
Thomson M, "Social Regimes and Gender Equality: Childcare in the EU – Parenting and Democracy in Contemporary Europe" in Mayes D and Thomson M (eds), *The Cost of Children* 27–45 (Cheltenham, UK/Northampton, MA, USA: Edward Elgar 2012).
Thornton M (ed), *Public and Private: Feminists Legal Debates* (Oxford: OUP 1995).
Thornton M, 'Work/life or Work/work? Corporate Legal Practice in the Twenty-first Century' (2016) 23 *Intl J Legal Profession* 13.
Tolmie J, Elizabeth V and Gavey N, "Imposing Gender Neutral Standards on a Gendered World: Parenting Arrangements in Family Law Post Separation" (2010) 16 *Canta L R* 302.
Towers J and Walby S, "Measuring the Impact of Cuts in Public Expenditure on the Provision of Services to Prevent Violence against Women" (Report for Northern Rock Foundation and Trust for London, 30 January 2012) http://eprints.lancs.ac.uk/55165/1/Measuring_the_impact_of_cuts_in_public_expenditure_on_the_provision_of_services_to_prevent_violence_against_women_and_girls_Full_report_3.pdf.
Tronto J, "Beyond Gender Difference to a Theory of Care" (1987) 12 *Signs: J Women in Culture and Society* 644.
Tronto J, *Moral Boundaries: A Political Argument for an Ethic of Care* (London/New York: Routledge 1993).
Tronto J, "The Value of Care" (*Boston Review*, 6 February 2002). http://bostonreview.net/BR27.1/tronto.html
Tronto J, "*Care* Démocratique Et Démocratie Du *Care*" in Molinier P, Laugier S and Paperman P (eds), *Qu'est-ce Que Le Care? Souci Des Autres, Sensibilité, Résponsibilité* 35–56 (Paris: Payot et Rivages 2009).
Trubek DM and Trubek LG, "Hard and Soft Law in the Construction of Social Europe: The Role of the Open Method of Co-ordination" (2005) 11 *European Law Journal* 343.
Tryfonidou A, "In Search of the Aim of the EC Free Movement of Persons Provisions: Has the Court of Justice Missed the Point?" (2009) 46 *CML Rev* 1591.
Twigg J, "Care Work as a Form of Body Work" (2000) 20 *Ageing and Society* 389.
Twigg J, *The Body in Health and Social Care* (Basingstoke: Palgrave McMillian 2006).
Ungerson C, "Cash in Care" in Harrington MM (ed), *Care Work: Gender, Labor and the Welfare State* 69–88 (London/New York: Routledge 2000).
UNICEF, *Child Poverty in Rich Countries*, Innocenti Report Card num 6, UNICEF, (Florence: Innocenti Research Centre 2005).
Velluti S, *New Governance and the European Employment Strategy* (London/New York: Routledge 2010).
Verbeek-Oudijk D and others, "Who Cares in Europe? A Comparison of Long-term Care for the Over 50s in Sixteen European Countries" (The Hague: Netherlands Institute for Social Research 2014).
Vigerust E, *Arbeid, Barn Og Likestilling* (Oslo: Tano Ashehoug 1998).
Villa P and Smith M, "Policy in the Time of Crisis: Employment Policy and Gender Equality in Europe" in Karamessini M and Rubery J (eds), *Women and Austerity: The Economic Crisis and the Future for Gender Equality* 273–294 (London/New York: Routledge 2014).
Visser J, "Neither Convergence nor Frozen Paths: Bounded Learning, International Diffusion of Reforms, and the Open Method of Coordination" in Heidenreich M and Zeitlin J (eds), *Changing European Employment and Welfare Regimes: The*

Influence of the Open Method of Coordination on National Reforms 37–60 (London/New York: Routledge 2009).
Vosko L, *Managing the Margins* (Oxford: OUP 2010).
Vosko L, MacDonald M and Campbell I (eds), *Gender and the Contours of Precarious Employment* (London/New York: Routledge 2010).
Waddington L, "Carers, Gender and Employment Discrimination: What Does EU Law Offer Europe's Carers" in Moreau M (ed), *Before and After the Economic Crisis: What Implications for the 'European Social Model'?* 101–128 (Cheltenham, UK/Northampton, MA, USA: Edward Elgar 2011).
Waddington L, and Hendriks A, "Expanding Concept of Employment Discrimination in Europe: From Direct and Indirect Discrimination to Reasonable Accommodation Discrimination" (2002) 18(4) *The International Journal of Comparative Labour Law & Industrial Relations* 403–427.
Walby S, "Enquête on the Current Financial Crisis: The UK" (2012) 14 *European Societies* 151.
Walby S, *Crisis* (Cambridge: Polity 2015).
Waldron J, *Theories of Rights* (Oxford: OUP 1984).
Walker M, "Amartya Sen's Capability Approach and Education" (2005) 13 *Educational Action Research* 103.
Wallbank J and Herring J, "Introduction: Vulnerabilities, Care and Family Law" in Wallbank J and Herring J (eds), *Vulnerability Care and Family Law* 1–21 (London/New York: Routledge 2014).
Wallbank J and Herring J (eds), *Vulnerability Care and Family Law* (London/New York: Routledge 2014).
Ward A, "A Judicial Perspective on the Place for Compassion in Family Law" (*Institute for Advance Legal Studies Symposium Compassion: Child and Family Law*, 13 July 2017).
Waring M, *Counting for Nothing: What Men Value and What Women are Worth* (Sydney: Allen and Unwin 1988).
West R, "Jurisprudence and Gender" (1988) 55 *U Chi L Rev* 1.
West R, *Caring for Justice* (New York: NYU Press 1999).
Westen P, "The Empty Idea of Equality" (1982) 95 Harv L Rev 537.
Wiggan J, "Telling Stories of 21st Century Welfare: The UK Coalition Government and the Neo-Liberal Discourse of Worklessness and Dependency" (2012) 32 *Critical Social Policy* 383.
Williams F, "The Presence of Feminism in the Future of Welfare" (2002) 31 *Economy and Society* 502.
Williams F, "A Good-Enough Life: Developing the Grounds for A Political Ethic of Care" (2005) 30 *Soundings* 17.
Williams J, *Unbending Gender: Why Family and Work Conflict and What to Do about It* (Oxford: OUP 2000).
Williams J, *Reshaping the Work-Family Debate* (Cambridge, Massachusetts, USA: Harvard University Press 2010).
Windebank J and Whitworth A, "Social Welfare and the Ethics of Austerity in Europe: Justice, Ideology and Equality" (2014) 22 *J Contemporary European Studies* 99.
Wittgenstein L, *Philosophical Investigations* (Chichester: Blackwell 1953).
Zbyszewska A, "Reshaping EU Working-Time Regulation: Towards a More Sustainable Regime" (2016) 7 *ELLJ* 331.
Zeitlin J and Vanhercke B, "Socializing the European Semester: EU Social and Economic Policy Co-ordination in Crisis and Beyond" (2017) 25 *J European Public Policy* 149.

Index

24/7 society 19, 35
2008 financial crisis 31–32, 64, 73–75, 88, 119, 152

absence of choice, as marker of caring relationship 9, 17–19, 143
access to care services 78, 95–96, 117
accountability of care 49–52
accounting for care 10, 50, 88, 152, 156
activation policies 22
adult care *see* long-term care (LTC)
affirmative action 35
affordability 55, 65, 69, 73, 78, 87, 96, 97, 123
ageing society 3, 19, 21, 83–85, 89, 93, 134, 147
Agency Work Directive 124
altruism 51
Amsterdam Treaty 68–69, 107, 108, 110
anti-discrimination law 37, 104–116, 128, 132
anti-social behaviour 61
Aristotle 105
associative discrimination 112–116
attachment 51
atypical work patterns 43–44, 124, 149
Augustine, St 44
austerity policies 32, 74, 77, 88, 101
autonomy: capability approach 42; and carers' rights 137; and the caring relationship 30; and choice 30; economic independence 58, 153; enabling recipient of care to have 8; long-term care (LTC) 95; policy making based around 47; relational autonomy 30; rights based around 27, 29–30; "weighted" autonomy 40
awareness-raising initiatives 151

Barcelona Council (2002) 63, 64, 70, 71, 73, 76, 77
bargaining powers 44
basic/human needs 24, 38, 42, 93
Becker, Gary 59
birth rates 19, 59–60, 84
borders, care transcends national 20–21, 92, 153–154
Borg, Tonio 102
brain-drain 21
breastfeeding 37, 118
Brexit 3
Busby, Nicole 44
business case for EU engagement in care 22–23
business organisations, care as overarching principle 5

capability approach 28, 38–52
capitalism, reliant on unpaid care 31
care crisis 19, 21–22, 34, 153
care feminism 36–37, 56
care jobs, creation of 76
"care penalty" 10
care support/care strategy measures 116
care-drain 21
care-gap 91
carers: caring for the carers 87, 91; defining 7, 138–144; future legal framework of 131–152; human dignity of 133; legal framework 100–129, 131–152, 154–155; non-discrimination and equality 104–116; numbers of 100; rights 137–151; strain placed on 102; support of 91
carers allowance 87n27
carers' leave 102–103, 117, 118, 122–127, 139, 142, 146–148
"caring about" versus "caring for" 5–6

Index

caring penalty 102
cash benefits 33
Cavaghan, Rosalind 65–66
Charter of Fundamental Rights (CFR) 1, 49, 97, 99, 105, 111, 116, 133, 134, 135, 137
child benefit 78
child poverty 19, 60–61, 78
child protection 55
childcare 53–82; "caring about" versus "caring for" 6; and children's rights 60–61, 75–81; defining 54–67; and the definition of carer 139; development history of EU strategy 67–81; differently regulated to long-term care 154; diversity across Member States 54–55; economic rationality 57–58; emerging EU strategy 53–82; fathers 16, 36, 142; and female paid employment 40; formal childcare 54–55, 71; full-time childcare 71; and gender equality 56–57; as a gendered activity 13–15; governance 61–67; institutional childcare 36; market orientations of 33; Member States responsibilities 53, 64, 72–73, 77, 82; vs. other types of care 11–13, 154; quantitative targets 62, 72; seen as service for women 75; supply-side versus demand-side considerations 72–73; targets for 70–71, 73; *see also* informal care arrangements
childcare facilities 19; *see also* formal childcare
Childcare Recommendation 1992 68
children's rights 60–61, 75–81
children's services 61
choice: absence of choice, as marker of caring relationship 9, 17–19, 143; and autonomy 30; capability approach 28; choice to care 17–19, 29, 143
Choudry, Shazia 29
chronically ill people *see* long-term care (LTC)
civil society 30, 151
cleaning 11
Clements, Luke 104
collaboration 50
Commission Communications 61, 65, 67n79, 77, 79, 82, 98, 103, 131, 150–151

Commission Roadmap 103
commodification of work 20, 21
Community First Action programme 67n79
community-based services 87
company/emotional support 87
compassion 45, 47–49, 135, 144
concepts of care 3–19
Confronting demographic change: a new solidarity between the generations (European Commission Green Paper) 134
consequentialism 45
constant ongoing responsibilities, as marker of caring relationship 8, 143–144
Convention on Workers with Family Responsibilities (ILO) 136
cooking 11, 87
core values, EU 64, 80–81, 97, 105, 134, 150, 152
Cosmas, Advocate General 102
costs of childrearing 59
Council Employment Guidelines 69
Council of the EU 2, 53, 61, 69, 76, 91–92
Court of Justice of the European Union (CJEU): care generally 20; carers 102, 111, 112, 113–114, 127, 128, 140–142, 144; and the Charter of Fundamental Rights 135; childcare 53–54, 64, 72; definition of carer 140–142, 144; definition of workers 143; economic rights versus social rights 31; emerging "care policy" 2; human dignity 133; indirect discrimination 107; leave provisions 120, 122; long-term care (LTC) 83; non-discrimination and equality 105–106; part-time employment 126; pregnancy 37, 145; work-life balance 39
Court of Session 113
cross-border elements of care 20–21, 92, 153–154
cultural attitudes 32–33, 150–151
culture of dependency 58

daily living activities 86, 87
Daly, Mary 7, 24, 79
data collection 55, 71, 94, 97, 151
definitions of care 3–19
democracy 38

Index

demographics 13–19, 59–60, 83–85, 89–90, 134, 147
deontological morality 45
dependency, as part of human existence 42, 58
dependency in old age 84–85, 92
developmental psychology 44–45
dignity 12–13, 24–25, 29, 43, 47–49, 97, 132–133, 144
diplomacy 50
direct discrimination 105–106, 107, 114, 145
disability 12, 86, 97, 111–113, 115–116, 135, 142, 144–145; *see also* long-term care (LTC)
Disability Rights Commission 147n99
disadvantaged children 61
discrimination: associative discrimination 112–116; carers 104–116, 124–125, 128, 138, 145, 157; direct discrimination 105–106, 107, 114, 145; discrimination by association 112–116; EU policies 23; indirect discrimination 105–106, 107, 109, 114–115, 125, 145; non-discrimination and equality 37, 104–116, 128, 132, 137, 138; part-time work 44; rights 44; sex discrimination 37, 111, 113, 125; *see also* gender equality
divorce 15
DIY 11
domestic tasks, equal sharing of 57, 64, 77, 79, 80, 119n119
dominant ideology of motherhood 80
dual earner/carer model 39–40, 41, 52, 58
duties, and rights 29
duty of care in tort law 5
Dworkin, Ronald 112

early education 61, 78
early interventions 61
economic activity: business case for EU engagement in care 22–23; caring falls outside of 19–20; childcare as economically productive 12; reliant on unpaid care 31; *see also* paid employment; unpaid care
economic independence 58
economic rationality: and care 19; and childcare 57–58, 71–72, 78; and the definition of carer 140; definitions of work 143; and human dignity 133; labour reform 129; long-term care (LTC) 91; Part-Time Work Directive 126; welfare 74
economic rights 31
education 54–55, 61, 78
eldercare, definition 85n17; *see also* long-term care (LTC)
emergency care 55, 72, 96, 117–118, 122–127, 146, 147
emotions: caring requires 7, 8; and compassion 47; emotional costs of caring 9–10; emotional wellbeing 49; emotionally sensitive personal connections 10, 144; law does not acknowledge emotional work 51–52; reconciling with rationality 52
empathy 45, 47
Employment Guidelines 69
employment law: business case for EU engagement in care 22–23; development history of EU childcare strategy 68–69; focus of book on 5; future legal framework for care 131, 142; historical development of EU 62–63; and legal aspects of care 4; women in paid employment 5; *see also* full-time employment; paid employment; part-time employment; precarious work
Employment Title (Treaty of Amsterdam) 68–69
Employment Tribunals 113
endurance 8
equal opportunity agenda 68–69, 72
equality: definitions of 105; equality legislation 115; equality promotion versus discrimination prohibition 105; formal equality 35, 105; protected characteristics 112–113, 114; substantive equality 35, 105, 145; *see also* gender equality
ethic of care 19, 28, 44–52, 79, 93, 132, 135–136, 144, 150, 157
ethic of justice 44
ethnicity 30, 34, 114–115
Eurobarometer 87n28
Europe 2020 Strategy 22, 57, 63, 64, 66, 76–77, 81, 89, 102
European Childcare Network 67
European Commission: carers 102–103; childcare 53, 65, 67, 70–71, 76, 94; concepts of care 15, 33; future

legal framework for care 134, 135; long-term care (LTC) 92; New Start Initiative 79–80; Social Investment Package (SIP) 77
European Convention on Human Rights (ECHR) 48, 136, 141, 157
European Court of Human Rights (ECtHR) 136
European Economic Area (EEA) 32
European Economic Community (EEC) Treaty 1, 108
European Employment Strategy (EES) 22, 62–63, 66, 69, 71
European Pact for Gender Equality (2011-2020) 76
European Parliament 2, 53, 64, 76, 103, 110
European Pillar of Social Rights (EPSR) 2, 66, 75–76, 80, 82, 87, 97, 99, 103–104, 111, 117, 127, 130–131, 135, 151, 154
European Platform for Investing in Children (EPIC) 76, 78
European Quality of Life Survey (EQLS) 100n4
European Semester 63, 64–66, 78, 95, 155
European Social Fund 65, 67n78
Eurostat 97
Eurozone 64
exchange relationships 9–10

families as bundles of caring relationships 39
family benefits 78
family economics 59
family law 4
family life, right to 136, 141
family reunification 140–141
family structure changes 59, 61, 85, 90, 140
family support 78
family-friendly policies 69; *see also* work-life balance
fathers: "caring about" versus "caring for" children 6; childcare 16; and the definition of carer 140; parental leave 121–122, 142; paternity leave 119–120, 139; primary carer status 142; sharing unpaid care work 36; time spent caring 16
feelings, care is more than 6

feminism: care feminism 36–37, 56; and childcare 66; and children's rights 79; employment feminism 22, 34, 56; feminist analysis of care 33–38, 39, 51–52, 56, 72; feminist political economic analysis 65; public/private dichotomy 30–31
fertility rates 19, 59–60, 84, 90, 153
financial costs of care 9–10
financial mechanisms for governance of care 66–67
Fineman, Martha 11, 15, 30, 39
Fischer, Berenice 6
Fixed-Term Directive 124
flexible working 43, 61, 97, 115n90, 117, 121, 125, 126–127, 144, 148–150
flexicurity 127
Folbre, Nancy 7, 51
force majeure leave provisions 122–127, 147
formal childcare 54–55, 71
formal equality 35, 105
formal long-term care 87, 90, 91, 94–95
frailty 84, 92, 96
Framework Directive 110, 112
France 33, 60
Fredman, Sandra 106
free markets: accounting for care 50; reliant on unpaid care 31; rights based around 27
free movement 20, 139, 141
freedom 42
friends, as carers 140, 146
full-time childcare 71
full-time employment 15, 71, 123–124
functionings (capabilities approach) 41–42
funding: childcare 54; childcare vs. other types of care 12; children's services 61; future legal framework for care 152, 155; long-term care (LTC) 87, 89–90
Future of Work Centenary Initiatives (ILO) 136

Gardner, John 112
gender: care as a gendered activity 13–19, 80, 109; cultural attitude shifts 150–151; flexible working 149–150; gender discrimination 107; gender justice 38–39; gender pay gap 75; gender-based leave provisions

117–118; moral development 45; most "prisoners of love" are women 51; and poverty 16–17; relational autonomy 30; versus sex 111; as social construct 111
gender equality: business case for EU engagement in care 22; capability approach 42; care as overarching principle 5; caregiving as main obstacle to 17; carers 107–110; and childcare 56–57, 66, 71–72, 79, 80; choice to care 18; Court of Justice of the European Union (CJEU) 2; development history of EU childcare strategy 68; economic rationality 108, 152; in EU employment strategies 62; EU institutions 64; Europe 2020 Strategy 77; European Pact for Gender Equality (2011-2020) 76; European Semester 64–65; feminist analysis of care 33–38; and flexicurity 127; fundamental right 108; long-term care (LTC) 97; moral case for EU engagement in care 25; New Start Initiative 80; policy goals/targets 57, 62, 66, 70–71, 73; post-2008 financial crisis 74; rights-based strategy 132, 137–138; sameness/difference debate 33–38; Work-Life Balance Directive 120, 138–144
gender-neutral provisions 57, 110, 117, 126
Gilligan, Carol 7, 28, 44–46, 49
global merchandise, care as 21
globalisation 19, 20, 21–22, 35
Glucksmann, Miriam 9
governance: childcare 61–67; long-term care (LTC) 96
grandparents 55, 139, 146
Growth 2020 Strategy 22, 57, 63, 64, 66, 76–77, 81, 89, 102

health and safety 37n75, 119, 137
health improvement strategies 96
health of carers 10
healthcare 87, 91, 94
heart, care work done with the 51; *see also* love
Herring, Jonathan 6, 8, 9, 29, 153
holistic approaches 13, 156–157
home-based care 87n28, 94
Honneth, Axel 50
human capital 12

human dignity 12–13, 24–25, 29, 43, 47–49, 97, 132–133, 144
human flourishing 41
human needs 24, 38, 42, 93
human rights 1, 48, 136, 152, 157

Iceland 32
inactivity traps 78
income, family, and number of children 59
income support 78
indirect discrimination 105–106, 107, 109, 114–115, 125, 145
individual rights 29, 46, 79
inequality: capability approach 41; social investment 80; structural inequality 35, 81, 105; *see also* equality; gender equality
informal care arrangements: childcare 55; emergency care 123; financial, physical and emotional costs of 9–10; gender of carers 110n63; as a gendered activity 15, 16; lack of carers available 90; long-term care (LTC) 87–88, 90, 94n63; part-time childcare 55; public/private dichotomy 30; supplementing full-time childcare 71; valuing of care 24; women's choice 18
information sharing 95, 130, 151
institutional childcare 36
institutional long-term care 87
interdependency 24, 46, 91
intergenerational solidarity 24–25, 97, 134
International Labour Organisation (ILO) 136, 157
intersectionality 13, 30, 151
investment in future generations 12, 24
invisibility of care work 50, 51; *see also* visibility
Italy 21n138, 85n15

Jacobs, Advocate General 133
job creation strategies 76, 91, 92
justice: capability approach 38–39; making care visible and accountable 49; male-biased traditional morality 45; redistributive justice 105; and rights 29; social justice 42, 81, 95, 105, 130, 154

Kant, Immanuel 29, 45
Kohlberg, Lawrence 45

"labour of love" perceptions 10, 18, 144
Lareau, Annette 6
laundry 8, 11
leave provisions 68, 69, 73, 97, 102–103, 116–127, 139, 142, 146–148; *see also specific types of leave*
legal aid 151
legal rights 29–30
Lewis, Jane 7
liberal markets 31
life cycle approach 146
life expectancy 59, 83–85
lifestyles, encouraging healthy 96
Lisbon Council (2000) 57, 60, 63, 69, 74, 77
Lisbon Treaty 22–23, 24–25, 57, 107, 133
long-term care (LTC) 83–99; care as a gendered activity 14; care-gap 91; carers' leave 123; vs. childcare 11–13; definitions of 86–87; differently regulated to childcare 154; EU work on 2; European Semester 65; features of 86–93; institutional long-term care 87; leave provisions 146–148; Member States responsibilities 33, 86, 88–89, 94–95, 97–98, 99; men doing 15–16; older people 83–99
long-term leave 146, 147
love 42, 43, 50, 51, 97, 137, 144
low paid care work 10, 31, 76
low pay 40, 75, 101, 125
low quality work 40, 125; *see also* precarious work
low skill work 8
low status 31
Luxembourg European Council (1999) 69

macroeconomics 65–66
Maduro, Advocate General 112, 133
"making work pay" 78
male breadwinner model 15, 35, 40, 61, 128
male norms of work 35, 37–38, 39
markers of the caring relationship 7–11
maternity leave 32n40, 116, 118–119
medical law 4
men: as carers 14, 15, 36, 39, 71–72, 109–110, 119n119, 120; carers for spouses 15; domestic tasks 57; equal sharing of domestic tasks 57, 64, 77, 79, 80, 119n119; flexible working 149; leave provisions 146; long-term care (LTC) 90; male breadwinner model 15, 35, 40, 61, 128; male norms of work 35, 37–38, 39; male-biased traditional morality 45; nurturing identity 38; seen as child-carers only in exceptional circumstances 71–72; sharing unpaid care work 36, 39; solidarity regarding care work 134; time spent caring 14, 15; *see also* fathers
mental disability 86
mental health 7, 84, 96, 134
middle classes 34
migration 20–21, 22, 34, 85, 85n15
Molinier, Pascale 18
moral case for EU engagement in care 24–25
moral development 45
moral rights 29–30
mothers: "caring about" versus "caring for" 6; choice to care 9n58; dominant ideology of motherhood 80; maternity leave 32n40, 116, 118–119; mothering roles 39; *see also* childcare; gender equality; women
mutual interdependence 24, 46
Mutual Learning Programme 98

nationality, discrimination on grounds of 107
neoliberalism 129
Netherlands 72
new social risks 23
New Start Initiative 79–80, 103–104, 131, 151
non-discrimination and equality 37, 104–116, 128, 132, 137, 138
nursing care 86
Nussbaum, Martha 28, 38, 42

O'Brien, Charlotte 9–10, 102, 144–145
old age, care in 83–99; *see also* long-term care (LTC)
Open Method of Coordination (OMC) 60, 63–64, 95, 155
Organisation for Economic Cooperation and Development (OECD) 86, 92
out-of-school care 65
outsourcing of care work 34, 36
overarching principle, care as 5

Index

paid employment: business case for EU engagement in care 22; capability approach 43; and childcare 55–58; considered the only form of work 43; dual earner/carer model 39–40, 41, 52, 58; feminist analysis of care 34–35; and fertility rates 59–60; male norms of work 35; old social risks versus new social risks 23; precarious and low-paid 40; removing barriers to 69; unencumbered worker model 35, 40, 101, 129; and welfare regimes 58; women 3, 5, 22, 57, 62, 71–72, 76, 77; women combining with care 14–15, 16–17; working classes 34
parental leave 32, 111, 117, 121–122, 139, 140, 142; *see also* maternity leave; paternity leave
Parental Leave Directive 117, 118, 121–122, 137, 149
Part-Time Directive 43–44
part-time employment: childcare 71; definitions of "work" 43; indirect discrimination 115; Part-Time Work Directive 124–127; value in economic terms 150; women more likely to undertake 15, 17, 19
Part-Time Work Directive 124–127, 137
paternity leave 32, 116, 119–120, 139, 140
pensions 23, 84, 102
personal autonomy 29–30
physical labour elements of caring 8, 9–10
policy making: about carers 102; childcare 54; ethic of care 46–47; horizontal 92; long-term care (LTC) 93–98; non-discrimination and equality 106; reactive versus proactive 55–56, 82, 89
population growth concerns 59–60; *see also* ageing society; demographics
positive action 35
positive duties 108
poverty: child poverty 19, 60–61, 78; and childcare 60–61, 80; future legal framework for care 148; and gender 16–17; and long-term care 96; new social risks 23; and women 74n119
precarious work 21, 34, 40, 76, 101, 129

pregnancy/maternity law 35, 37, 113, 145
Pregnant Workers Directive 37, 73n113, 103n24, 117, 118–119, 120, 137
preschool education 55, 61, 70
prevention strategies 96
primary carer status 112, 140, 141–142
private childcare provision 54–55
private sphere, caring takes place in the 30–31
professional care work 51, 87
Programme for Employment and Social Innovation 98
promotion, women passed over for 107
protected characteristics 112–113, 114
psychodynamics 18
psychological care 8
psychological wellbeing 49
public goods, childcare as 12
public sector childcare 33, 54–55
public/private dichotomy 25, 30–31, 35, 39, 49

quality of care 51, 55, 72–73, 78, 96
quantification of care 50–51, 55, 71

race 22, 30, 114–115
Race Directive 110, 114–115
rationality 19, 27, 47, 52; *see also* economic rationality
Raz, Joseph 30, 112
reasonable adjustments 115, 118, 144–145
Recast Directive 106, 113, 118, 119–120
reciprocal, care is 24
Recommendation on Childcare 1–2
Recommendation on Investing in Children 2
reconciliation provisions *see* work-family reconciliation
redistributive justice 105
re-enablement 96
Regional Fund 65
regulation, of childcare 61–67
rehabilitation 96
relational autonomy 30
relational work, law does not acknowledge 51–52
relationship, caring is a 24, 143–144, 154
relationship breakdown 5
reproductive biology 17, 37, 66, 81, 146

residency 89, 140–142
residential care 94
responsibilities 46, 49
reunification of families 140–141
rewards and satisfaction from caring 10
Right to Reconcile Work and Family Life (Article 33 EUCHR) 49
rights: carers' rights 144–151; and the caring relationship 27–28, 29–38; children's rights 60–61, 75–81; and duties 29; and EU legislation 27; future legal framework for care 132; human rights 1, 48, 136, 152, 157; individual rights 29, 46, 79; legal rights 29–30; long-term care (LTC) 95, 97, 99; moral rights 29–30; right to care 23, 29; rights-based strategy for carers 137–151

sameness/difference debate 33–38
same-sex couples 15
Scandinavia 88
Second Action Program (1986-1989) 67
second shift 16, 57, 80
Self-Employed Directive 73n113, 103n24
self-sacrifice 8
Sen, Amartya 28, 41
service-based economies 61
sex discrimination 37, 111, 113, 125
sex versus gender 111
shopping 8, 11, 87
sickness law 37, 118, 148
Silver Economy 91–92, 93
single parents 40, 58, 61
skills of care work 50–51
Smart, Carol 6
Soares, Angelo 50
social capital 24, 78, 93
social care 4–5, 87, 91, 94
social class 22, 30, 34
social cohesion 77
social contract 44
social disdain 50
social exclusion 10, 60, 74n119, 80–81
social infrastructure 91
social investment 78, 79, 80–81
Social Investment Package (SIP) 77, 79, 80–81
social justice 42, 81, 95, 105, 130, 154
social protection 94, 96
Social Protection Committee 33, 86, 94
social rights 31

social risks 23
social security coverage 23
soft law 61–62, 63, 94, 155
solidarity 24–25, 35, 47, 49, 97, 132, 134, 137
sovereign debt crisis 64
spouses 15
state as carer 4–5
statutory definitions of care (lack of) 3–4
stigmatisation 78, 106
stress 134
Structural Funds 66–67
structural inequality 35, 81, 105
subconscious 51
subsidiarity principle 103
substantive equality 35, 105, 145
sui generis 32–33
surrogate parents 118, 146
sustainability: carers 102–103; long-term care (LTC) 90, 96; Silver Economy 92
Sweden 33

taxation 55
technology 19, 96–97, 118, 134, 149
third country migrants 21, 89, 135, 141
third shift 16
time measures 116
time provisions 117, 123–127, 148
time to work 23
tort law 5
transactions 9–10, 24, 51
transgender people 133
Treaty of Amsterdam 68–69, 107, 108, 110
Treaty of Lisbon 22–23, 24–25, 57, 107, 133
Treaty on European Union (TEU) 54, 60, 69n88, 97, 99, 105, 132, 134, 137–138, 142
Treaty on the Functioning of the European Union (TFEU) 1, 97, 107, 111, 113, 132, 137–138, 152
Tronto, Joan 6
trust 50
24/7 society 19, 35
2008 financial crisis 31–32, 64, 73–75, 88, 119, 152

unemployment 23, 69, 74
unencumbered worker model 35, 40, 101, 129
unfair dismissal 113, 115, 118

unfair labour practices 23
Universal Declaration on Human Rights 48
universal experience, caring/being cared for as 1–26
universal vulnerability 11
unpaid care: capability approach 43–44; care feminism 36–37; challenging traditional valuation of 138; and childcare 57; in the definition of "carer" 7; definitions of 20; as a gendered activity 16; long-term care (LTC) 87; not considered work 43, 143; transferring to the formal paid sector 58–59; and the unencumbered worker model 35; value in economic terms 23; valuing of care 152
unpaid leave 121, 123, 147, 148
unskilled "body work" 8
utilitarianism 45

valuing of care: accounting for care 10, 50, 88, 152, 156; business case for EU engagement in care 22–23; capability approach 38–39, 42–43; care professions 8; and the choice to care 19; Court of Justice of the European Union (CJEU) 54; definitions of "work" 43; future legal framework for care 130–152; importance of carers 102; making care visible and accountable 49–52; moral case for EU engagement in care 24–25; valuing care *per se* not just as investment 12–13, 19
violence 106
visibility: of care to policy makers 46; childcare vs. other types of care 12; making care visible and accountable 49–52; of not-done care work 51
vulnerability 10–11, 91, 110, 112, 135, 145, 157

Wahl, Advocate General 126
welfare: austerity policies 32; and childcare 54; long-term care (LTC) 87; and old age 85; post-2008 financial crisis 74; reform of inefficient 58; and rights 29; of society 24, 27; welfare economics 41
welfare benefits 78
wellbeing: capability approach 41, 42; compassion, dignity and solidarity 49; ethic of care 46; future legal framework for care 132, 144; and human dignity 133; importance of carers 102; long-term care (LTC) 93, 97; Treaty on European Union (TEU) 134
women: austerity policies 74–75; business case for EU engagement in care 22; care as a gendered activity 13–19; careers 17; caring as "women's nature" 36–37; in EU employment strategies 62; fertility rates 59–60; flexible working 149; indirect discrimination 106, 107; long-term care (LTC) 87–88; maternity leave 118–119; paid employment 3, 5, 22, 57, 62, 71–72, 76, 77; parental leave 121; part-time employment 115, 125; refusal by employers to take on 17; and social exclusion 74n119; "special ability" of care 17–18, 36–37; wellbeing 134; *see also* feminism; gender equality; mothers
Women at Work initiative 136
work, definitions of 19–20, 43, 143
work-family reconciliation 60, 68, 73–74, 77, 78, 102–103, 109, 116–127, 146–147
working classes 34
Working Time Directive 124
working time regulations 73, 124
work-life balance 39–40, 60, 68–69, 73–75, 77, 79, 134
Work-Life Balance Directive 39, 65, 80, 104, 117, 118, 119, 120, 121, 123, 126–127, 128–129, 131, 137, 138–144, 154, 155, 157
Work-Life Balance Package 73, 103, 119, 152
workplace/home divide, blurring of 35

Zbyszewska, Ania 124